Berklee CONTEMPORARY MUSIC NOTATION

JONATHAN FEIST

Dedicated to Matt Marvuglio, my Berklee guru, grounding rock, and sometime coconspirator, who has helped me become hip to so much jive, and to Rhoda Forte, my childhood piano teacher, who taught me a great many things, including the fact that the piano pedal symbol looks very much like a sheep.

𝆮

Write it right. Rewrite.
Wring its rot, and wright it wrought.
Edit and end it.

BERKLEE PRESS
Editor in Chief: Jonathan Feist
Senior Vice President of Online Learning and Continuing Education/CEO of Berklee Online: Debbie Cavalier
Vice President of Enrollment Marketing and Management: Mike King
Vice President of Online Education: Carin Nuernberg
Editor: Susan Gedutis Lindsay
Editorial Assistants: Emily Jones, Eloise Kelsey
Cover Designer: Ranya Karafilly

ISBN 978-0-87639-178-5

1140 Boylston Street
Boston, MA 02215-3693 USA
(617) 747-2146

Visit Berklee Press Online at
www.berkleepress.com

Berklee Online

Study music online at
online.berklee.edu

DISTRIBUTED BY

HAL•LEONARD®
7777 W. BLUEMOUND RD. P.O. BOX 13819
MILWAUKEE, WISCONSIN 53213

Visit Hal Leonard Online
www.halleonard.com

Berklee Press, a publishing activity of Berklee College of Music, is a not-for-profit educational publisher. Available proceeds from the sales of our products are contributed to the scholarship funds of the college.

CONTENTS

ACKNOWLEDGMENTS

This book has been informed and assisted by a great number of people. At Berklee College of Music, I have worked with more than two hundred authors to prepare books, videos, recordings, and online courses about music, and each one has provided insights in new dimensions of musicianship and notation. Similarly, in my *Music Notation and Score Preparation Using Finale* class at Berklee Online, I have taught many hundreds of students, and graded approximately 10,000 notation assignments, as of this writing. It's an old saw, that we learn more from our students than they learn from us, but I have found this to be the case. I am particularly grateful to those pesky students who ask the most challenging questions.

At an existential level, this book could only exist thanks to the work and insight of Carin Nuernberg, Debbie Cavalier, Jeff Schroedl, J. Mark Baker, Jackie Muth, Marilyn Bliss, Emily Jones, Eloise Kelsey, and the staff of production and engraving elves at Hal Leonard Corp. Additionally, at Berklee and beyond, I have long relied on a group of sage advisors who have been my sounding board and "voices from the street" about which notation practices are in use and which ones are preferred. I hesitate before I start naming individuals because I'm sure to leave out someone critical, but my thoughts about notation and the better parts of this book were profoundly shaped by the wisdom of Matthew Nicholl, Matt Marvuglio, Ben Newhouse, David Wallace, Casey Driessen, Mike Block, Joe Mulholland, Kari Juusela, Larry Baione, Kim Perlak, Rich Appleman, Allan Chase, Casey Scheuerell, and Felice Pomeranz. In a separate phrase marked *molto espress.*, Charys Schuler, David Patterson, Shane Adams, and Susan Gedutis Lindsay. Also, my mentors in composition, Arthur Cunningham, William Thomas McKinley, and Arthur Berger.

And finally, my parents Addie and Lee Feist, and to Marci, Merlin, Forrest, and Cricket. Okay, Lola too.

I am grateful for all of your wisdom, support, friendship, and love.

FOREWORD

Matthew Nicholl is a composer, arranger, coauthor of ***Music Notation: Preparing Scores and Parts****, and Associate Vice President for Global Studies of Global Initiatives at Berklee College of Music, where he previously served as chair of the Contemporary Writing and Production department for many years.*

Music notation is highly developed visual language that describes a complex aural event as it unfolds in time, providing a set of directions for its recreation through performance. Over hundreds of years, the language has evolved a vocabulary, grammar, and syntax that are applied in specific contexts to communicate profound artistic intent. It is not an easy subject to present in a comprehensive manner, but it is an essential study for the contemporary musician of any level and writing in any style.

Jonathan Feist has done something quite unusual with this text: he has created a book that is readable, engaging—at times witty, at times thought provoking—and that covers the topic from the most elemental material to the most complex. The book will be immediately useful to any musician who wants to create written parts and scores, for music in any style, and for any purpose.

Like Jonathan, I find the subject of notation endlessly fascinating. As a writer, I seek the best possible way to communicate my musical ideas efficiently, clearly, and succinctly. Every musical creation requires a specific application of notational principles to best communicate musical ideas and intent. As these ideas grow more refined and comprehensive, so should their written expression.

Like a great film score, music notation should be so well executed that it becomes transparent to the reader. And so, great music notation is not simply a craft but a task that requires the extension of musical artistry to the written page. Thanks to Jonathan's expertise and hard work, this text is an essential guide in that endeavor.

—Matthew Nicholl

INTRODUCTION

Music is magic, and every score, lead sheet, and songbook is a grimoire. Just as any language has its common practices and its dialects, music notation—the written form in which these mystical recipes are rendered—has myriad forms and styles. As much as we teachers and editors like to present tidy rules, the rough reality of the creative human spirit sometimes proves reluctant to conform to our style books—either to the notation itself or the tidy genre boundaries of the art at which it hints.

In the wild, music often misbehaves. While some might prefer that there be universally acceptable standards for notation that all artists follow as gospel, in fact, deviation is the norm. Compare a Hollywood film score to a Nashville chord chart, to a *Guitar Player* magazine tablature example, to a hip-hop drum machine chart, to a rendering of Bach's *Mass in B Minor*, to a contemporary aleatoric duet for prepared piano and improvising Theremin, to a grid for djembe ensemble, and you might wonder if the practitioners of these expressions called "music" have anything in common at all. Books of notation standards promulgate opposing preferences, and volumes released even by the same music publisher will vary.

It's tempting, then, to simply throw up our hands and admit that there is no standard. Let's let chaos reign and do as we please, shall we?

This vast divergence of practice is easily misinterpreted as ignorance or carelessness, on the part of music writers. On the contrary, though, in my forty-odd years of grappling with notation standards, I've found that most music writers care quite a bit about these details. Further, there are, in fact, consequences to the resulting musical performances that will result from inattention to detail—that is, careless notation. A simple example is the handling of page turns. A carelessly rendered page turn can lead to dropped notes and other mistakes, while a thoughtful page turn can be executed relatively seamlessly. A cleverly sadistic music publisher could make every page turn resemble a Victor Borge routine.

So, the way notation is rendered will affect the outcome of the art. The details can be argued from one publisher or musician's culture to the next. However, there are some relatively universal standards, beyond the placement of our precious dots and squiggles, that we can likely agree upon, as we consider relatively "standard" or dare I say "best" practices: clarity, consistency, and ergonomics. We want our scores to be as easy as possible for our readers to understand. We want our notation to be correct. But what, exactly, does that mean? Who gets to decide these matters of right and wrong? Authors of notation books? If only it were so.

Matthew Nicholl, who kindly wrote the foreword to this book and was chair of Berklee's Contemporary Writing Department for many years, speaks of "Four Levels of Notation Correctness," which I have found to be a useful framework for parsing these murky matters. Here they are:

1. **Universally Accepted Practices.** Some aspects of notation are essentially settled law and universally accepted. For example, you cannot put more than four beats' worth of note durations in a 4/4 measure. It would simply be wrong. End of story.
2. **Cultural Preferences.** There is some variation across musical cultures and time periods for how to render certain types of information. For example, a pop piano/vocal score will set measure numbers once per system, above the staff, while a Hollywood film score will set them in every measure, at the bottom of the score, enclosed in a square. Similarly, practices evolve over time and across instrument groups. To a violinist, a slur indicates a specific bowing choice, but to a pianist, a slur is an expressive nuance. We live in a diverse world, and we waste time when we don't understand the language and conventions used by our readers.
3. **Client-Specific Preferences.** Publishers and other clients have individual house standards, and musicians of different capability levels sometimes require different choices. For example, some publishers use parentheses around courtesy accidentals, and others do not. Some publishers use dots on rests; others prohibit them. A beginning trombone part may avoid tenor clef, whereas a part for a professional would use it easily. Smart people can disagree. In the end, the client is always right.
4. **Personal Preferences.** There are often multiple ways to handle a notation element, and nobody will really care much how you do it except you. For example, you can choose to abbreviate a minor chord symbol as mi or min. Right vs. wrong here is really a matter of consistency. And that matters a lot.

Some practices fall in grey areas, between these classifications, but the framework is helpful for considering many conundrums.

The editor in me would prefer tidier and more definitive answers to some of the practices to be discussed in this book. If every score, every method book, and every writer used exactly the same symbols in the same way, my job would be so much simpler. Coordinating all the people who work on a publication—composer, engraver, editor, proofreaders, production manager, indexer, etc.—would be a breeze. See one, seen 'em all, we'd say. But that isn't the world we live in, and the diversity of notation in some ways mirrors the diversity of music and human expression itself.

So, we must muddle through, and attempt to be clear and easy to read, in hopes of serving the music as best we can.

Notation is not music. Notation is a haphazard Frankenstein soup of tangentially related alphabets and hieroglyphics via which music is occasionally discussed amongst its wonkier creators. The music itself towers infinitely over the anemic scribbles that attempt to describe it. The best that notation can and should do is to be a good servant and get the hell out of the music's way and not confuse it into a monkey-brawl of an inky mess.

It's approaching twenty years that I've been editing music books at Berklee Press, trying to find consensus on notation among the world's best artists, music educators, and thinkers. Berklee is an interesting place. People come to teach here and publish books with Berklee Press from everywhere: all corners of the globe, from the Hollywood sound stages to the recording studios of Nashville, from Broadway to the Boston Pops, from the grunge clubs of Seattle to Carnegie Hall—from Korea, Peru, Mexico, Japan, and yes, even from rural Massachusetts. I've worked on books with luminaries such as Lalo Schifrin and Gary Burton, as well as many who have performed alongside the more "household names," with artists such as John Scofield, Stan Getz, Bob Dylan, Alison Krauss, Liberace, Miles Davis, the New York Philharmonic, Chaka Khan, Leonard Bernstein, Johnny Cash, Béla Fleck, Earl Scruggs, and Grandmixer DXT.

Then, of course, there are Berklee's legendary teachers, such as the late John LaPorta and Ray Santisi, each of whom taught many thousands of students over more than fifty years. At Berklee Press, we just published a book coauthored by three bass players who had a combined 130 years of teaching experience! Berklee is an extraordinary place, bringing together a diverse wealth and depth of experience. I am fortunate, in my role here, to frequently find myself deep in discussion about nuances of notation with them, while we create our books.

In this arena where giants gather, alas, often there is no clear agreement about notation standards. But there is one kernel of insight that I believe nearly everyone here will agree with: Diversity of human expression is more important than conformity to editorial standards. So, we serve, rather than prescribe.

Humbled but not hobbled, let's do the best we can do to support what matters most: the music itself, and consider what notation practices are likely to serve the music best.

To all who try to communicate the magic of music in this abstract and imperfect symbology—whether you are composing, songwriting, arranging, orchestrating, teaching, theorizing, or writing prose or poetry about music—this book is for you.

Jonathan Feist
Boston, 2017

CHAPTER 1

Rhythm

Most essentially, music notation communicates rhythm and pitch. This information is commonly indicated by a series of symbols called "notes," set on a "staff," which is a type of graph. The characteristics of a note's shape and its placement on a staff define pitch and rhythm, such as this G eighth note.

FIG. 1.1. Note on a Staff

Note symbols may have the following parts.

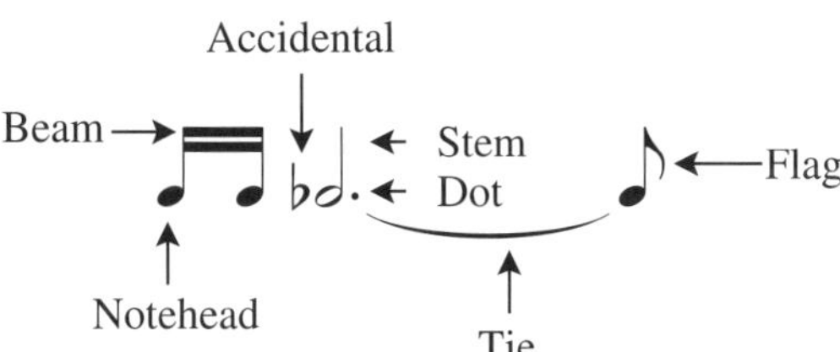

FIG. 1.2. Parts of a Note

In this chapter, we will discuss the symbols and conventions for these core components of notation. Additional aspects of their appearance and use will be discussed throughout this book.

NOTE DURATIONS

Here are the most common symbols for note durations and their corresponding rests. We'll discuss others later, particularly the shapes for percussion notation. Each note value has a corresponding rest, indicating silence for the same duration as the note. A note means "play," and a rest means "don't play."

Note	Rest	Name	Notehead	Stem, Flag/Beam
		Double Whole Note and Rest (*Br.* Breve)	Large, open head framed by vertical lines	None
		Whole Note and Rest (*Br.* Semi-Breve)	Large, open head. The rest hangs downward from a staff line	None
		Half Note and Rest (*Br.* Minim)	Regular, open head. The rest sits on top of a staff line	Stem, no flag
		Quarter Note and Rest (*Br.* Crotchet)	Regular, closed head	Stem, no flag
		Eighth Note and Rest (*Br.* Quaver)	Regular, closed head	Stem, one flag
		Sixteenth Note and Rest (*Br.* Semiquaver)	Regular, closed head	Stem, two flags
		Thirty-Second Note and Rest (*Br.* Demisemiquaver)	Regular, closed head	Stem, three flags
		Sixty-Fourth Note and Rest (*Br.* Hemidemisemiquaver)	Regular, closed head	Stem, four flags

FIG. 1.3. Note Durations

In the United States, the whole note is the "standard" by which all other note durations are defined. It has the larger, open (hollow) notehead. The other notes are described as fractions relating to one whole note.

- A half note lasts half as long as a whole note; two halves equal one whole. The half-note symbol has a regular-sized open notehead, and it also has a stem.
- A quarter note lasts a quarter of the duration of a whole note. It has a closed (solid) notehead and a stem.
- An eighth note lasts an eighth of the duration of a whole note. It has a closed notehead, a stem, and either a flag or a beam.
- A sixteenth note lasts a sixteenth of the duration of a whole note. It has a closed notehead, stem, and two flags or two beams.

The durations of the notes are self-referential fractions; how long they actually last depends on their context. One of the great structural flaws in music notation is that the notes are built on divisions of four. Music with a triplet rather than a duple rhythm requires various retrofits. If the music's meter is divided into three rather than four (such as the 3/4 or 9/4 time signatures), a "whole" note (i.e., a semi-breve) might not relate well to what will fit in the measure. What's whole? The notation element itself, rather than anything to do with the actual music.

A whole rest serves a secondary function: appearing in an empty measure, with no other activity. In this case, it means "rest for the whole measure," whatever the time signature or however many beats the measure holds.

Using Flags and Beams

Flags or *beams* (used to connect a series of notes that would otherwise be flagged) indicate note durations of an eighth note or shorter. Each flag/beam halves the note duration, similar to the way in which a stem on an open notehead cuts a whole note in half to become a half note. So, an eighth note (one flag) is half the length of a quarter note (no flags). A sixteenth note has two flags/beams, a thirty-second note has three flags, and so on. A beam indicates the same thing as a flag, and using beams greatly reduces the busyness of a page.

Figure 1.4 shows the most common note durations, with each group lasting for the same amount of time. Notice how much tidier the "beamed together" versions are.

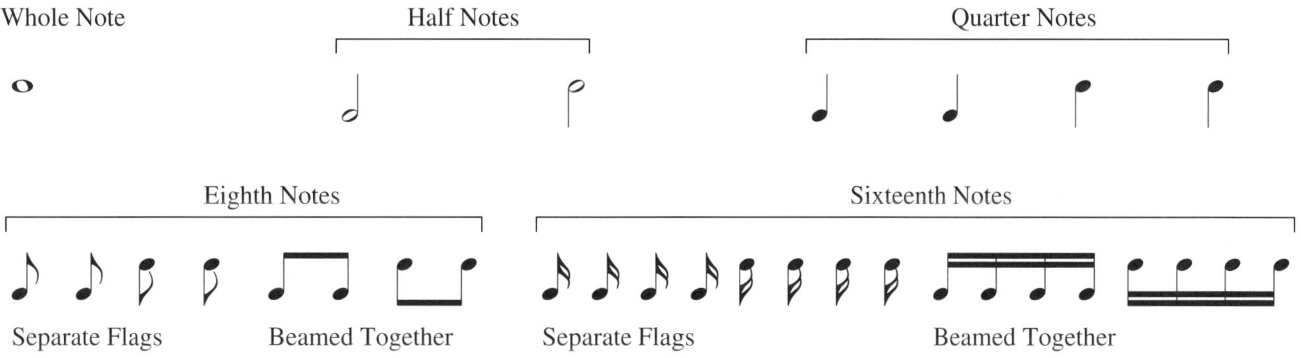

FIG. 1.4. Stems and Beams for Common Note Durations

You can keep adding flags/beams to cut the duration of a note in half. Thirty-second notes are relatively rare, and sixty-fourth notes, one hundred twenty-eighth notes, or smaller, are even rarer, but theoretically possible. On the other end of the spectrum, double whole notes are relatively rare, though you see them sometimes. Most music is in 4/4 meter, where the double whole note simply does not fit.

The nuances of beaming varies between publishers. Some publishers will beam together eighth notes on beats 1 and 2, and beats 3 and 4, in 4/4 time. Others will always beam the beats individually. The beam never crosses the "imaginary barline" (discussed later this chapter), though, between beats 2 and 3.

FIG. 1.5. Beaming in 4/4

Beams also clarify meters such as 7/8, regarding whether they are felt as 2+2+3, 2+3+2, or as 3+2+2.

FIG. 1.6. Beaming in 7/8 (2+3+2)

Older vocal music notation avoided beams, sometimes with all stems pointing up. This practice has faded and is generally considered archaic. In contemporary notation practice, vocal music follows most of the same conventions as notation for other instruments.

FIG. 1.7. Vocal Notation: Not Beamed (Archaic) and Beamed (Contemporary)

When there are multiple beams, the outermost one (farthest from the notehead) is called the "primary beam," and the others are all "secondary beams." To clarify subdivisions of beats, such as long strings of thirty-second notes or triplet sixteenths sharing beams with other sixteenths, you can break all the beams except the primary beam. This can greatly clarify the rhythms and feel of complex figures.

FIG. 1.8. Broken Secondary Beams

A beam's angle ideally follows the music's melodic contour. So, if the melody clearly ascends during the beamed group of notes, the beam's angle should ideally mimic this contour, ascending from left to right, and vice versa for descending. Sometimes, though, it is best to just keep the beam horizontal to avoid busying the page with awkward lines. General rule: keep the stem length of the beamed group's first and last notes an octave high. However, the resulting beam angle might be better off softened by violating this rule and implying a generally similar contour rather than being too literal.

FIG. 1.9. Beam Angle Follows Melodic Contour

On piano, harp, vibraphone, or other instruments that read a grand staff, a beamed group might include notes set on both staves. This is sometimes called "cross-staff beaming." It indicates that a single hand is playing on notes set on both staves, and it is a good way to reduce ledger lines and general complexity on the page—particularly when the notes are all part of the same phrase.

FIG. 1.10. Cross-Staff Beaming

Feathered beams indicate accelerating or decelerating series of notes. Generally speaking, they start at a single point and then expand to three beams. You'll see some scores with them expanding to four or five beams, but honestly, from a performance perspective, that's unnecessary and just adds clutter to the page. Feathered beams are intended as a free sort of acceleration/deceleration, so getting overly specific or extreme here seems against the spirit of the thing. It gets to be a bit like using five exclamation points to communicate your exuberance. Three are enough.

Feathered beams are a relatively contemporary notation practice, primarily used among classical musicians. They are not universally understood, so their use should be predicated on knowledge of your reader's level.

FIG. 1.11. Feathered Beams

Rhythm Notation

Rhythm notation is sometimes used in lead sheets and pedagogical notation to indicate purely rhythmic concepts, dissociated from pitch. The difference is the noteheads, which are either set without a staff or on the middle line of a staff. It could be interpreted to mean that any notes can be selected, that a known note or chord should be repeated, that the rhythm should be played on a percussion instrument, or other generic rhythm concept, such as "kicks over time."

FIG. 1.12. Rhythm Notation

Ties and Dots

Note durations can be expanded with ties and dots. A *tie* combines two note values of the same pitch; instead of playing two attacks for each duration shown, the note is held through both. Ties are particularly helpful in combining note durations across a barline.

FIG. 1.13. Ties

A *dot* increases the note duration by half. For example, half of a quarter-note value is an eighth note. A dotted quarter note is the same, then, as a quarter note tied to an eighth note.

FIG. 1.14. Dotted Quarter vs. Tied Quarter/Eighth

Rests also can have dots, though not all publishers use them. The rules are the same as for dotted notes. Here, then, are the most common dotted note and rest durations, with how many beats are contained in each, assuming that a quarter note gets one beat.

Note	Rest	Number of Beats (Quarter Note = 1 beat)
𝅜 .	𝄺 .	12
𝅝 .	𝄻 .	6
𝅗𝅥 .	𝄼 .	3
𝅘𝅥 .	𝄽 .	1.5
𝅘𝅥𝅮 .	𝄾 .	.75
𝅘𝅥𝅯 .	𝄿 .	.375

FIG. 1.15. Dotted Notes and Rests

A dotted single note is usually preferred to the tied pair, though tied notes are sometimes preferred in order to clarify rhythmic syncopations, imaginary barlines, or changing articulations. In figure 1.16, the two measures sound identical, but only the first measure is correct, as it reveals beat 3 and doesn't cross the *imaginary barline*—the sense of metric subdivision between beats 2 and 3.

FIG. 1.16. Use of Dots vs. Ties

Less common, but still sometimes found: a *double dot* increases the duration of a note by half, and then half again. So, a double-dotted half note is like a half note tied to a quarter tied to an eighth. Not all publishers use double dots, but they can be an elegant way to render a rhythmic concept. (Theoretically, you might see more than two dots, but in practice, three or more dots are exceptionally rare because they can be difficult to interpret.)

FIG. 1.17. Double Dot

Grace Notes

Grace notes are small notes set before a regular-sized note, often phrased with the target (or "primary") note. In contemporary usage, grace notes are widely held to indicate a note or series of notes to be played as quickly as possible, preceding the beat on which the regular-sized primary note is set, but their precise rhythmic interpretation varies. In some cases, a slashed grace note is interpreted as an *anticipation* (preceding the beat on which the regular-sized target note is played) and a grace note without a slash as an *appoggiatura* (on the beat, delaying the target note, lasting for half the duration of the indicated primary note), but this is not a universal contemporary practice.

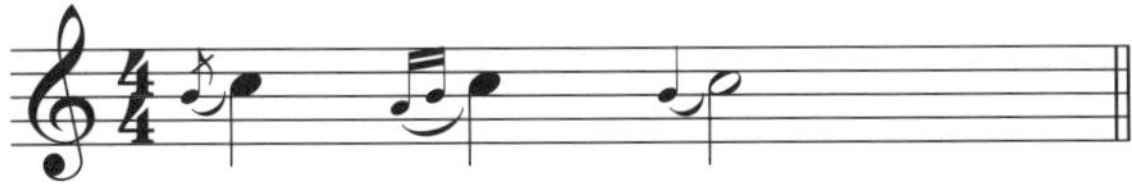

FIG. 1.18. Grace Notes

Syncopation

Here are two general rules of notation that are often at odds with each other and may lead to confusion and debate.

1. Use as few characters as possible to express a duration. So, instead of a tied quarter/eighth, we generally use a dotted quarter.

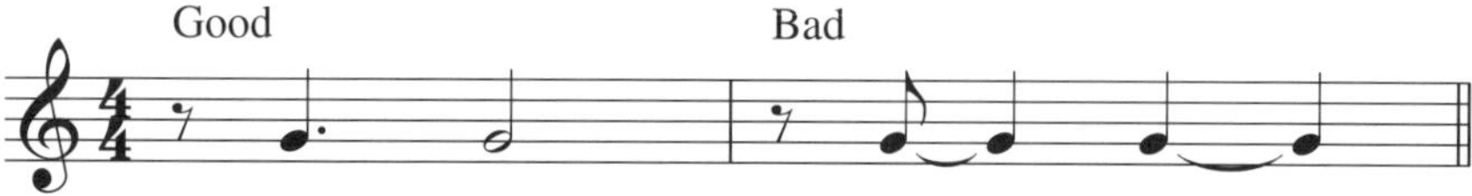

FIG. 1.19. Using Fewer Notes

2. When a syncopated rhythm starts less than half a beat before the target downbeat, the notes are set as tied pairs of notes. The target note of the tie clarifies the anticipated beat. Similarly, a syncopation should not cross an imaginary barline.

FIG. 1.20. Clarifying Syncopations

There are a few widely accepted exceptions to these rules. In most music set in 4/4 time, a quarter note can begin on the "and" of beats 1 and 3, but not on the "and" of beat 2.

FIG. 1.21. Quarter-Note Anticipation

However, in various Latin and South American notation traditions, the figure shown in figure 1.22 ♪ ♩ ♩ ♩ ♪ is commonly accepted, particularly when it recurs, as in a repeated bass figure.

FIG. 1.22. Latin Bass Rhythm

To summarize, these rhythms are correctly rendered.

FIG. 1.23. Correctly Notated Rhythms

Here are some common duration notation mistakes, followed by the correct notation. Note how much easier it is to interpret the syncopations of the corrected versions, where the anticipated beats are clearly visible.

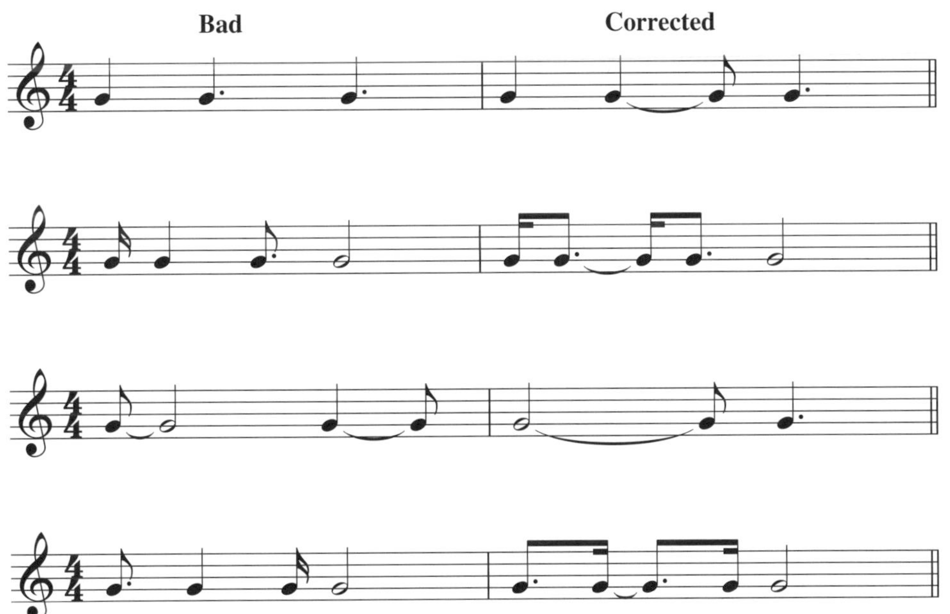

FIG. 1.24. Common Mistakes, Corrected

There are some nuances in how rhythms may be rendered. We will return to this point frequently.

PULSE, METER, AND TIME SIGNATURE

Rhythm happens in the context of pulse. A pulse is a steady division of time, which we measure in "beats per minute," abbreviated "bpm." A helpful device for measuring these is a metronome, and these days, you might as well get a free metronome app for your phone. There are many good ones. Go ahead and grab one now, if you don't already have one.

The basic pulse of the music is among its most profound attributes. To wax speculative and philosophical for a moment, music likely ties into certain cyclical patterns common in the human body. We have a pulse that is essentially steady, though it speeds up or slows down depending on our activity level. Try taking your own pulse now by feeling a vein on your wrist or on the sides of your throat. Tap your foot to your own pulse. Or try tapping on every other pulse. Instant music!

We breathe in and out, and that has a "two feel," meaning, a recurring pattern of two different, equally timed actions. Similarly, when we walk, we have a "two feel" with a left and right foot. If we skip, though, our cadence has a three feel, or "triplet feel." A human heartbeat also has a triplet feel. And if you ride a horse, as humans have done for thousands of years, you'll find repeating patterns of two, three, four, and six, depending on the cadence.

This sense of pattern is both profoundly primal and abstractly intellectual and subjective. Turn on a steady click on your metronome, or feel your pulse, and count along. First, count in two: 1-2, 1-2, and so on. Then, count in three: 1-2-3, 1-2-3, 1-2-3, and so on. Imagine the "1" stronger than the rest. Even count the "1" aloud and just think the other two to yourself. Then move on to a pattern of four, five, six, and twelve. Do any subdivisions seem to emerge within each beat? Twelve, for example, is usually felt as four groups of three. The pulse doesn't actually change, but the way we perceive it certainly does, depending on the meter we are imagining. Once we are in the habit of "hearing" a steady pulse one way, it seems difficult to imagine it organized differently—even though the objective reality is that every click is the same.

These are all regular pulses. Our proclivity towards music and beat is likely related to the fact that we have these rhythms built into our bodies, so they come across as deep and profoundly human. The heartbeat of someone we love is the most magical music of all.

Music imitates all these patterns, which we call "meters." Nearly all meters are felt in patterns of two and three: breath or heartbeat. Most commonly, we have 4/4 meter, which is felt as two groups of two beats. A meter in six is generally felt as two groups of three or three groups of two. A meter in twelve is typically felt as four triplet pulses. And odd time signatures, such as five, are generally felt in adjacent groupings of two and three. While music is sometimes written to deliberately avoid a sense of meter, such as ambient music, film background music, and so on, most music that people listen to for pleasure has a clear meter.

We have, then, the mathematical concept of meter as a number, paired with the human concept of feeling pulse ultimately as either two or three. In notation, this is reflected and reinforced in various ways.

First, we indicate meter with a time signature. This symbol is set at the very beginning to set up the context within which the meters exist. Here is the 4/4 time signature, which is the most common one. In fact, it is sometimes called "common time" and abbreviated with a C. The C and 4/4 mean the same thing.

FIG. 1.25. 4/4 and Common Time

Fun fact: the C symbol was originally an incomplete circle, rather than the letter C. A complete circle indicated triplet meter. The circle is a "perfect" shape, and represented the Holy Trinity—three pulses, symbolizing perfection. Then, if music was in four, the imperfect/broken circle indicated that. Then later, a slash through the C indicated "cut time," which is 2/2 meter.

When we are writing out the time signature, rather than using the abbreviations, the meter is expressed as a two-part symbol. The bottom number indicates which note value gets the pulse, or the "beat." It will be 1 (whole note), 2 (half note), 4 (quarter note), 8 (eighth note), and so on. Most time signatures will have a 4 or 8 below for a quarter or eighth note, but any note duration can get the beat. Then, the top number tells how many beats are in a measure—the recurring pattern of emphasized beats. Typically, a waltz is 3/4, a march is 2/4, a rock beat is usually 4/4, and a blues is 12/8.

Here are some frequently used time signatures. I've filled the measures with some rhythms so that you see what they can contain, but obviously, there are a great number of other possibilities. Notice that a time signature might change during a piece of music.

FIG. 1.26. Time Signatures

Two things to point out here. First, notice that when the time signature changes on the next line, we have a "courtesy time signature" at the end of the preceding line, as a warning. These are only used when the time signature changes during a piece. In a series of exercises or theoretical examples that start and stop, such as figure 1.27, you can leave off the courtesy time signature.

Second, in the two 5/8 measures, notice how the beams group the eighth notes in a pattern first of three plus two and then in two (combined as the quarter) plus three. In this way, beaming can help clarify the feel of the music, which can be otherwise ambiguous.

The common-time symbol is still widely used. However, if the meter changes to anything but cut time, use numerals for all the time signatures, rather than mixing the shortcuts with the numeric version. Keep the logic of your "time signature narrative" consistent.

Imaginary Barline

An *imaginary barline* is a notation convention designed to clarify a measure's organization and hierarchy of beats. The idea is that measures have beat subdivisions that are felt and supported with certain notation practices for note durations and beaming, rather than explicitly notated with an actual barline. Within most meters are felt subgroupings of two or three beats: walking or skipping, your breath or your heartbeat. In 4/4, the imaginary barline is felt between beats 2 and 3; we can describe this organization of two groups of two beats as 2+2. In 5/8 or 5/4 meters, the subdivision can be felt as either 2+3 or 3+2. In 6/8, it can be felt as 123+456, 12+34+56, or in a grand feeling of 1: 123456. And so on.

While these subdivisions are not notated with actual barlines, they are indicated in notation by use of beaming and other notation conventions, as discussed. Careful notation of syncopations, as described earlier, should clarify all imaginary barlines as a byproduct of clarifying the syncopation, regarding weaker and stronger beats. When a syncopation occurs, the first beat after the imaginary barline must be rearticulated with a tie, rather than having a single note crossing over.

Some imaginary barline violations are universally considered "wrong," others are simply confusing because they are inconsistent, and others will be considered "okay" by some readers and abhorrent to others. The goal is always to help the reader clarify the music's feel.

So, in 4/4 meter, on beat 1, obviously, you can have a whole note or dotted half note cross the imaginary barline between beats 2 and 3. The half note can start on beat 2 as well; there is not obscured syncopation. But a half note beginning on the second eighth note of beat 1 (the "and" of 1) is a problem because beat 3 (a strong beat) would then be buried in the note duration, and the syncopation of a note starting on the "and" of beat 3 wouldn't be obvious.

Here are some of the conventions for imaginary barline crossings, both in 4/4 and 6/8, and some examples of how beaming clarifies the way in which the beat groupings are felt.

FIG. 1.27. Imaginary Barlines in 4/4 and 6/8

Thus, we have three related considerations, regarding the rules of using note durations and their boundaries.

1. The real barline. Note durations cannot exceed the meter and cross a barline. If you are in 3/4, you cannot have a whole note in a measure.
2. The imaginary barline. Syncopated durations that can't be broken down evenly can't cross the imaginary barline, as in the examples in figure 1.27.
3. The beat line. Any note duration can start a beat, but per figure 1.24, syncopations can't be obfuscated by note durations such as quarter notes beginning on the last sixteenth of a beat.

Triplets and Other Tuplets

The time signature sets up a basic metrical organization, and the note duration symbols let us subdivide each beat into even multiples. Often, though, the music doesn't adhere nicely to that duple-based math that defines our note durations: whole, half, quarter, eighth, etc. What if we want to subdivide a beat into three notes? That's where "triplets" come in.

Here, on beat 4, the sax has an eighth-note triplet, indicated by the numeral 3 centered in its beam. Text below shows how you would count this rhythm.

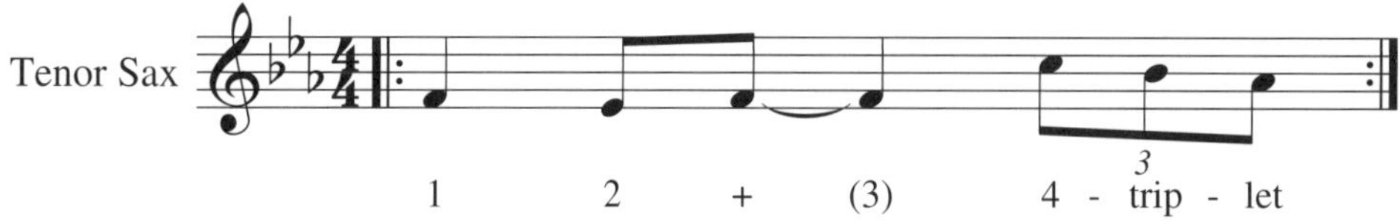

FIG. 1.28. Triplet

Here is that measure in the context of a score. The bass plays quarter notes (beats), and the ride cymbal of the drum set plays eighth notes. You can thus see how the triplet relates to other beats and beat subdivisions.

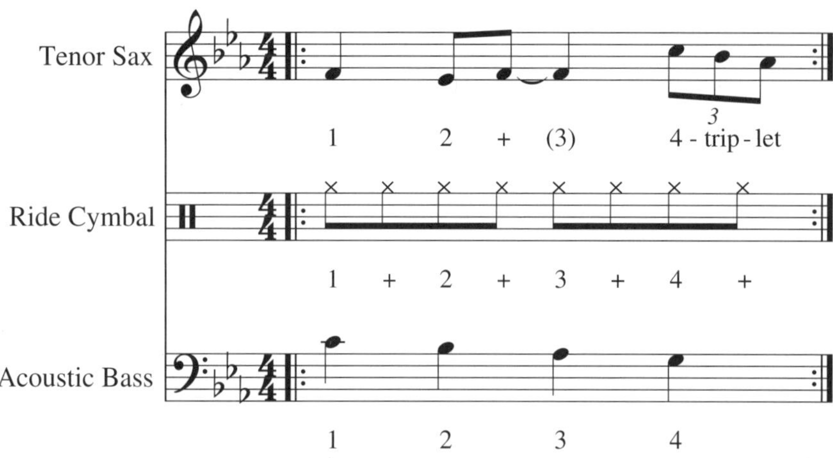

FIG. 1.29. Triplet in a Score

We can also divide greater or lesser numbers of beats into three. Here, the first two beats of the sax part feature quarter-note triplets. Three quarter notes take up the space normally occupied by two quarter notes, or a half note (two beats in 4/4). Then, on the "and" of beat 4 of the first measure, the sax has sixteenth note triplets, taking up the space of one eighth note. Notice here that the quarter note triplets have a bracket above them, showing what's included. The bracket is only necessary when a beam isn't connecting the first and last notes of the triplet.

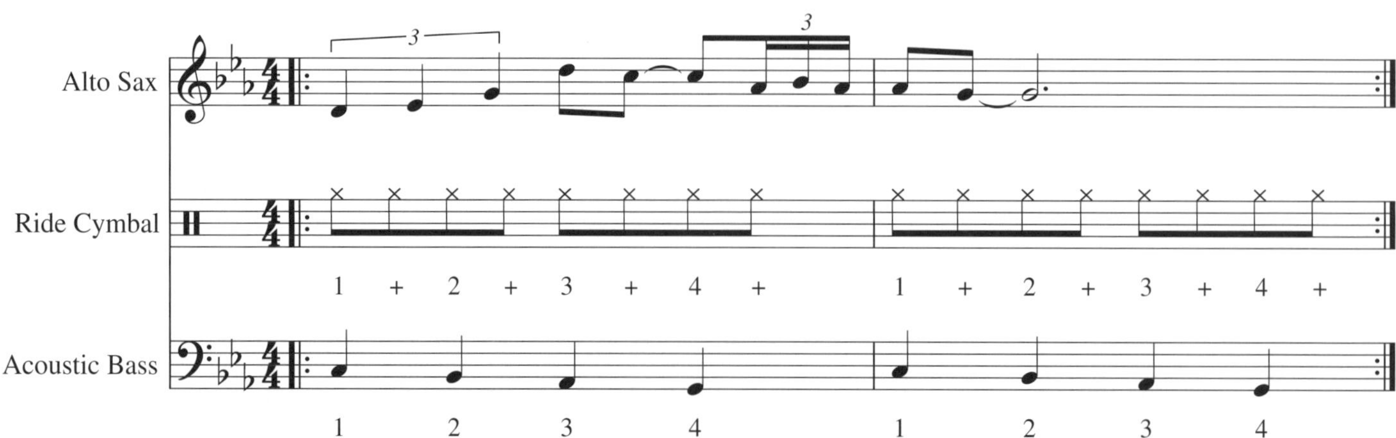

FIG. 1.30. Bracketed and Unbracketed Triplets

Brackets also help clarify the triplet when either the first or last note is a rest, and so the beam isn't any help. You can't see the boundary without that bracket, in this case.

FIG. 1.31. Triplet with Initial Rest

Besides triplets (three in the space of two), you can squeeze other numbers of notes into a beat or over a series of beats. But triplets are the most common.

FIG. 1.32. Tuplets

"Four against three" is another relatively common tuplet. Below, four quarter notes in the quartuplet are set against three beats in the meter. Tip: to feel this sense of 4:3, say "NO, I don't THINK i WILL" where the uppercase syllables are notes performed against the 3/4 meter. To feel 3:4, say, "PASS the GOSH-darn BUT-ter." (Nobody really says "gosh darn.")

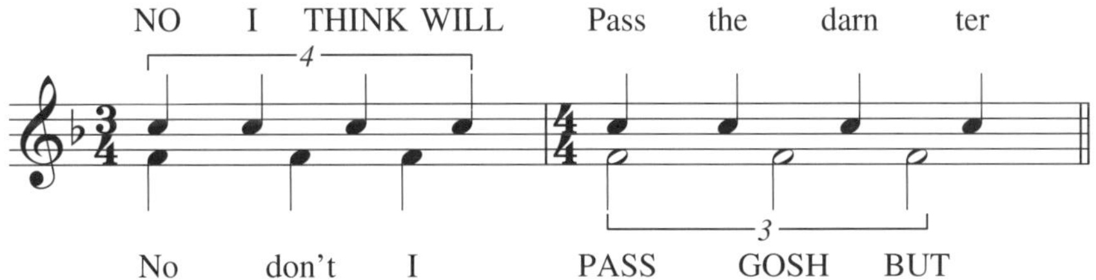

FIG. 1.33. 3:4 vs. 4:3

It can clarify a complex tuplet to set the numeral as a ratio, such as 4:3 in this case. The ratio translates to "four beats in the space of three." In the first measure, the ratio is not necessary because the first beat is a quarter note (the basis for the tuplet), but in the more awkward second measure, the ratio format helps.

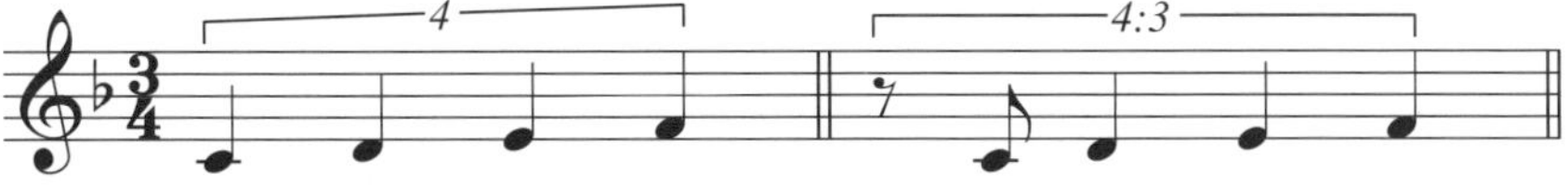

FIG. 1.34. Tuplet as a Ratio

Remember, a bracket is used to clarify the tuplet grouping when either the first or last notes of the group are a rest or when there isn't a beam present to group all the notes together. If all the notes of the tuplet are beamed nicely together, you don't need the bracket. But if there isn't a beam connecting them, or the first or last item in a beamed group is a rest, then the bracket is helpful.

In some rare circumstances, though, the bracket can help clarify the notation. Here is an example of harp notation, which uses brackets to indicate hand direction, and the presence for fingerings 1, 2, 3, 4 further opened the door to potential confusion regarding what a "3" for a triplet might indicate. In this case, we chose to bracket the triplet, despite that beam. You sometimes need to bend the "rules" in favor of clarity.

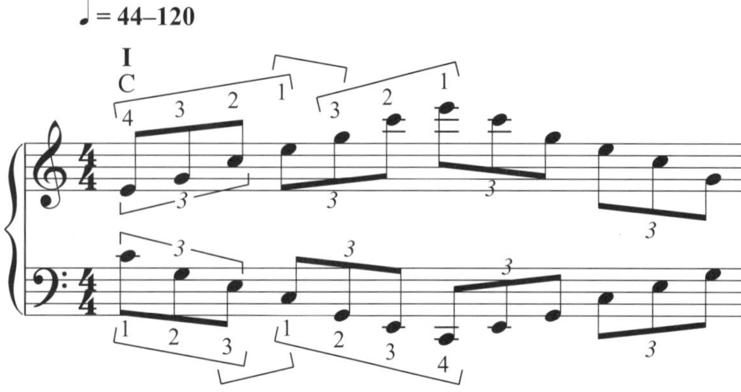

FIG. 1.35. Tuplet Bracket Exception

Omitted Tuplet Numerals

When music has an extended series of beamed tuplets, and it is obvious that the rhythm recurs, the tuplet numeral is sometimes left off after the initial rendering. This is playing with fire, and it should only be done when you are certain that there is no chance of confusion, such as in a scale or arpeggio exercise.

FIG. 1.36. Omitted Triplet Numeral

Swing Rhythms

In most jazz and other styles of music with a "swing" feel, it is common practice to write pairs of notes that have the typical triplet feel as simple eighth notes. This can greatly simplify the notation and omit a lot of ink from the page. *Swing eighth notes* are interpreted essentially as triplets with a quarter note and eighth note. However, if all three notes of the triplet are sounded, the triplet numeral is included.

FIG. 1.37. Swing Eighths

(Note: Reducing the concept of "swing feel" to being a triplet subdivision is an oversimplification, and there are many nuances to describing this fully, but that is a discussion for another book.)

When the music is to be interpreted with this feel, the word "Swing" or "Swing Feel" (or some other variant, such as "Jazz Swing," etc.) should appear at the first bar in order to clarify how this subdivision should be felt. Alternatively, rather than the word "Swing," the notation symbols for two eighths equaling the triplet feel can be indicated. This is particularly common midway through a piece, where there's an actual shift from a straight feel to a swing feel, but it can also be an opening indication at the first bar.

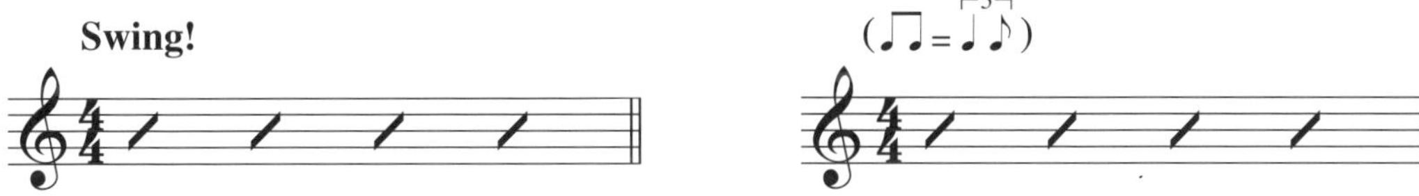

FIG. 1.38. Indicating Swing

A few additional points about tuplets:

- In some scores, you'll see a slur instead of a bracket. Personally, I think this makes more sense as a handwriting convention than in an engraved score. Brackets are simpler shapes, so I recommend those, but you'll see the slurs used by well-respected publishers as well. You will also see respectable publishers either set the numeral inside the bracket or above it, but nobody respectable will ever set the bracket through the numeral.
- It is best to set the numeral on the beam side, and this is nearly always possible. However, if for some reason, you must set the tuplet numeral on the notehead side, use a bracket or a slur. Otherwise, it is easily mistaken for a fingering.
- The angle of the tuplet bracket ideally follows the melodic contour of the melody, running parallel to the beam, if there is one.

Here's a roundup of "the good, the bad, and the ugly" of tuplet notation. "Ugly" means that it is done, out in the field, but I don't think it's the best choice. (Maybe, "ugly" is too strong a word in some cases, but you get the drift.)

FIG. 1.39. Good, Bad, and Ugly Ways to Render Triplets

Notice that the bracket above the complete beam group (first measure, third triplet) is labeled "ugly," not "bad." Some publishers do use brackets on all tuplets, including beamed groups. Again, I don't recommend this, as it needlessly adds complexity to the score. But the practice is still sometimes promulgated by otherwise intelligent, knowledgeable, kind-hearted music publishers. It doesn't mean that they are bad people.

CHAPTER 2

Pitch

STAVES

Music notation is usually written on a five-line staff. The staff is essentially a graph, where each line or space represents a note, arranged low to high. Time is represented from left to right, with rhythms represented by the note duration symbols discussed in chapter 1.

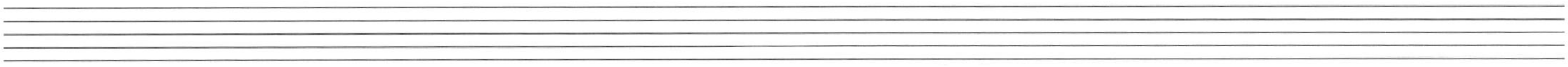

FIG. 2.1. Staff

The staff evolved over many centuries, primarily coming out of European monasteries in the Medieval and Renaissance periods. Notation was originally an extension of text, where relatively informal and nonstandardized small lines and squiggles were added above the words, showing the melodic direction. Later, these markings were separated to a line above the text. Additional staff lines were added, over centuries, varying in number from monastery to monastery and region to region. In the early Renaissance, the staff stabilized at five lines.

This five-line staff isn't the only variation still in use. Percussion notation is often set on a one-line staff, or sometimes, two or three lines. In tablature for guitar and other string instruments (which also dates back many centuries), the lines represent strings, not notes, and their quantity varies from instrument to instrument: six lines for guitar tablature, four lines for bass, five for ukulele, and so on. We will delve into these possibilities in chapter 8.

FIG. 2.2. A One-Line Staff and a Tablature Staff

Most notated music is set on a five-line staff, so that will be our focus in this chapter. This staff has been in common use for about a thousand years, or so; it is the staff for "traditional notation" in what many call "standard practice," and it is not going to go anywhere despite its shortcomings.

Again, the staff is a graph. Noteheads are set either on a line or on a space between the lines, which each represent a specific pitch, described with a letter from A to G and representing a specific frequency (in science, described in Hertz, or Hz), perhaps modified with an accidental (sharp, flat, etc.), and describing note duration/rhythm as well. Low notes to high notes are plotted from bottom to top.

So, we've got five lines, and one of those lines will have an indication on it that reveals what pitch corresponds to that line. We call that indication a "clef" symbol.

A *clef* (transliterating as "key") indicates a specific pitch on a staff. Figure 2.3 shows a "treble clef" staff, which indicates the note G is on the second line from the bottom. (G clef's inside curly cue terminates just below that G line.) The staff's five lines, four spaces, and the space above and below the outside lines most easily support eleven notes, which (perhaps not by accident) is roughly analogous to the singing range of quite a lot of humans. Again, each line or space maps to a note one letter name, A to G, away from its neighbors.

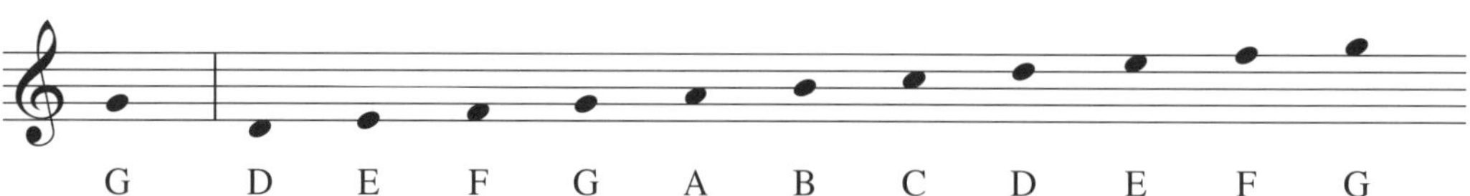

FIG. 2.3. Notes on a G Clef

Depending on what mode or scale you are in, these distances between notes could be either half or whole steps apart.

In the monasteries, the nuns and monks knew the sound of the chants that they were reading, and the notation served as a reminder of the pitches. They could recall the rhythms by ear, much like how modern users of guitar tablature do. (Medieval monk, meet your kindred spirit, the shredder metal guitarist. How do you do....) The way we use notation has changed, though, and "standard" notation has evolved to include more nuance over the centuries. It's gotten much more specific.

For example, different instruments and singers have different ranges, and most performers can sound more notes than there are lines or spaces, so we extend the staff with "ledger lines." These are temporary additional staff lines that just house one note. Here are the most commonly used ledger lines, but we can keep going!

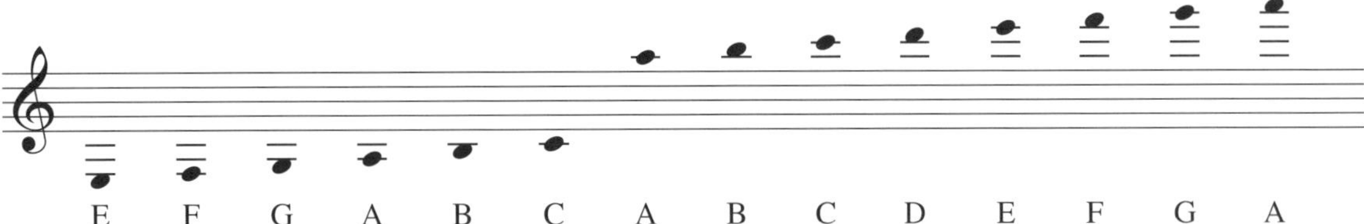

FIG. 2.4. Ledger Lines

Too many ledger lines get a bit difficult to read, and so various modifications to the staff have been developed to simplify the reader's task. Let's explore some of these standards and options.

CLEFS

Different instruments have different ranges, and these ranges don't always fit nicely on the same staff. While an amateur's singing voice might have a range of just an octave, a standard piano has a range seven times that! And face it, reading those ledger lines gets difficult, so we want to minimize their usage. A beginning musician can tolerate one or two ledger lines, but beyond that, they freak out. A more experienced musician can read up to four ledger lines, comfortably.

A solution to this is to use different clefs to change the reference point for the staff notes so that we can reduce some ledger lines and have the most common range of instruments rest primarily on the staff lines. Three clef symbols have emerged as most useful: G, F, and C.

We saw how the treble clef (G on the second-to-bottom line) staff easily accommodated the notes D (above middle C) to G an octave and a half above that. With a few ledger lines, that's terrific for a soprano singer and many high instruments. For example, here is a typical working range for a soprano singer: middle C (called C4) to C6, which is two octaves above that.

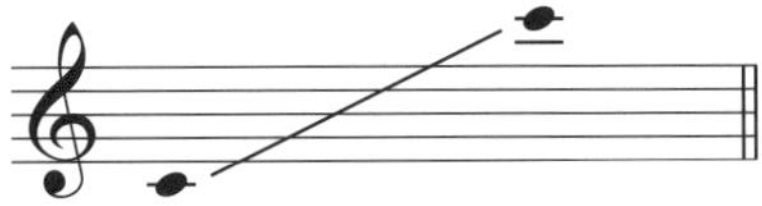

FIG. 2.5. Soprano Range

Now, let me tell you about my own personal plight. I sing low bass. My working vocal range is D2 (right above "great C") up to an E4, above middle C. Plotted on a treble staff, my highest, screechiest note at the top of my range would be on the lowest line on that staff. Then, for me to sing down in the rumbly bottom where I belong, I would have to look at a preposterous number of ledger lines, if some sadist were to force me to sing from the treble clef staff.

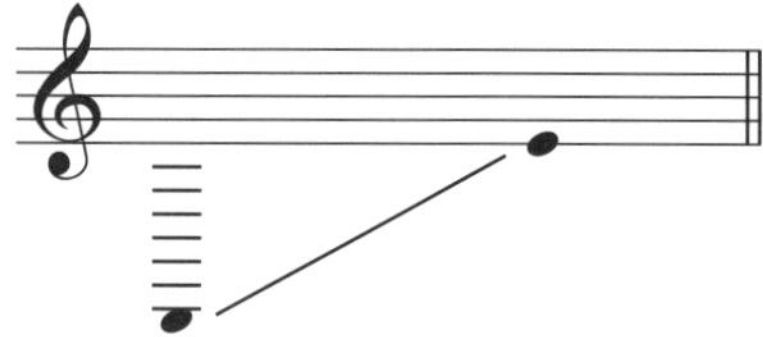

FIG. 2.6. Low Bass Singer's Range in Treble Clef

One of music theory's great innovations to address this issue was the invention of the clef symbols. A clef can shift the pitches to different lines, and thus make reading easier for different ranges. Here's how I read my range on the staff orientation that bass singers use: the bass clef, where the two dots of the F clef symbol indicate the line that is F, and set in an octave where the top line of the staff is the pitch A at 220 Hz. Much easier, without so many ledger lines!

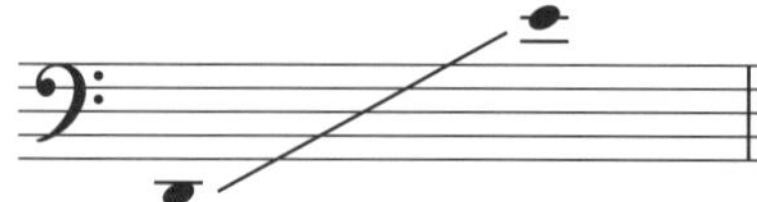

FIG. 2.7. Low Bass Range in Bass Clef

As you can see, clefs make the staff readable by a diversity of voices and instruments with various ranges. Today, the treble and bass clef are the most common clefs. There are others, though. Let's take a closer look at clefs, and how/why they are used.

Three pitches are commonly used as reference points in discussions about music and notation:

- A440. The note A at 440 Hz. Commonly used as a tuning note.
- Middle C. The central note of a piano keyboard. It is the C below A440. In treble clef, it is one ledger line below the staff. In bass clef, it is one ledger line above the staff.
- Great C. Two octaves below middle C.

FIG. 2.8. Specially Named Notes

Treble clef is the most common instance of the G clef symbol, which indicates that the note G is on the second to bottom line of the staff. It is the most common clef in contemporary usage. However, it is possible for the G clef to move around to different lines. For example, the French violin clef (rarely used today) indicates that the bottom line was for the note G. The indicating feature of the G clef is the end of its inside curly-cue, resting just below its target line for the note G. Figure 2.9 shows middle C on both the treble clef and the French violin clef. (French violin clef was used in France in the Baroque and early Classical eras, but today, it is considered obsolete.)

FIG. 2.9. Two G Clefs

You might notice that the French violin note yields the same note name (C) as would bass clef, though in a different octave. The names of lines and spaces are identical, though, for French violin clef and bass clef.

So, the G clef indicates the G line with its inside curly-cue. The F clef, such as the bass clef (figure 2.7), indicates the F line with its two dots. The third clef of this type is the C clef, which has two curves converging on a line that it designates as the note C. And of course, there's the tablature clef and percussion clef, and we'll look at those in a later lesson. You can see all the clef symbols in figure 2.14.

Depending on where these clefs are situated, they give specific names and orientations to the staff. Treble and bass clefs are in the widest use. Some clefs are still commonly used among a relatively small group of instruments, such as the alto clef, where the C clef is on the middle line. Violas nearly always use that, but pretty much nobody else touches it. Some clefs are used primarily in certain academic environments, particularly among conductors and composers, because it helps them sight-read scores with transposing instruments. And a few clefs aren't used at all in contemporary publishing.

Here's the note G and a C major triad on a treble clef staff. Treble clef is usually assumed to indicate the G above middle C, found a step below A at 440 Hz. However, some instruments (most notably tenor saxophone and guitar) actually sound an octave below that.

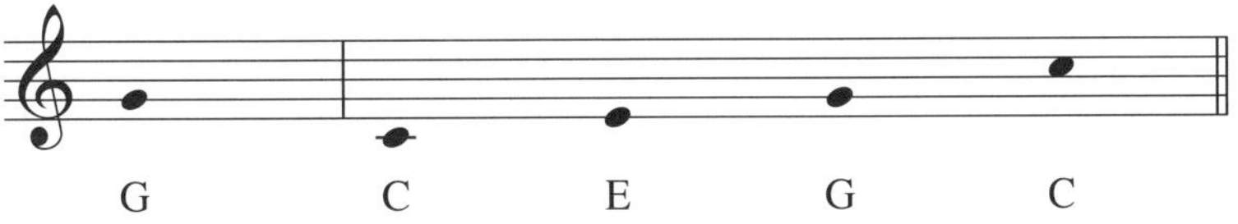

FIG. 2.10. Treble Clef and C Triad

The second most common clef is the bass clef, which is an orientation of the F clef symbol. The most common usage of F clef is the bass clef, with F set at the second to top line of the staff. Here are the same notes as in figure 2.10 but in bass clef. So, if you're Leonard Cohen, rather than Mariah Carey, you'd likely want to read bass clef. It's usually assumed that the indicated F is one fifth below middle C, though some instruments (such as double bass) may play the note that sounds an octave below.

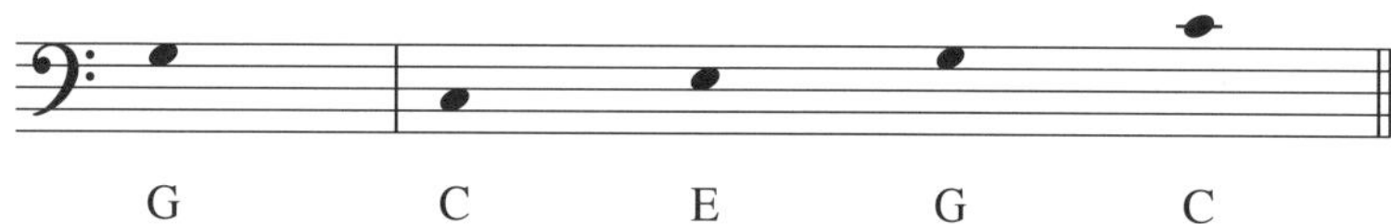

FIG. 2.11. Bass Clef and C Triad

Commonly, bass clef is used for lower-pitched instruments, such as bass singers, double bass, trombone, tuba, and so on. In addition to the notes being oriented on different staff lines, bass clef notes are generally set in a lower octave than are treble clef notes. Here are the exact pitches of the treble clef example in the bass clef, without that octave transposition. Lots of ledger lines! Leonard Cohen and I really don't want to read this!

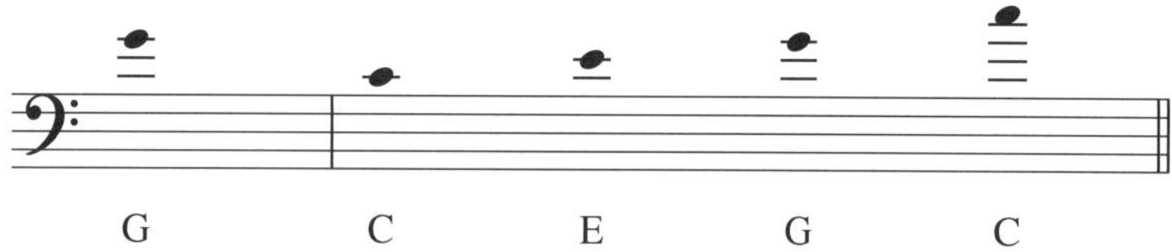

FIG. 2.12. Bass Clef with Exact Transposition of Figure 2.10

The C clef indicates which line is C by centering its two curves around it. It would seem the most logical clef, but for various reasons, it is less common today than it was in centuries past. Violas still read it, set on the middle line of the staff and called "alto clef" (sometimes, "viola clef"). Trombones, bassoons, cellos, and some others sometimes use a C clef too, but set on the second-to-top line where it is called "tenor clef."

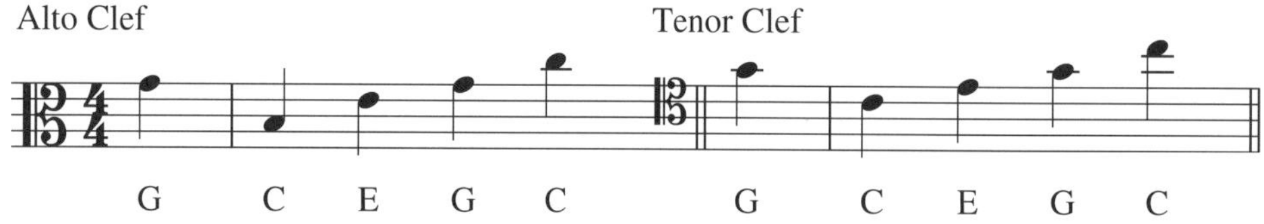

FIG. 2.13. C Clefs: Alto and Tenor

Here is a chart showing the various clefs, each with the note middle C. If you were to play this piece, it would be the exact same note, over and over. Notice that the numeral 8 changes the octave transposition of the clef; above the staff means it sounds higher than written, and below the staff means it sounds lower. You might also see a 15 in these positions, indicating a two-octave transposition.

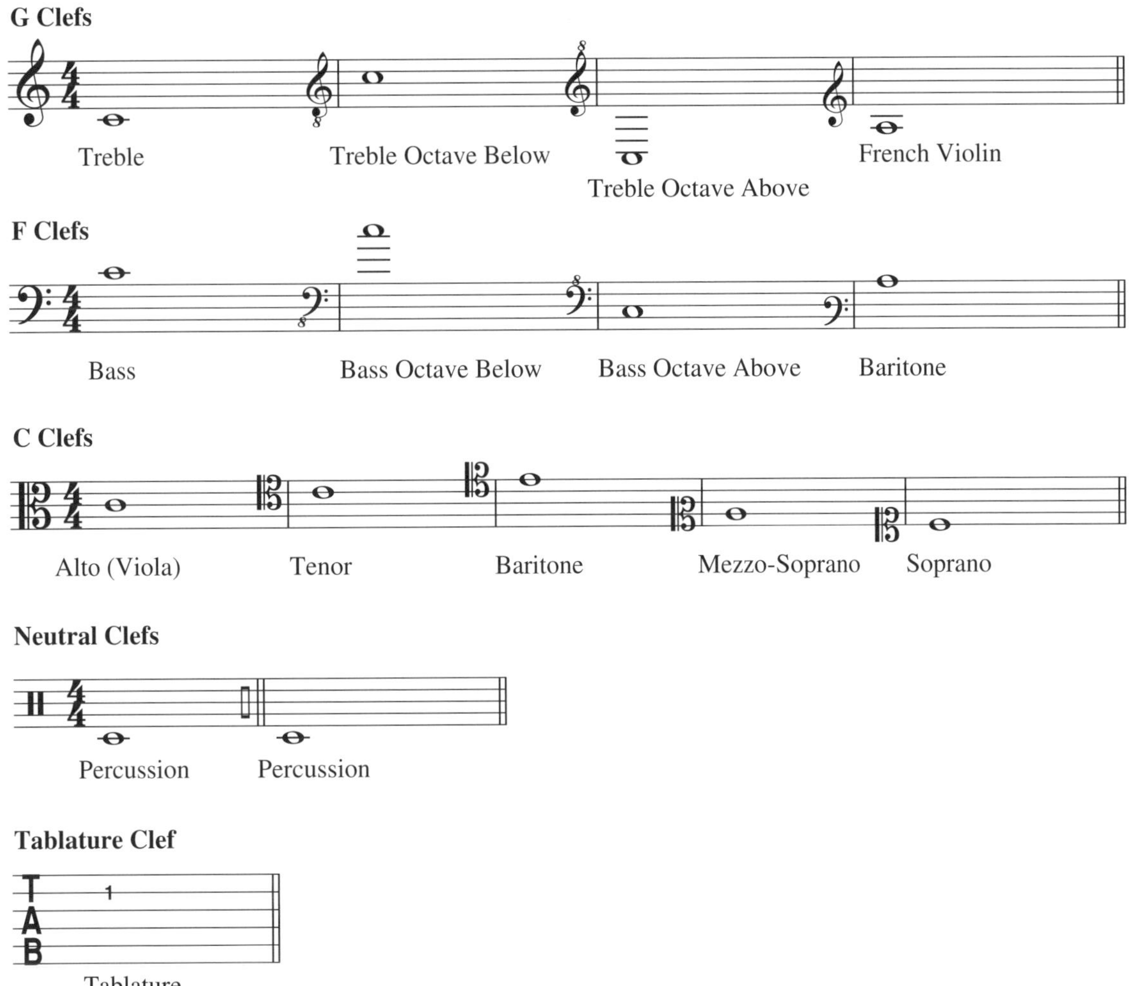

FIG. 2.14. Various Clefs and Middle C

In many music schools, students spend a great deal of time in their ear training classes becoming comfortable with various clefs. Facility reading clefs helps us to read ensemble scores—notation with multiple instruments shown all at once, often in different transpositions. Getting comfortable reading different clefs takes some practice, but the good news is that the omnipresence of the five-line staff makes the clefs all fairly analogous. You just need to change the orientation of what pitches are indicated by the different lines. Key to this is spotting how intervals relate to the staff. Adjacent lines and spaces are seconds, adjacent lines or spaces are thirds, skipping lines or spaces are fifths, and skipping two lines or spaces are sevenths. Once you drill these relationships and patterns into your memory, reading scores becomes much easier.

Instruments and Clefs

The clef or clefs associated with each instrument tends to stay consistent. Higher instruments (flute, female and high male voices, guitar) favor treble clef, while lower pitched instruments (trombone, bass male voices, bass guitar) favor bass clef. Piano, organ, vibraphone, harp, and some others use a "grand staff," which includes both treble and bass clefs, with the right hand usually playing high notes and reading treble clef, and the left hand usually playing low notes, reading the bass clef.

Here's a *grand staff*: a connected pair of treble and bass clef staves.

FIG. 2.15. Grand Staff

For some instruments, the clef may change within a staff to accommodate unusually high or low music.

- Viola generally reads alto clef, but may switch to treble clef for extended higher passages.
- Trombone and bassoon read bass clef, but might switch to tenor clef for extended higher passages.
- Piano reads a grand staff, but either staff might change to the clef of the other.

It's helpful to the reader to place clef changes at logical positions in the score, where they don't disrupt a musical pattern or idea. In this example of ascending arpeggios (figure 2.16), the clef changes occur at the beginning of a new triad, each time, rather than being placed to omit all possible ledger lines. This placement reinforces the concept behind the notation: practicing chords.

FIG. 2.16. Changing Clefs

OCTAVE TRANSPOSITION SYMBOLS

Clefs reduce the need for ledger lines, alleviating clutter and complexity, and generally make for an easier read. Some instruments, though, never switch clefs. Flute, for example, only reads treble clef. Its lowest note is usually a B below the middle C, so going to bass clef wouldn't help. Most flautists would loathe reading bass clef.

On the other hand, some flute parts are set way up high in the screechy stratosphere, presumably as an attempt to irritate dogs. Similarly, instruments such as the piano and organ have very wide ranges and are capable of playing notes far above and below the treble and bass clef staves, which are really the only two clefs typically read for these instruments.

The handy, traditional way to reduce ledger lines in this type of situation is to use the various octave transposition symbols. These should be set above or below the notes, depending on the direction of transposition. Now, there are some common shorthands for these, such as leaving off *va* and *vb*, or using *e* instead (e.g., 8e), and letting the placement indicate the direction of transposition, but using va, vb, etc., is clearest.

Symbol	Name	Meaning
8va	Ottava	Play an octave above
8vb	Ottava basso	Play an octave below
15ma	Double Ottava	Play two octaves above
15mb	Double Ottava basso	Play two octaves below

FIG. 2.17. Octave Transposition Symbols

A dashed line/bracket shows the notes to which these symbols apply. In the absence of a line, the word *loco* is a common alternative, but the bracket is generally clearest, with the hook pointing towards the staff.

These two measures sound exactly the same.

FIG. 2.18. Use of 8va and 8vb

Transposing Staves

Another way we avoid ledger lines is by having instruments transpose to a different octave or different key than where the notation normally sounds, and there are standard, universal transposition practices for all instruments.

Some instruments routinely read a treble or bass clef but play other notes, either in other octaves or other keys, than what are written. A common example is the guitar. Guitar reads treble clef, but the notes sound an octave below the typical orientation of the treble clef staff, with its A440 orientation on the second to top space. The guitar is therefore a "transposing instrument." (We'll look at this more closely when we discuss score layout.)

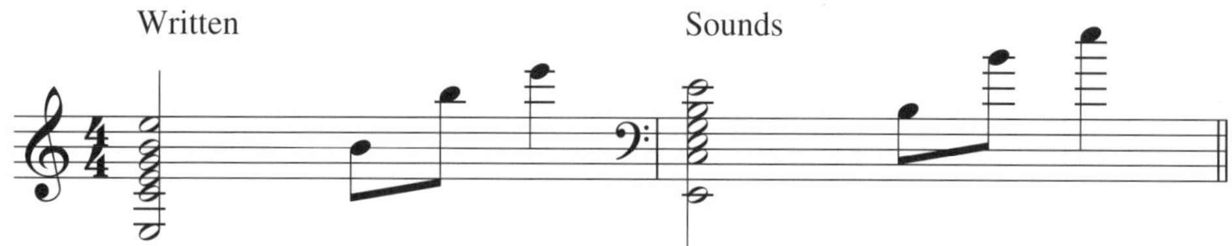

FIG. 2.19. Guitar Transposition

Some clefs have an 8 built into it, which indicates an octave transposition, and the 8 can be either on the top or on the bottom of the usual clef symbol. For example, the "treble octave" clef is used by tenor singers in choral music. What the tenors sing sounds an octave below where it is written on treble clef. Similarly, the piccolo reads a treble clef staff modified with an 8 on top to indicate that it sounds an octave higher than where it is written. The measures below sound the same (for each staff).

FIG. 2.20. Octave-Modified Treble Clefs

So, there are three basic ways that we have come to reduce the number of ledger lines: clefs, octave transposition symbols, and transposition.

ACCIDENTALS

A note can be modified by an *accidental*: a flat, sharp, double flat, or double sharp. These symbols raise or lower the pitch. (A natural symbol cancels the accidental.) Accidentals are necessary when a flat or sharp note is not specified by the key signature.

♭	Flat	Half step lower
♯	Sharp	Half step higher
𝄫	Double Flat	Whole step lower
𝄪	Double Sharp	Whole step higher
♮	Natural	Cancels the accidental for a note

FIG. 2.21. Accidentals

Accidentals are set to the left of the notehead, with the enclosed part of the accidental shape aligned on the line or space of that note (figure 2.22a). When multiple simultaneous notes have accidentals, the accidentals follow the same "uphill" direction as the noteheads; the higher note's accidental is closer to the notes, the lower note's accidental is set to the left. The exception is when the interval is spread wide enough (usually at a sixth or seventh, depending on the font) that the two accidentals can fit in a single column without touching (figure 2.22b).

On *clusters* (stacked seconds) with accidentals on notes of adjacent lines and spaces (figure 2.22c), the highest and lowest notes have the accidentals closest to them, and the inner voices' accidentals are set farther left, again in ascending pairs, left to right.

Even if there are two simultaneous voices, all the accidentals are set to the left of *all* the notes, following the same rules as for chords that are not split into multiple voices (figure 2.22d).

A note tied over a barline from a previous measure does not need to restate its accidental (2.22e). However, if the tie is across a page break, a second ending, or other potentially confusing circumstance, a courtesy accidental may be warranted on the tie's target note.

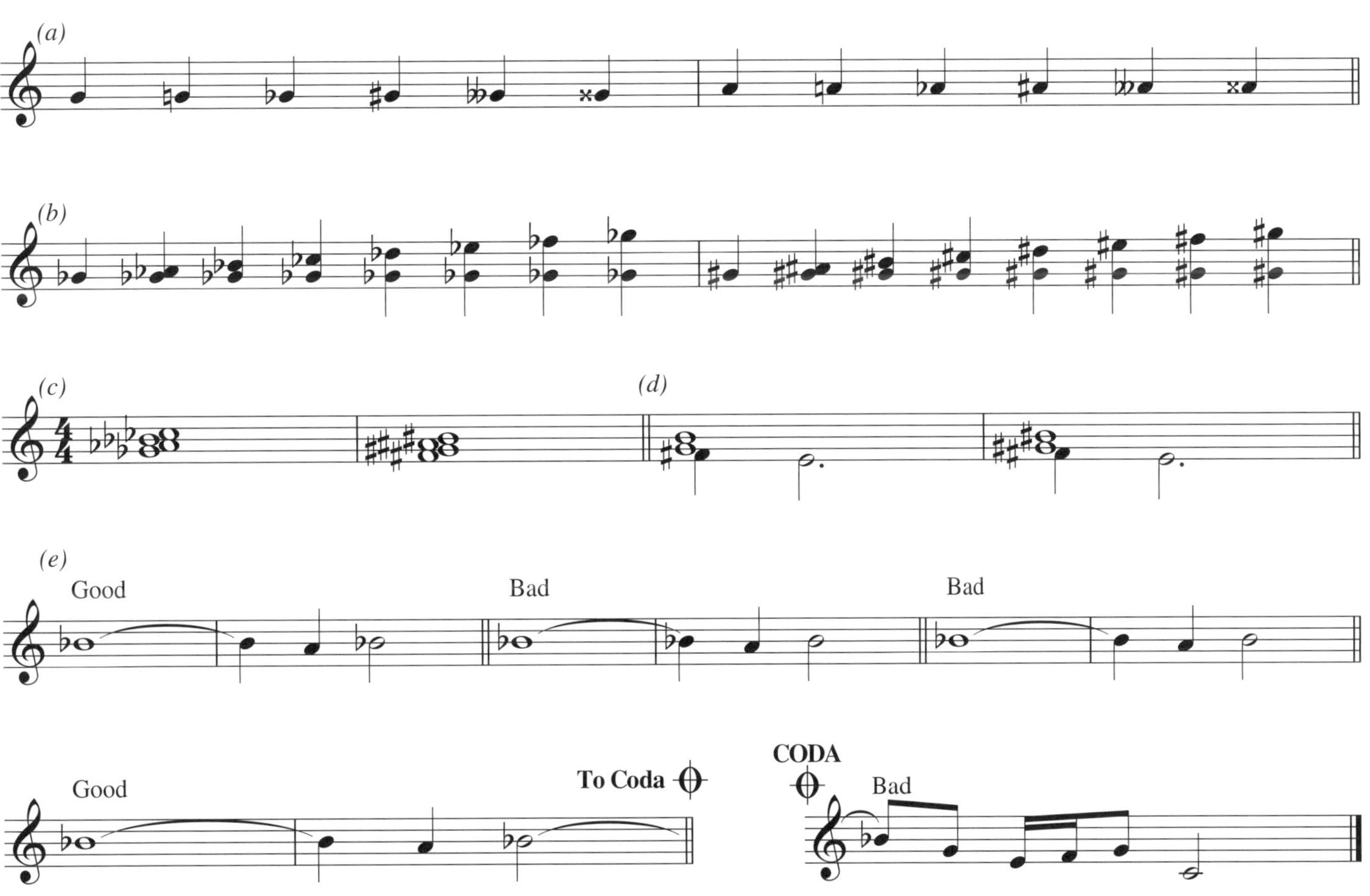

FIG. 2.22. Placing Accidentals

Enharmonics (different spelling of the same pitch) can help clarify musical intent. Altered notes are generally spelled in accordance with the key signature, chord, or melodic direction. As a very general and often-broken rule, a note in a sharp key is more likely to favor additional sharps, and flat key is more likely to favor flats.

Similarly, sharps are to be favored for ascending melodic lines and flats are favored for descending melodic lines. However, each note in a figure will have a distinct note name/staff position, and so these guidelines are often at odds with each other. Clarity of musical intent and conciseness of symbology should guide your decision, and there is often no perfect solution.

FIG. 2.23. Enharmonics

Ideally, a chord is spelled using only sharps or only flats. Sometimes, though, it is clearest and most logical to violate this rule. For example, if there's a recurring exchange between two notes a half step apart, the notation is far simpler if they are set as two different notes, rather than two different alterations of the same note. In figure 2.24, notice also that the melody is more intuitively rendered with the F♯ to A as a clear third, as opposed to a G♭ to an A. By spelling the note F♯, we can omit the natural on the whole note G, the natural on the second eighth note, the flat sixteenth note, and the natural on the half note.

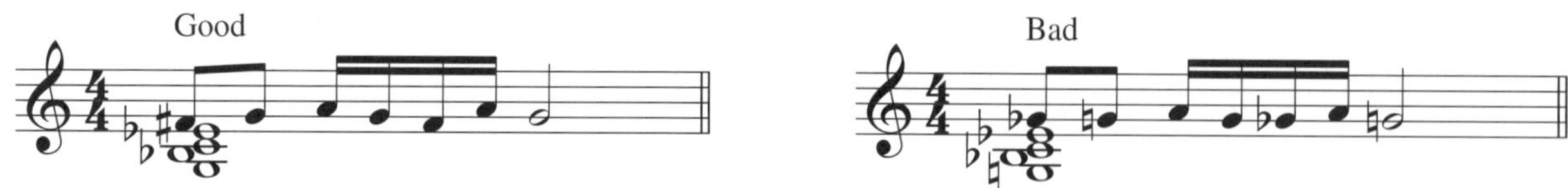

FIG. 2.24. Mixing Accidentals in Chords

MICROTONES

Microtones are notes at an interval of less than a half step above or below a given note. Notation isn't standard for these, and they are often notated only approximately, with lines to indicate pitch bends. However, there are some accidentals in common use for *quartertones*—microtonal pitches halfway to a regular sharp or flat.

Here are some of the accidental symbols in common use for quartertones. (And by in common use, I mean commonly used among the uncommon writers who use them.)

𝄳	¼ Tone Flat
𝄲	¼ Tone Sharp
◖	¾ Tone Flat
𝄰	¾ Tone Sharp

FIG. 2.25. Quartertone Symbols

Here are two descending quartertone series. The notes in each corresponding staff are enharmonics of each other, going from G to F.

FIG. 2.26. Quarter Tones

KEY SIGNATURES

A *key signature* is a set of sharps or flats at the beginning of the score that indicates the music's key—its tonal center, with the required sharps and flats used by the notes to fulfill the music's intended diatonic quality (major, minor, modes, etc.). A key signature is set between the clef and time signature. It appears on every system—unlike a time signature, which only appears once at the beginning of the score.

Unless otherwise marked, every note in the piece is played with that accidental. In this way, key signatures simplify the page by relieving the need to set accidentals on every note.

FIG. 2.27. Melody with and without a Key Signature

The "circle of fifths" is a common tool for organizing key signatures. Starting from the note C, we go a fifth (clockwise) or a fourth (counterclockwise), adding sharps or flats to the signature, respectively, yielding the indicated major keys and their relative minor keys.

Notice the placement of each additional flat or sharp. Flats are added in pairs; sharps have two, then three in a row, and then back to two. It is different for every clef. Just make sure you stay within the staff, rather than using ledger lines, and it will come out right.

Here is a quick way to translate key signatures into major scales.

- In sharp keys, the right-most sharp is a half step below the scale's tonic.

- In flat keys, the right-most flat is a fourth above the scale's tonic.

Minor-scale key signatures are based on a tonic a minor third lower than that key signature's related (i.e., "relative") major scale's tonic.

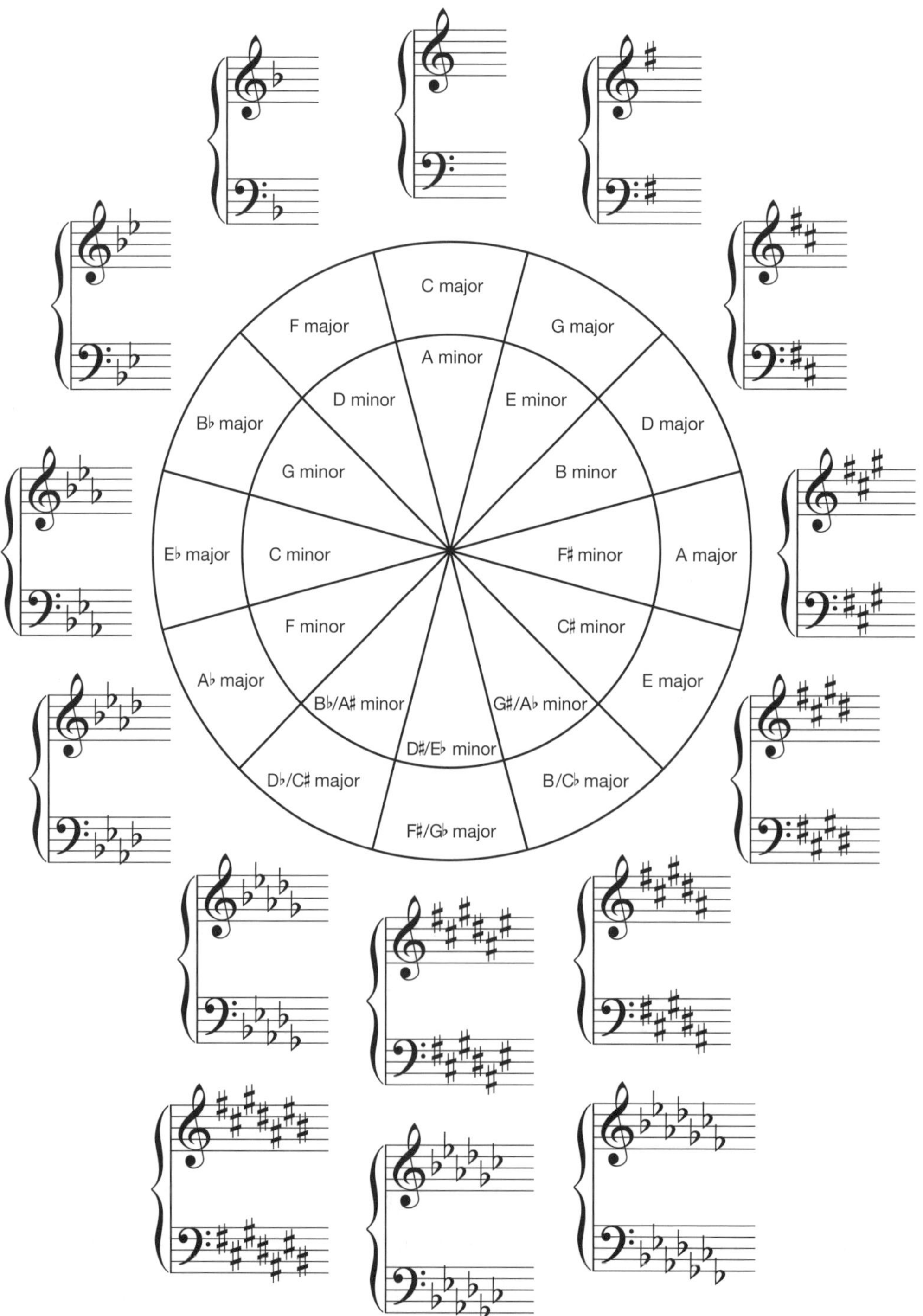

FIG. 2.28. Circle of Fifths with Key Signatures

Courtesy Accidentals

An accidental holds for only the measure in which it appears, and only for the octave shown.

Many publishers will clarify the musical intention by stating an accidental after that altered note, even if it is technically redundant to do so. This "courtesy accidental" is used both within a measure, or in the following measure of the altered note. They are sometimes set in parentheses. However, a more contemporary style is to omit the parentheses, so as to omit some clutter from the page.

The accidental only refers to the note in its own octave, not for all notes of the same scale degree in all octaves; it must be set on the octave too, if that's the intention. It is common, though, to add a "courtesy accidental" at the octave to clarify what is intended.

Once set, it holds for all remaining notes in that measure. Future measures return to the flavor of that note as dictated by the key signature.

FIG. 2.29. Using Accidentals

Another place where courtesy accidentals are used to clarify the indicated pitch is in the measure immediately following the one with the accidental. They are also sometimes used to clarify that an octave of an altered note is not affected (as in figure 2.29), or that a note does not adhere to what's indicated by a chord symbol (see chapter 4). Again, courtesy accidentals are sometimes set in parentheses (as in "Octave" in figure 2.30), though this is not a universal preference among all publishers.

FIG. 2.30. Courtesy Accidentals

Courtesy accidentals are a kindness to your reader, and their use is often subjective. They can be cluttering, though. It is sometimes worth considering whether using enharmonics instead is a better way to clarify the musical intention.

Often, the harmonic context and stylistic convention dictates how a note should be spelled, and thus, the best accidental approach. For example, few jazz composers would spell a half-diminished chord (minor 7♭5) as a sharp 4 rather than a flat 5, even if it did tidy the page or keep the chord consistent. It would be harmonically abhorrent to do that, and all the other cats would make fun of you. However, someone from the contemporary classical world whose priorities were more melodic than harmonic might write that ♯4 without hesitation or regret. So, cultural context is again an important consideration, here.

Modulation and Courtesy Key Signatures

If the music permanently modulates to a new key, it should probably change the key signature as well. Many publishers precede a new key signature with a double barline. When the key change begins on a new system, add a courtesy key signature change to the end of the previous system.

A practice that is growing obsolete is that if there are fewer sharps or flats in a new key signature, natural signs would cancel out the ones that are no longer in effect. This is fading, and most publishers are now just setting the new key signature. (Some are dropping the double barlines too.) However, if the new key is C major or A minor (no sharps or flats), use naturals to cancel out the old key.

If there is a courtesy key signature, the natural signs appear there only, not both there and in the new key signature.

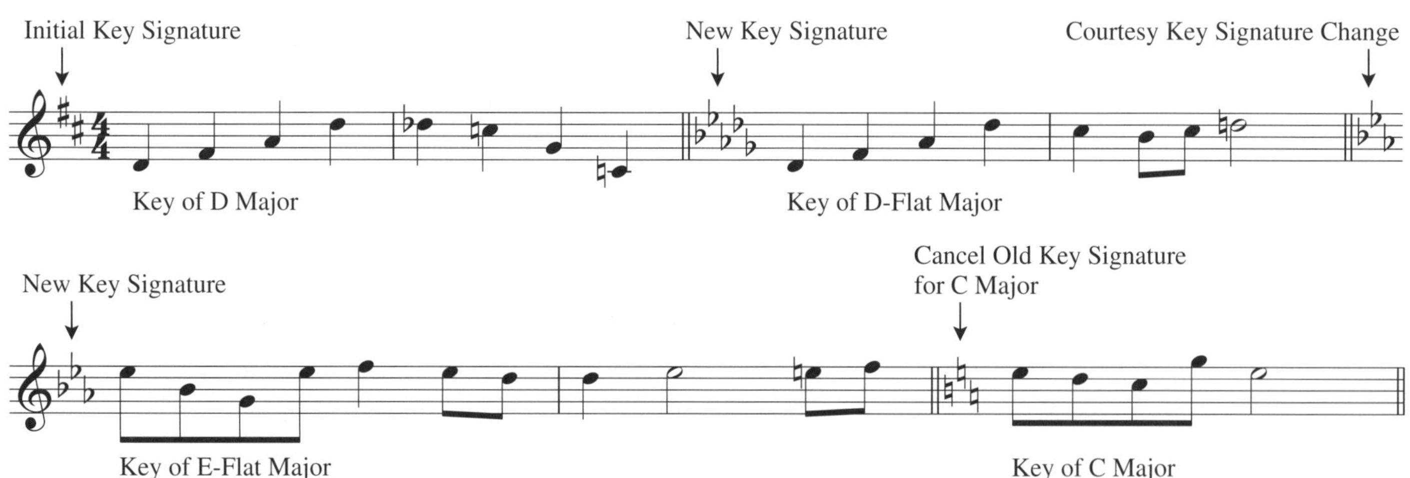

FIG. 2.31. Modulations and Courtesy Key Signatures

Modal Key Signatures

There are three accepted approaches to notating key signatures in modal music, such as for a tune set in F Dorian.

1. Use the "parent tonic" of the mode (figure 2.32a). For F Dorian, the parent is E♭ major, so the key signature would be three flats. There would be no need for future alterations.

2. Use the mode's parallel major as the key signature (b). For F Dorian, that would mean a key signature of one flat (like F major), and then every E and A in the tune would have a flat sign.
3. Omit the key signature (c). It would look like C major. Then, every B, E, and A in the tune would get a flat.

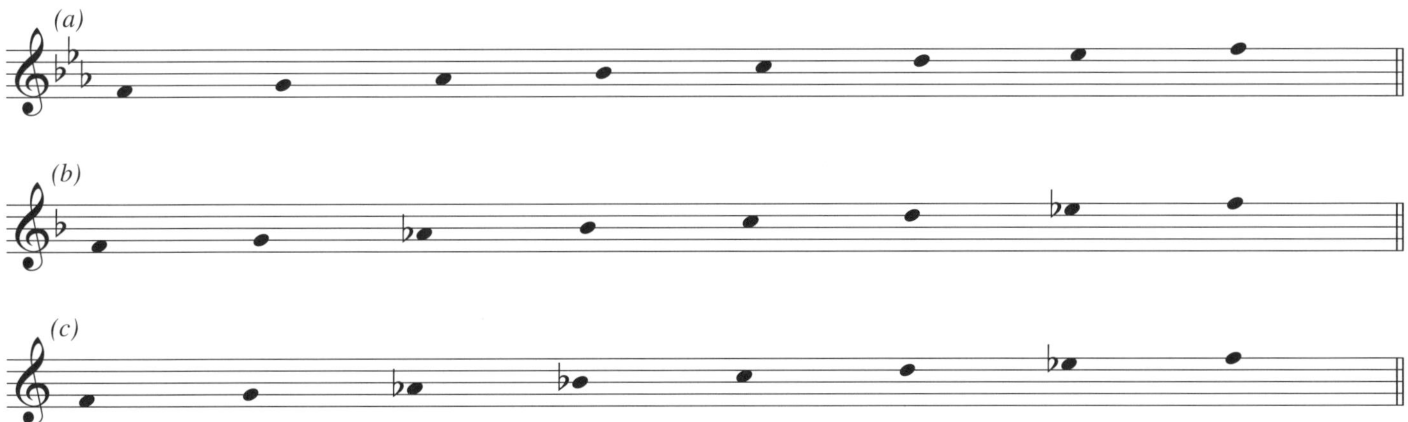

FIG. 2.32. Modes Three Ways

Atonal Notation

Atonal music generally avoids key signatures, as in the modal example figure 2.32c. Accidentals are shown on every note. While there may not be an assumption that the accidental holds throughout the bar, many publishers prefer to clarify the intent by using courtesy accidentals. As usual, sharps are generally favored for upward moving lines, and flats for downward examples.

PITCHES AND DURATIONS: STEMS, FLAGS, AND BEAMS

In chapter 1, we saw how note stems are used to represent different durations. You saw that a stem just touches the side of a notehead, blending into the edge of the oval without sticking out like a sharp elbow.

With the addition of pitch, we come to another consideration regarding the look of the stem: the stem's direction, i.e., whether it points up or down, and the side of the note where the stem connects.

- On notes on or *below* the middle staff line, the stem points up and touches the notehead on the right.
- On notes on or *above* the middle staff line, the stem points down and touches the notehead on the left.
- In beamed groups, the note the farthest away from the staff determines the overall stem direction of the group.
- On an upstem note, the flag curves outward.
- On a downstem note, the flag curves inward.

Notes on the middle line usually have downstems, but that stem might point up if it best suits a melodic line or phrase. Similarly, if a beamed group of notes has notes above or below, the stem direction decision is usually based on the first and last notes of the beam group (such as the triplet in bar 4 vs. bar 5 in figure 2.33).

FIG. 2.33. Stem and Flag Directions

Stem length is usually an octave (three and a half staff spaces) high. However, there are a few exceptions to this recommendation. In a beam group, the first and last notes are an octave high, but what happens between them can be pretty much anything, as long as nobody gets crushed. Beams can follow the melodic contour. That said, it is sometimes better to keep them horizontal and further away from the notes, in order to make every note within the group easily readable.

FIG. 2.34. Stem Length within Beamed Groups

When there are two notes on the same beat, sharing the same stem, the lower note goes on the left and the higher note goes on the right. However, if there are two independent voices on the staff, then the stems go in the middle. The higher voice's stems go up, and the lower voice's stems go down.

FIG. 2.35. Stems with Multiple Notes or Voices

We have now covered the standard rules and commonly accepted practices for writing melodies. You might notice that notation decisions often have to take into account competing rules of thumb. Multiple factors often have to be considered when determining the clearest way to render a musical idea, but most music readily adheres to the most common rules. We are fortunate to live in an age where notation software automatically makes many of these standard-practice decisions for us. It is important to review software-generated notation, however, as the default settings might not always be the best choice for the music at hand, particularly as trends and individual publishing house practices evolve.

CHAPTER 3

Meter, Measures, and Systems

In chapter 1, we discussed how most music is based on a regular pulse: a recurring division of time at a specific tempo. Some ambient soundscapes avoid the use of pulse, but most music has some sort of regular ticking or thump, which we generally call the "beat." Beats tend to be organized and felt in recurring groups, usually perceived in some multiple of two or three beats. In notation, these are described in a number of ways. A "triple feel," for example, can be written as an eighth-note triplet, a quarter-note triplet, or a measure of three, and tempos can be adjusted so that any of the notated options will sound the same. Or, "a sense of four" can mean beats within a measure or measures within a phrase.

As notation engravers, we have decisions to make regarding all these elements. In this chapter, we will look at the various tools for describing these musical constructs.

MEASURES

A *measure*, informally called a "bar," is a grouping of beats. It is framed by vertical barlines that connect the top to bottom staff lines, and also simultaneously sounding staves.

Single barlines frame a measure, and they are referenced as "left" and "right" barlines; the right barline of one measure can be called the left barline of the next measure.

The staff in figure 3.1 includes three measures.

FIG. 3.1. Three Measures

A *staff system* is the set of measures across a page. A system includes all staves for all instruments of the ensemble. Figure 3.1 shows just one system. Figure 3.2 shows examples of two systems, first for (a) a single-staff score and then for (b) a multiple-staff score.

FIG. 3.2. Two Systems. (a) Single-Staff Score. (b) Multiple-Staff Score.

A single-staff score (figure 3.2a) need not have a barline on the left of each system, particularly if every system begins with a clef and time signature. However, if the house style is to leave off the clef after the first system, include the left-hand system barline.

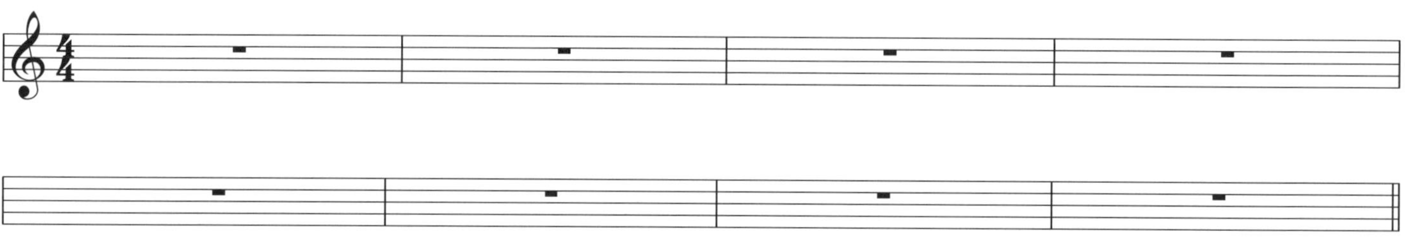

FIG. 3.3. Left Barline on Single-Staff Score with Hidden Clefs

Systems usually end with a complete measure, so there is usually a barline on the right.

A score with multiple staffs will have a left barline, showing the relationships of the staffs or instruments. The staffs within a system will be further organized with brackets and braces.

- A *bracket* connects instruments within the same family, sometimes nesting multiple brackets to show further groupings.

- A *brace* connects two staffs played by the same person (such as a pianist) or a temporary division of an instrumental section that would ordinarily read just one staff (e.g., the violin I section breaking into two subsections).

In a score with more than one staff, barlines can connect staves to show their relationships. For example, measures for a grand staff's treble and bass clef staffs are connected with barlines, as well as a brace on the left of each system. Similarly, in ensemble scores, instruments of a family are often grouped together via barlines connecting their staves, and brackets beginning each system.

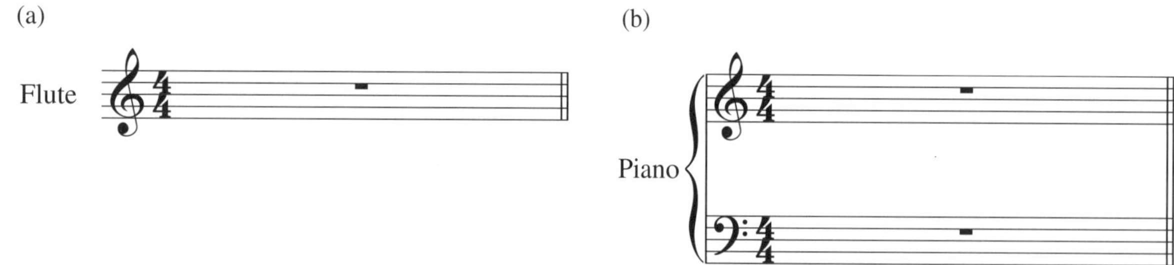

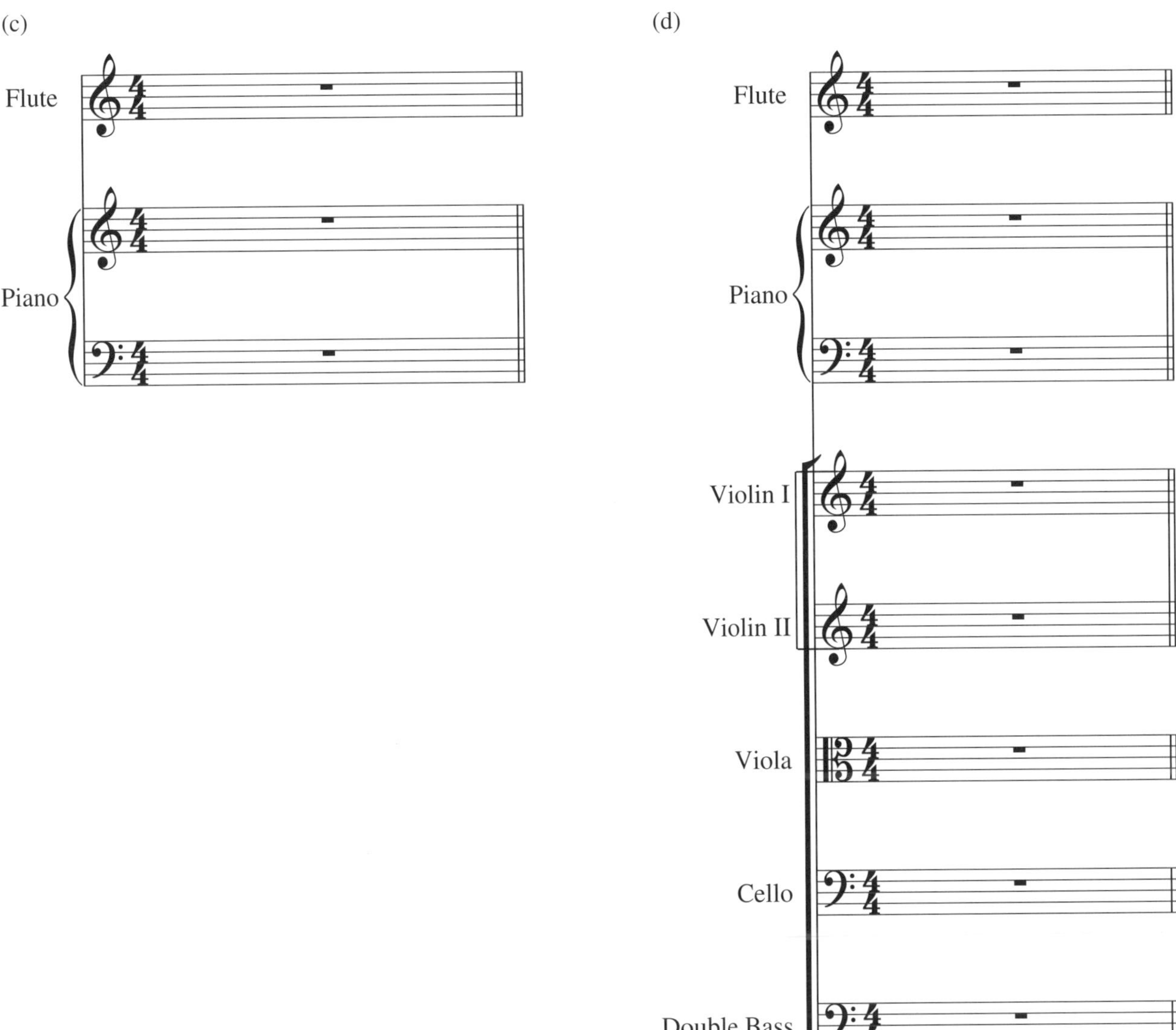

FIG. 3.4. Barlines with Multiple Staves. (a) Flute (b) Piano (c) Flute and Piano (d) Flute, Piano, and String Section.

In addition to simple barlines, which consist of a single "thin" line, other barline configurations are used for various purposes. Here are some common barlines. In figure 3.5, the following barlines are used.

a. Single barline (one thin). Separates measures normally.
b. Double barlines (two thins). Separate formal sections, such as a verse and chorus. They are also sometimes used in writing about music to indicate the end of a short illustration or an example that is not the end of a piece. Sometimes they are used to separate a pickup measure from measure 1.
c. Broken barline (single dashed line). End of a partial measure or an imaginary barline within complex meters.
d. Final barline (thin/thick). End of a piece.
e. No barline. Shows a partial measure.

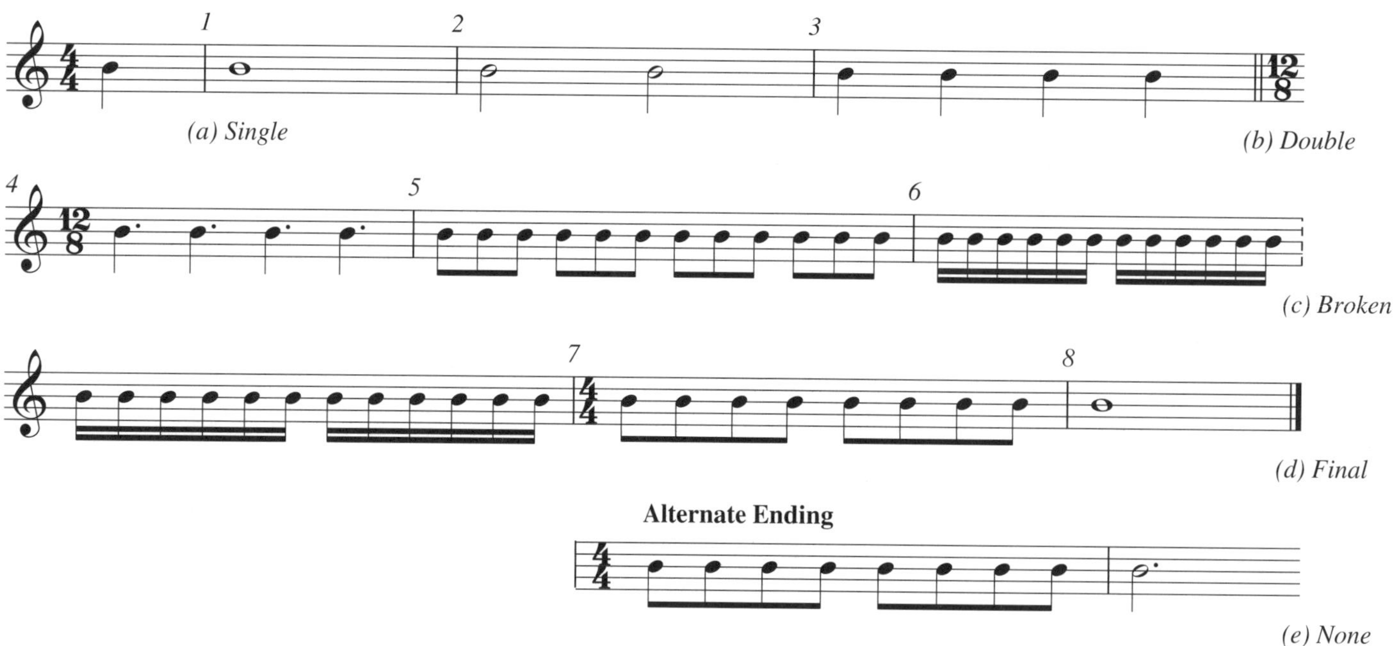

FIG. 3.5. Types of Barlines

A system may end with a partial measure, such as figure 3.5e. Particularly in lead sheets and hymn music, where it's common to repeat the whole form, the page might end with a partial measure at the bottom. This means repeat from the top, taking any pickup beats into account. If it's vocal music, sing the next verse.

Rarely, a complex measure might be divided across a system break (see figure 3.5c), the first part ending with a broken barline. This is generally to be avoided, but sometimes necessary.

System dividers (⫽) separate multiple systems on a page. They are only necessary for large ensembles, such as orchestras or concert bands.

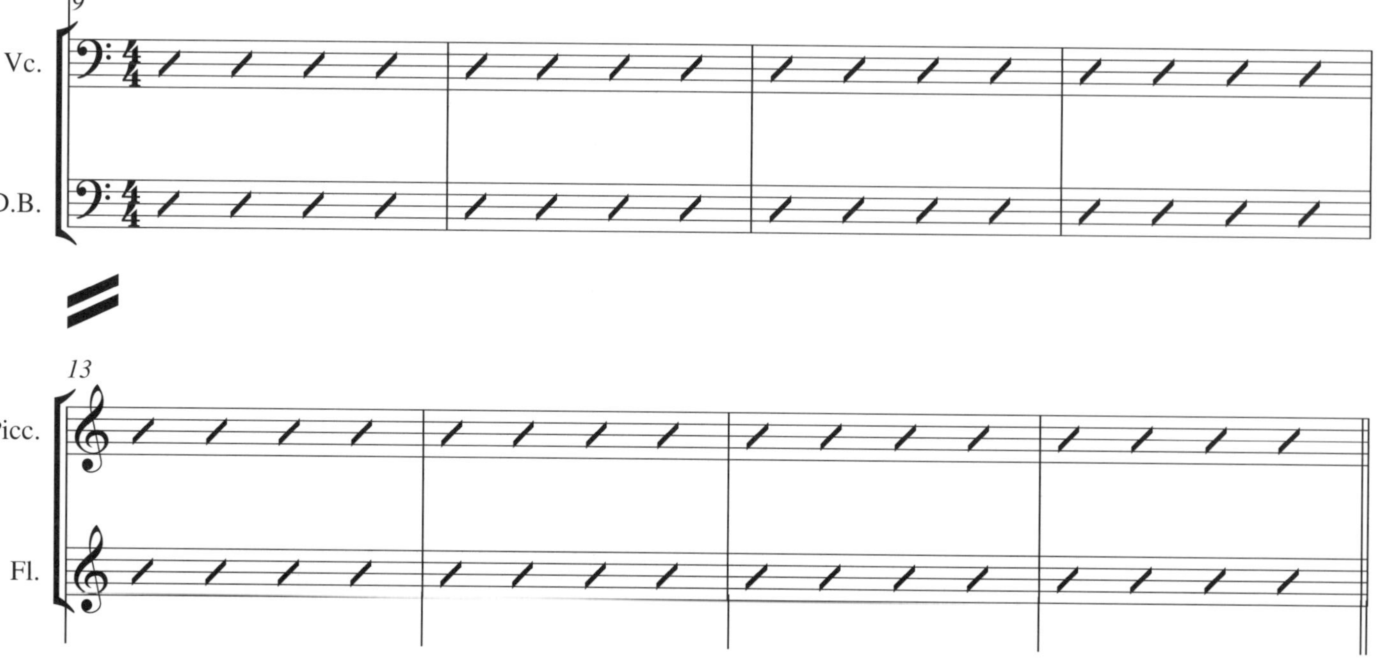

FIG. 3.6. System Divider

TIME SIGNATURES

A time signature indicates the music's meter: how the beats are grouped, and what note duration gets the beat. To clarify terms, a "time signature" is a notation element. A "meter" is a musical effect, as indicated by a time signature.

The top number (numerator) of a time signature indicates how many beats are in a measure. This can be any positive whole number, but 1 to 12 are the most common, and 4 is the most common of all.

The bottom number (denominator) indicates which note duration value gets one beat. These may be 1 (whole note), 2 (half note), 4 (quarter note), 8 (eighth note), 16 (sixteenth note), and rarely any higher exponent of 2. Again, 4 is the most common; usually, the quarter note gets the beat. Most music is written in 4/4 time. In this example, each measure is filled with note durations as simply and as idiomatically as possible.

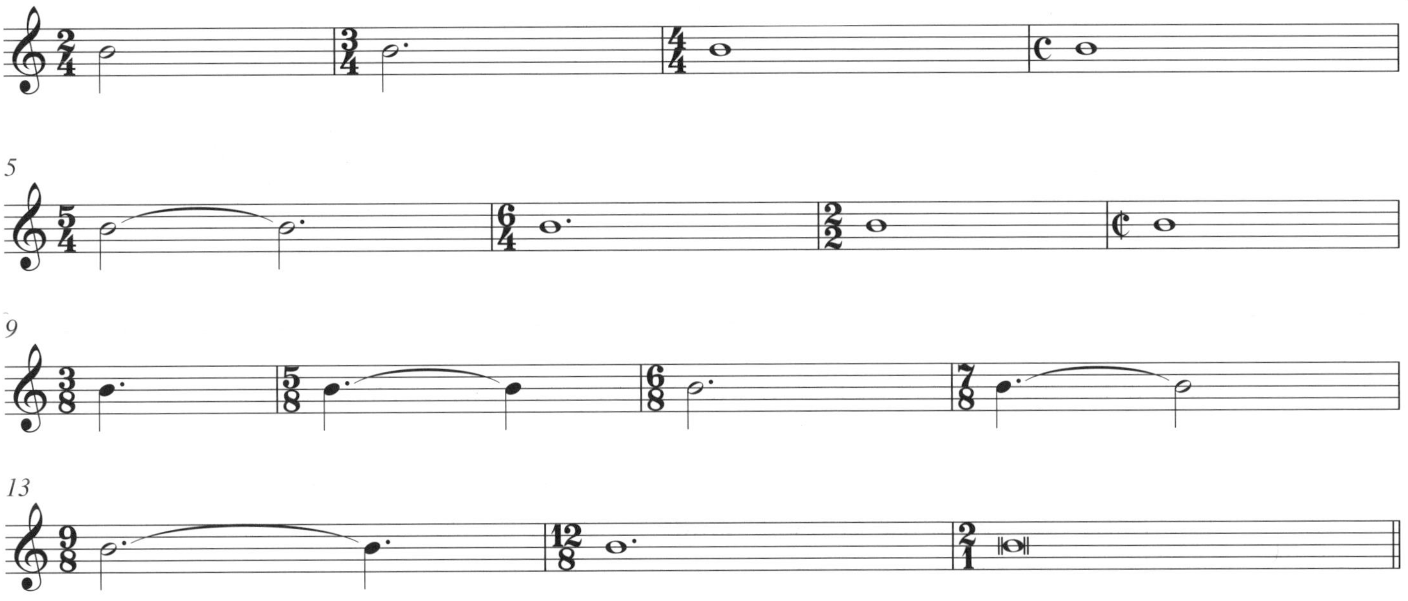

FIG. 3.7. Time Signatures

Measures without any notes have a whole rest, whatever their time signature. So, the whole rest symbol has two different meanings: a rhythmic value that relates to other note durations, and a "whole measure rest" symbol.

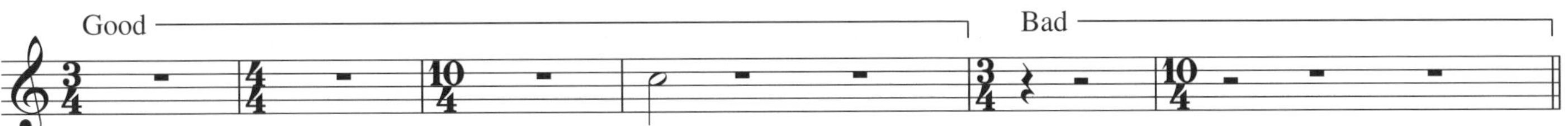

FIG. 3.8. Whole Rest

Time signatures are set to the right of the clef and key signature at the beginning of the piece. A given time signature stays in effect until a new time signature is indicated. Time signatures are not restated after the first system. Every staff has the same time signature (except in rare cases of multiple concurrent meters).

When a time signature changes on a new system, a *courtesy time signature* is set at the end of the preceding system, with a left barline before it. (If the meter change coincides with a new formal section, this should be a double barline.) If the time signature changes mid system, no courtesy time signature should appear. (Note: Figure 3.7 was deliberately written without courtesy time signatures, as it is a theoretical example, rather than music to be performed.)

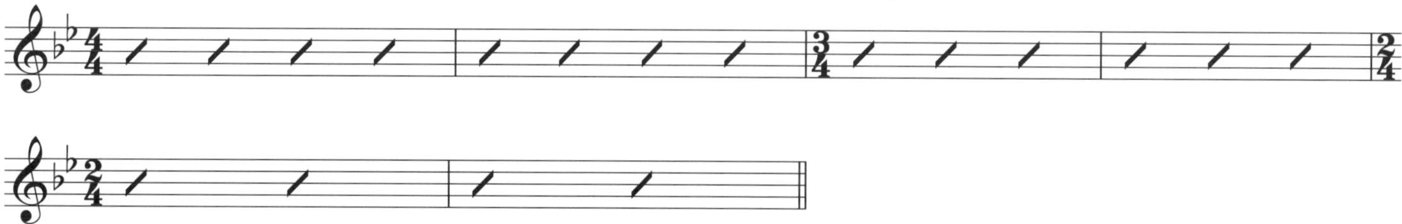

FIG. 3.9. Changing Time Signatures

Time signatures reference musical effects, and which one to select can be a subjective call. Here are three different ways we might notate "Amazing Grace." The differences in how each will sound and feel are subtle, and you could make a good argument for any of the creative options. The choice often comes down to what makes for the clearest page.

FIG. 3.10. "Amazing Grace" Three Ways

How to choose a time signature? The most common meters are 3/4 and 4/4, and the easiest note values to read are whole notes through sixteenth notes. There's something a little frenetic about sixteenth notes, so I'd go with the first rendering in figure 3.10. It's the most laid-back. But the other two aren't bad or incorrect.

Composite Time Signature

A *composite time signature* features multiple numbers in the numerator, separated by a + symbol. This further clarifies how the beats are subdivided. Composite time signatures are generally only used for odd meters—by which we mean uncommon meters that are odd numbers such as 7/8, 11/8, and so on, but excluding 3/4 and 3/8, which are mathematically "odd" but commonly used. In figure 3.11, the composite time signatures show how the seven beats are grouped. It is arguably redundant with the other notation elements that inform how the music is to be felt, but sometimes a helpful practice, particularly in relatively complex contemporary "classical" music, or some folk traditions, or to indicate changes in how a meter is to be felt.

FIG. 3.11. Composite Time Signatures

MEASURE LAYOUT ON A SYSTEM/PAGE

The number of measures set in a system affects the legibility of the score and can clarify the form. A common rule of thumb is that a system should have four measures so that it follows the common four-bar structure, but this is often impractical. Some of the issues that should inform the decision:

1. The density of the music. If each measure has dense activity, with sixteenth notes and smaller, chord symbols, lyrics, and so on, fewer measures per system will help avoid collisions and let you keep the relative proportional spacing consistent. Similarly, if the density is very light, such as only whole notes, a greater number of measures per system might better support the music's legibility.
2. Phrases. Keeping a phrase intact on a system can make it easier to read, particularly if there are slurs or hairpins that would otherwise break across a system.
3. Form. Begin a new section on a new system, if you can.
4. Page turns. Page turns are disruptive, and the measure layout can be helpful by setting the last measure of a page as one that is relatively simple to play, perhaps with a rest in it, or playable by one hand. A related point: a good way to alleviate page turns is to have fewer pages. Measure layout can help omit the need for extra pages, and some greater density of notation can be a good trade to reduce the page count.
5. Orphan measures. Avoid having systems (and especially pages) with just a single measure in them—particularly, those common last measures that contain just a single whole note. Instead, bring that "goose egg" up to the previous system.
6. Consistency of note spacing. Keep a roughly similar number of bars between systems, so as to promote a general consistency of note durations as related to horizontal spacing throughout the score. Notes of longer values should command relatively more horizontal space, and this amount of space is ideally reasonably consistent throughout the score. This helps make the score intuitive to read.

While the "rule" is frequently broken, setting four bars per system does often help clarify the musical content. A twelve-bar blues, for example, is much more intuitive to read if it is three systems of four measures, as opposed to four systems of three measures. In the first 4-4-4 rendering, it is easy to see the three harmonic phrases. In the 3-3-3-3 version, these patterns are disrupted, which will make the notation more difficult to understand.

FIG. 3.12. Twelve-Bar Blues

Supporting the song form is indeed an important consideration. It is not, however, the only one. Consider the "four bars per system" rule of thumb more of an "ideal if you can manage it" rather than a true "rule."

PICKUP MEASURES

A *pickup measure* is a partial measure at the very beginning of a piece of music, leading into measure 1. It does not have a measure number. Some publishers set a double barline between the pickup measure and measure 1. If a pickup measure begins off a beat, many publishers include rests for just that beat. These examples are all "correct," with variations common across publishing house styles.

FIG. 3.13. Pickup Measures. (a) Pickup on the Beat (b) Pickup off a Beat (c) Pickup off a Beat with Rest (d) Pickup with Double Barline.

On lead sheets, chord symbols are generally set at bar 1, not above the pickup measure, which could well belong to a different harmonic region.

FIG. 3.14. Chord Symbols and Pickup Measures

MEASURE NUMBERS

Measure numbers are great clarifiers during rehearsals and recording sessions. They are also useful for analysis and generally help musicians understand the form and keep their place. Here are some common contemporary conventions, but there are many variations.

1. Set them above the top staff of a score at the beginning of each system. Most scores don't need a number in every measure, but film scores and other high-intensity recording session scores do.
2. Omit the measure number for the first bar and for wherever there is a rehearsal letter, number, or similar symbol.
3. The pickup measure does not get a measure; it precedes measure 1.

If a section is repeated with multiple endings, the measure following it may either proceed sequentially, or it could take the sum of the repeated measures and start there. So, in the AAB form in figure 3.15, the second system might either start at measure 5 or 9, depending on what seems clearest.

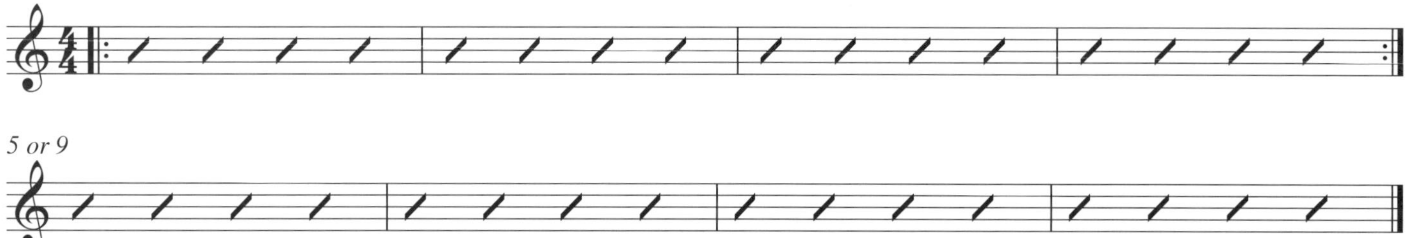

FIG. 3.15. AAB with Measure Number Options

4. In orchestra, wind ensemble, or other large ensemble scores, the top staff of each instrument family (woodwinds, brass, strings, percussion, rhythm section) gets a measure number. A common malpractice is to post numbers on every staff, but this is redundant and clutters the page. Notice that the bass clef staff in figure 3.16 doesn't have measure numbers.

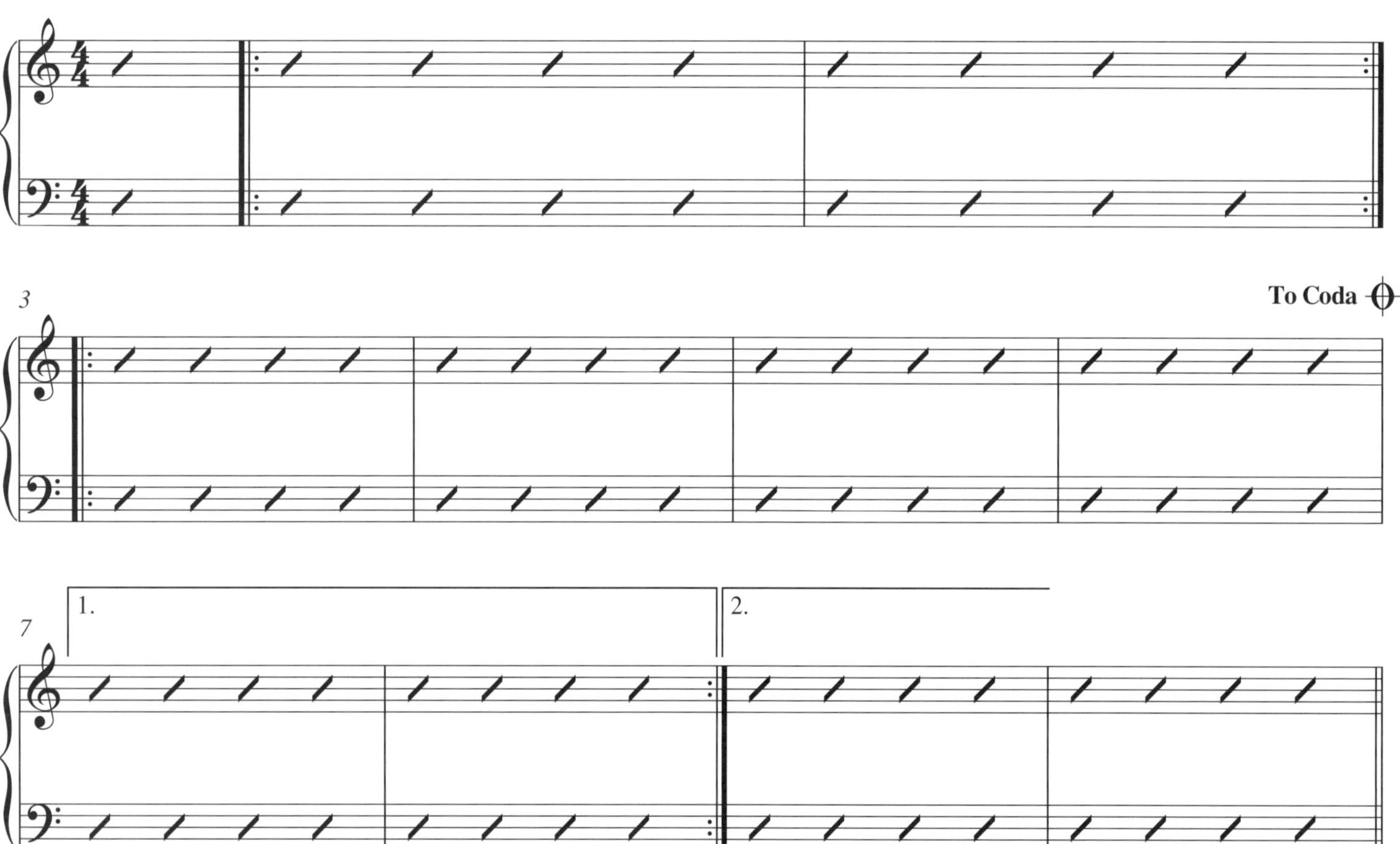

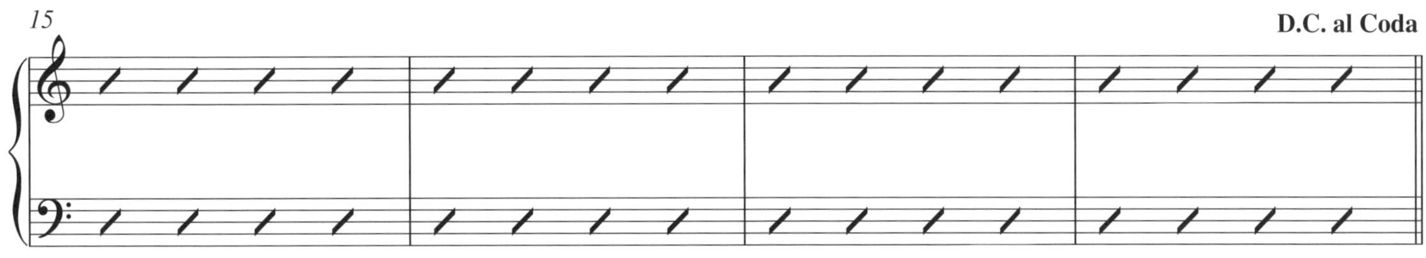

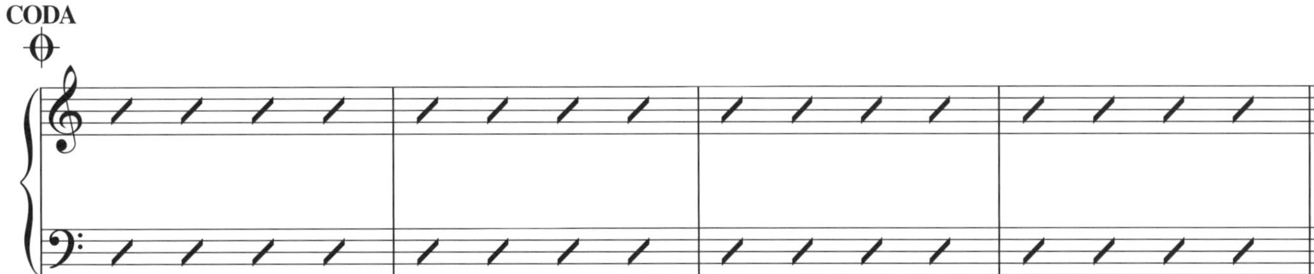

FIG. 3.16. Measure Numbers

Film scores and other scores intended for recording often feature measure numbers on every bar. In Hollywood, they are often enclosed in boxes and set below the bottom staff of the system, centered, rather than above the top staff.

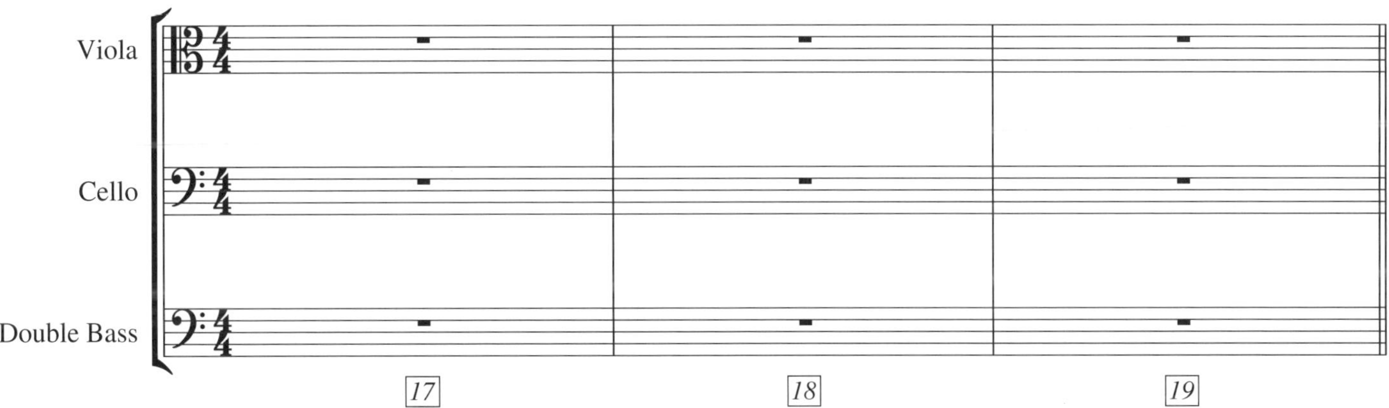

FIG. 3.17. Film Score Measure Numbers

Drum parts also sometimes number every bar, particularly for long, repetitive sections.

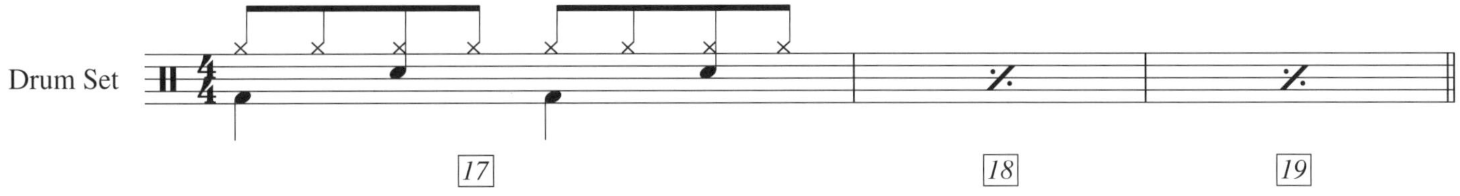

FIG. 3.18. Drum Set Measure Numbers

Measure numbers are sometimes used to indicate sections of a score. Those may be set larger than the other measure numbers and enclosed in a square. They might appear as form markers or periodically, say every eight bars.

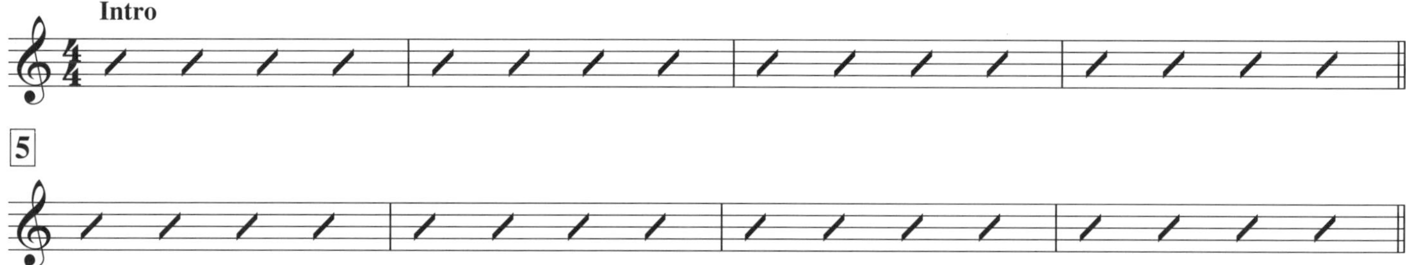

FIG. 3.19. Measure Numbers as Section Beginning

Extended sections of identical measures that are marked with slash notation or measure repeat symbols sometimes have "bar count" numbers in addition to measure numbers to help the player keep their place in the form. They are often numbered every four measures, centered over the measure, and in parentheses, to distinguish them from measure numbers.

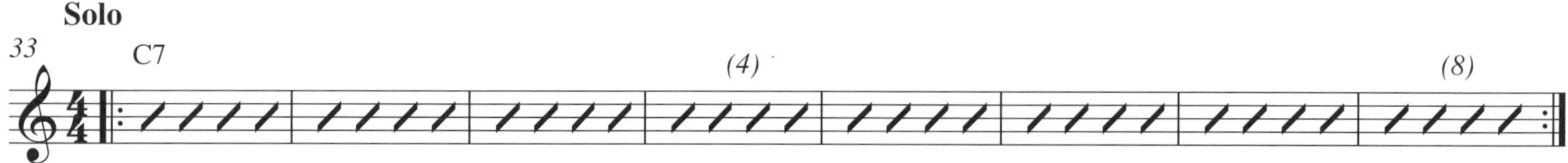

FIG. 3.20. Bar Count Numbers

The symbols and practices discussed in this chapter can greatly increase the readability of a score. Musical form and phrasing—and thus, the dramatic narrative of the music itself—are clarified by a thoughtful setup of measures per system.

Judicious use of double barlines further clarifies formal musical sections, whether they are intro/verse/chorus combinations, or exposition/development/recapitulation. In pedagogical materials, these sections are sometimes explicitly labeled with the names of the types of formal sections, such as "Verse" or "Exposition," or analysis letters for A sections, B sections, and so on. Commercial scores aimed at professionals typically don't have such explicit labeling, and instead rely on double barlines, rehearsal letters/numbers, and/or style or tempo markings.

Start new sections on new systems whenever possible, and organize measures per system so that the musical integrity is preserved and the score layout looks balanced and deliberate.

CHAPTER 4

Lead Sheets

Lead sheet notation consists of just the melody ("lead line") and chord symbols, in its purest form. Here are a few bars from a lead sheet to a tune I wrote, "No Time."

FIG. 4.1. Lead Sheet Notation

Whereas the notation paradigm for classical music is to specify every note so that musicians perform the composer's explicit intent, in jazz and other rhythm section–based forms of music that use lead sheets, it's more common for players to develop their own unique parts for the tune. What they play will be based on the melody and harmony, as well as the musical genre, the traditional roles that instruments play, the primary artist's current creative intention, and various other criteria. The lead sheet provides "just enough" information for everyone to be on the same page, literally, so that they can develop a unique interpretation of the tune as a band.

Everyone in the band might work from the same lead sheet. The sax player will play the melody (or improvise based on the chord symbols), the keyboard player will play chords developed from the chord symbols, the drummer will play a beat, and the bass player will create a bass line that focuses mostly on chord roots and fifths, with some added notes in between. In some situations, transposed lead sheets are provided to different instruments, but more commonly, everyone receives the same "concert" lead sheet.

There are many style variations in lead sheets, in terms of what information is included. Besides this "pure form" of the lead sheet, you might see lead sheets with lyrics, guitar diagrams, written chords, transpositions to different keys (for transposing instruments), or cue notation (or "kicks over time") in the margins. There are many shortcuts and special conventions.

CHORD SYMBOLS

The defining component of a lead sheet is its chord symbols. A chord symbol describes the current harmonic region, like a key signature, and it stays in effect until the next chord symbol—until the chord symbol "changes," hence the terms "chord changes" or just "changes" as hip synonyms for "lead sheet." Chord symbols are set above the staff, centered over the beat where they take effect.

There are two approaches to locating chord symbols, rhythmically:

1. At the start of a new harmonic region.
2. Coinciding with a specific note's attack, particularly on an anticipation.

Most authors at Berklee Press prefer to set them to define the harmonic region. Remember, the whole band will interpret the same lead sheet. Usually, anticipations are only played by some instruments, not everyone, so it is more universally applicable to set the chord symbols in this more general way.

FIG. 4.2. Harmonic Region vs. Note Attack

A chord symbol consists of up to five parts:

1. The chord root is indicated by a letter for the note name. The other information provided is in (usually) diatonic relationship to the given note.
2. The triad quality other than major is indicated with a suffix: minor (mi, min, –), augmented (aug, +), or diminished (dim, °). Major triads do not have suffixes indicating their quality; it is understood.
3. Whether there is a 6 or 7. The 6 and 7 are considered basic chord tones, rather than tensions (extensions). A major 7 chord will have a suffix, such as Maj7 or Ma7. This is an example of a logical incongruity with chord symbol notation; the quality suffix in this case refers to the 7, not the 3, as it does in all other cases. Without the "Maj," the 7 is a ♭7, not a diatonic 7.
4. Chord tensions 9, 11, and 13. At Berklee, we set tensions in parentheses. Usually. There is also the common shortcut to leave out the 7 and just use the tensions, such as C9 and C13.
5. More advanced structural information, such as specific bass notes, polychords, or upper-structure triads.

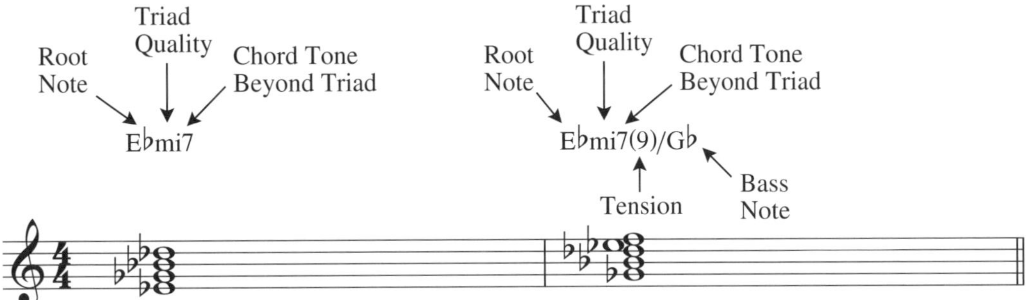

FIG. 4.3. Parts of a Chord Symbol

The style standards with which these elements are rendered are not universal. There are many abbreviations and practices for chord symbol suffixes. Consider, for example, a C minor 7 flat 5 chord (often called "half-diminished" by classical theorists), which consists of the notes C, E♭, G♭, B♭. At Berklee, we are likely to abbreviate this Cmi7♭5 or C–7♭5, but not Cmi7(♭5). This is because we use parentheses to indicate tensions and the ♭5 is considered a chord tone. But some cultures or publishers will use parentheses to mean "logically separate," and they would cheerfully use Cmi7(♭5).

There are also often multiple ways to indicate the same chord. A pop writer might unapologetically write a sus2 chord, from which a jazz artist might recoil and insist that it is more properly spelled as a 9. Some writers prefer ♯5; others lean towards calling that triad "augmented."

Figure 4.4 indicates the most common abbreviations. There are some others out there. Some, I recommend not using, such as lowercase m and uppercase M for minor and major—which you will certainly see published. My personal beef with m and M is that in some fonts, the characters look the same, except that the sizes are different, and this leads to confusion, particularly because in my work, we trade files a lot, and fonts are frequently changed. Similarly, the 7 to indicate "major" is one to avoid, in part because it is so much at the mercy of the font used to render it.

Quality	Abbreviations	Examples	Notes for C Root (Bottom to Top)
Major	(none, triad only) Ma, Maj, M, Δ	C CMa7	C E G C E G B
Minor	mi, min, m, –	Cmi or C–	C E♭ G
Suspended 2	sus2	Csus2	C D G
Suspended 4	sus4, sus	Csus4	C F G
Diminished	dim, °	Cdim	C E♭ G♭
Augmented	aug, +	Caug	C E G♯
Five	5	C5	C G
Sixth	6	C6 C–6	C E G A C E♭ G A
Seventh	7	CMaj7 C7 C7♭5 Caug7 C–7 C–(Maj7) Cdim7 Cdim(Maj7) C7sus4	C E G B C E G B♭ C E G♭ B♭ C E G♯ B♭ C E♭ G B♭ C E♭ G B C E♭ G♭ B♭♭ C E♭ G♭ B C F G B♭
Half Diminished	mi7♭5, –7♭5, ø	C–7♭5	C E♭ G♭ B♭
Tensions	♭9, 9, ♯9, 10, 11, ♯11, ♭13, 13 Note: A + can be used in place of a ♯ for raised tensions.	Note: Usage is subject to context. Not all tensions are available on all chords. C7(9,♯11,13)	C E G B♭ D F♯ A
Altered	alt, (alt)	C7(alt)	Use tension substitutions per personal preference: D E A B♭, D♭ E A♭ B♭, D♭ E G♭ B♭, etc.
Chord with Designated Bass Note	/	C/D	D C E G
Chord with Upper-Structure Triad	___	B♭ C7	C E G B♭ D F
Polychord	/	C7/D7	D F♯ A C E G B♭
No chord	N/C	N/C	Melody without harmonic context.

FIG. 4.4. Chord Symbol Abbreviations

A few items of note:

- If an accidental follows the root's letter name, it applies to the root, not to the tones after it. So, an A♭7 chord includes the notes A♭C E♭G♭, rather than A C♯ E G (or A C♯E G♭).
- The number 7 is understood to mean a dominant 7 (♭7), not a diatonic 7. C7 means C E G **B♭**, not C E G B-natural. For major 7, use Maj7 or Ma7.
- The suffix "sus" means substitute either the 4 or 2 for the 3. It goes after a 7, if present. If neither the 4 or 2 is specified, it is assumed to be a sus4. C7sus4 and C7sus are both C F G B♭.
- N/C means that there is no harmonic context at work, such as for an atonal or purely percussive section.
- Alterations to the 3 or 5 go after the 7: C7sus4, C7no3, Cmi7♭5, C7♯5

Chord symbols stay in effect until the chord changes. They should not be repeated every measure. Some writers add a chord symbol repeat sign to clarify that a chord symbol repeats on subsequent measures, but most feel that this adds unecessary clutter to the score.

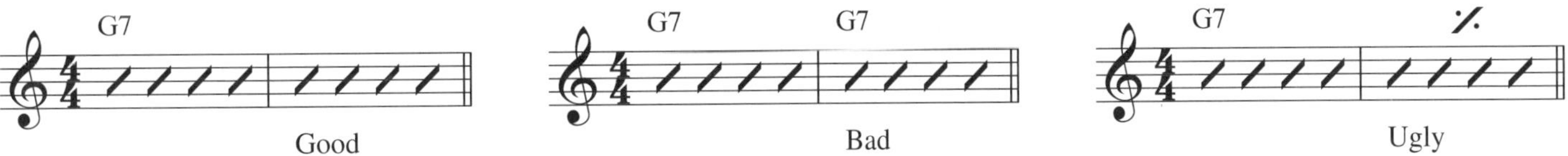

FIG. 4.5. Indicating Continuing Harmonic Regions

The chord symbol should be restated, though, at the beginning of a new section or on the top of a new page. When the harmonic region crosses a page break, parentheses help clarify that this is a courtesy symbol, rather than a new chord.

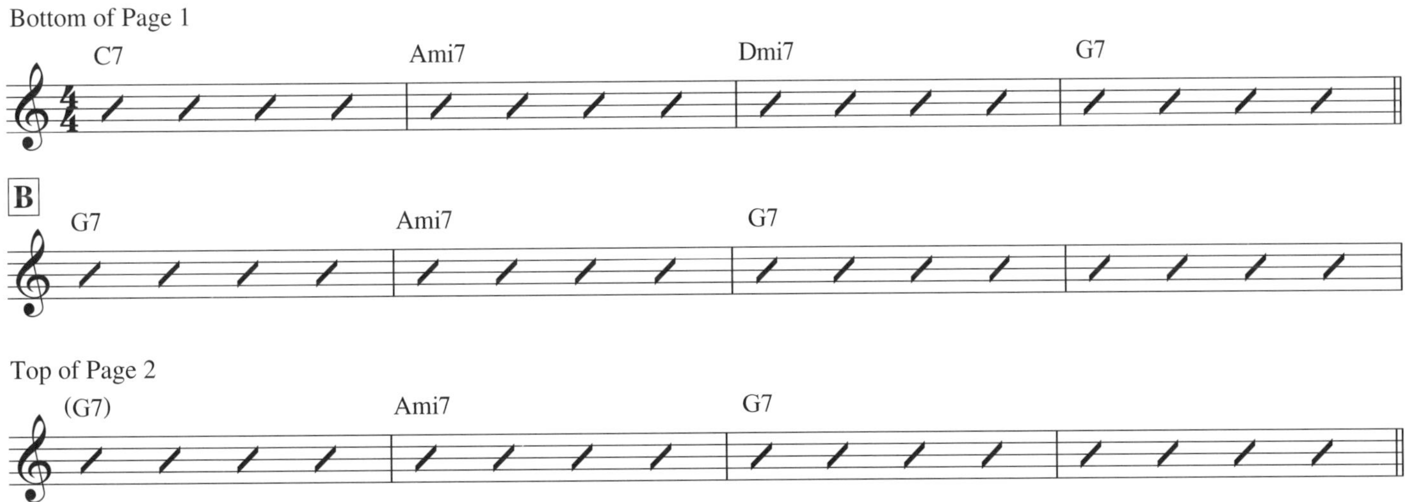

FIG. 4.6. Restating Chord Symbols

Tensions

Chord extensions (tensions) 9, 10, 11, and 13 are often set in parentheses. If multiple tensions are present, such as C7(9,13), they may be arranged either vertically or horizontally. If they are arranged vertically, the numbers should ascend from bottom to top. If they are arranged horizontally, they should ascend from left to right and be separated by commas.

E♭7$\binom{13}{9}$ E♭7(9,13)

FIG. 4.7. Vertical and Horizontal Tensions

For stand-alone lead sheets, there is an advantage to the vertical orientation. Vertical tensions take up less space and do not require commas, and particularly if there are chord symbols on eighth notes or quarter notes, the thinner width makes for less awkward music spacing. However, for annotated lead sheets in books, there is an advantage to the horizontal orientation, because that rendering is easier in running text—such as in this chord symbol: E♭7(9,13). It would be awkward to set that vertically, within a paragraph, and it would likely make the text's graphic designer crabby. By keeping it horizontal in the notation also, the chord symbol looks the same in both locations, and is thus immediately recognizable. So, there could be a reading comprehension benefit to the horizontal format, in some analytical music writing.

Another potential point of confusion relates to vertical orientation of tensions, regarding specific voicing practices. In thoroughbass (or "figured bass") notation, which is a baroque/early classical notation style—arguably the historical precursor to lead sheet notation—the vertical orientation of such numerals also indicated specific voicing directions. Lead sheets do not typically indicate specific voicings, so this potential conceptual ambiguity may be present in the vertical orientation, depending on how the reader was educated.

When a tension is present, it is understood that it can replace the less interesting notes of the triad (the root and 5). Again, chord symbols are meant to be interpreted by the whole band. So, a bass player will focus on the root and 5, no matter what tensions are specified. A melody player will be particularly interested in tensions, as well as the 3 and the 7. Comping instruments will choose what they play based on what other instruments are in the band, and drummers will likely be less oriented to the specific notes as they are to where the chord symbols are located rhythmically.

Abbreviations and Customs

There are a number of common practices for abbreviating chord symbols. Not all fit into a tidy, logically consistent system, but their use is widespread and idiomatic among jazz musicians, and at a point, we must observe and marvel, rather than prescribe.

1. Leave out the 7. Many jazz players routinely omit the 7 from a symbol when diatonic tensions are present. So, a C9 is commonly understood to be the same as C7(9), rather than C(add9). It is assumed that the 7 is present. This is jazz, after all; the ♭7 is nearly ubiquitous. There is a common assumption that lower available tensions may also be used. So, C13 would include the 9 as well.

   If tensions are altered, such as ♭13, the 7 is included in the symbol in order to avoid confusion with accidentals on the root: A7(♭13), not A♭13. Parentheses, A(♭13), would similarly clarify the altered tension.

   Tension ♯11 is often listed to the right of a 13: C13(♯11).

2. Leave out everything else, when the root stays the same but tensions change. In figure 4.8, we start with a C7 chord but then shift to a C7(9) chord.

FIG. 4.8. Leaving Out the Root

3. Leave out the tensions. Some writers simply indicate seventh chords and assume that the players will reharmonize them with tensions to their taste.

The Slash (/)

A slash ("virgule") in a chord symbol has multiple functions. Most commonly, it separates the primary symbol on the left from a specified bass note on the right. So, Ami/D means an A minor triad (A C E) above the note D.

However, the slash is also sometimes used to indicate *polychords,* where one chord is on top of another chord. In our example, an Ami/D would then be the notes A C E and D F♯ A, all combined. A vertical line is also sometimes used for this: Ami | D.

The slash can also indicate an upper-structure triad: a triad that contains at least one tension. This becomes more obvious when the left-hand symbol is a triad and the right-hand chord is a seventh chord that includes a tension in the triad to the left, such as Ami/D7, or the notes D F♯ A C E (where the E is the tension 9 of D7). Because of the potential ambiguity of the symbol, rather than the slash, Berklee Press uses a horizontal line to indicate USTs (upper-structure triads: triads built on seventh chords that include at least one tension). Read this as "A minor triad over a D7 chord." While the notes of a UST structure are the same as those of indicated polychords, USTs come from a different perspective of looking at harmony, and so can imply different interpretive practices.

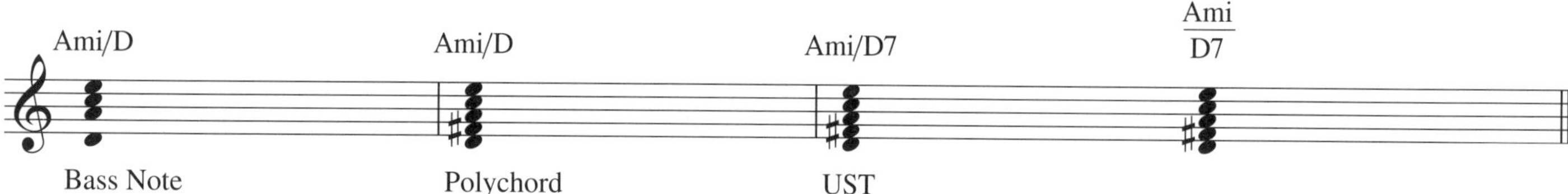

FIG. 4.9. Different Uses of the Slash

Now and then, you see the slash creep in other places, and since we are already saturated with ambiguous meanings, I recommend avoiding these constructions. Some use the suffix 6/9, for example, as in G6/9. This isn't universally understood, though. Asking my team of reputable advisors resulted in many different interpretations of this symbol, including it being the same as G6(9), G6/A, and G7(9,13). Everyone was mad at everyone who had a different opinion. So, I say, avoid that construction.

How do you know what's intended by the slash? Alas, it isn't always one hundred percent possible to be certain. Its most common usage is to indicate the bass note, so that's the safest guess, particularly if the lower part is an unmodified letter. If there are tensions or 7s in both chords, it's probably a polychord. If there's a triad on top and a 7 in the bottom note, there's a good chance it's a UST.

If the composer is available, ask him or her. If not, discuss it with your band and come to consensus. At least, you will all go down together.

Mi(Maj7)9

As mentioned, the parentheses are often understood to mean "tensions." However, there is a pesky exception to this logic, and that is the minor-major 7 chords—such as C E♭ G B—or even worse, the minor-major 7(9) chord, which is C E♭ G B D.

There is no perfect solution. To follow the rule about tensions, the symbol would be the hideous CmiMa7(9). More common, though, is to set the major 7 in parentheses: Cmi(Ma7)9, even though it adds an inconsistency to the system.

Oh well. At a point, we must choose clarity. Or, we must accept the world as we find it, no matter how nonsensical it may seem, and simply get on with our lives.

no/omit, add, alt

The following words/abbreviations are also common in chord symbols.

- The word "no" or "omit" means that a note is omitted. C7no5 means C E B♭. It follows the 7.
- The suffix "add" means that the tension is included but the 7 is left out.
- The suffix "alt" means use available tension substitutions to your taste. It also follows the 7: C7alt or C7(alt).

Parentheses on Turnarounds

A *turnaround* is a progression of chords designed to create harmonic instability at the end of a song form, so that the progression's tonal gravity leads back to the beginning of the form, such as using the chords IImi7 V7. A common notation convention is to set the turnaround chords in parentheses, which means that when the form is to repeat, those chords are played, but when the tune ends, they are not. In this way, the parentheses and repeat function similarly to bracketed multiple-repeat endings (see chapter 7).

Since the chords within the parentheses might have tensions that are also in parentheses, the turnaround parentheses are usually considerably larger so that there is no confusion.

FIG. 4.10. Turnaround Chords in Parentheses

Nashville Notation

The *Nashville numbering system* is attributed to Neal Matthews Jr. of the Jordanaires, who were best known as the backup singers for Elvis Presley, but who also worked with thousands of other artists. It is a style of chord chart, but instead of indicating specific chords, it presents chord *functions* as numerals, based on the scale (in C major, 1 for C, 2 for D, 3 for E, etc.). Some writers will indicate suffixes for minor or diminished chords, such as m for minor (e.g., 6m for A minor in the key of C major), but many do not. Using numbers like this facilitates transposition—common practice for session musicians who frequently adapt song keys for specific singers. A line under multiple chords indicates that they share a measure, and rhythm notation helps reveal irregular harmonic rhythms. Chord qualities beyond triads are indicated with superscripts (1^{Maj7}), or to clarify nondiatonic harmonies. You might see other symbols, such as a diamond shape to indicate "let it ring," a caret for "choke it short," slash marks (/) for chord repetitions, and others. There are many variations, with additional symbols and nuances. Essentially, though, it's a system that uses numerals instead of specific letters for chords.

Here is the Nashville-style chart for "No Time." The original jazz harmonies are a little complex for Nashville notation and would have required some finicky superscripts that would have revealed me to be the Yankee that I am, so I simplified it in order to give a more idiomatic example. For country or rock harmonies, which tend to be triadic, Nashville notation comes into its own, with simple numerals summarizing the score. It is designed to be very quick, convenient notation in a recording studio. While much detail is avoided, it provides "just enough" information for a seasoned Nashville session musician to understand what's needed.

This chart begins with a key and time signature: a jazz waltz in C. Thus, 1 means that the first chord here is C major, 5 means G major, 6 means A minor, and so on. If that proved too low/high for the singer and he or she decided to transpose it to, say, D major, then only one character on the chart would change (the C changing to D). Song sections, such as "intro" and "head" (once through the form) are indicated in boxes. Repeated sections don't require a restatement of the chords.

Figure 4.11 is a relatively formal Nashville chart. Often, it is handwritten on a scrap of paper or a napkin. A smudge of barbeque sauce would make this chart more authentic. Maybe we'll add that to the upcoming scratch-'n'-sniff edition of this book.

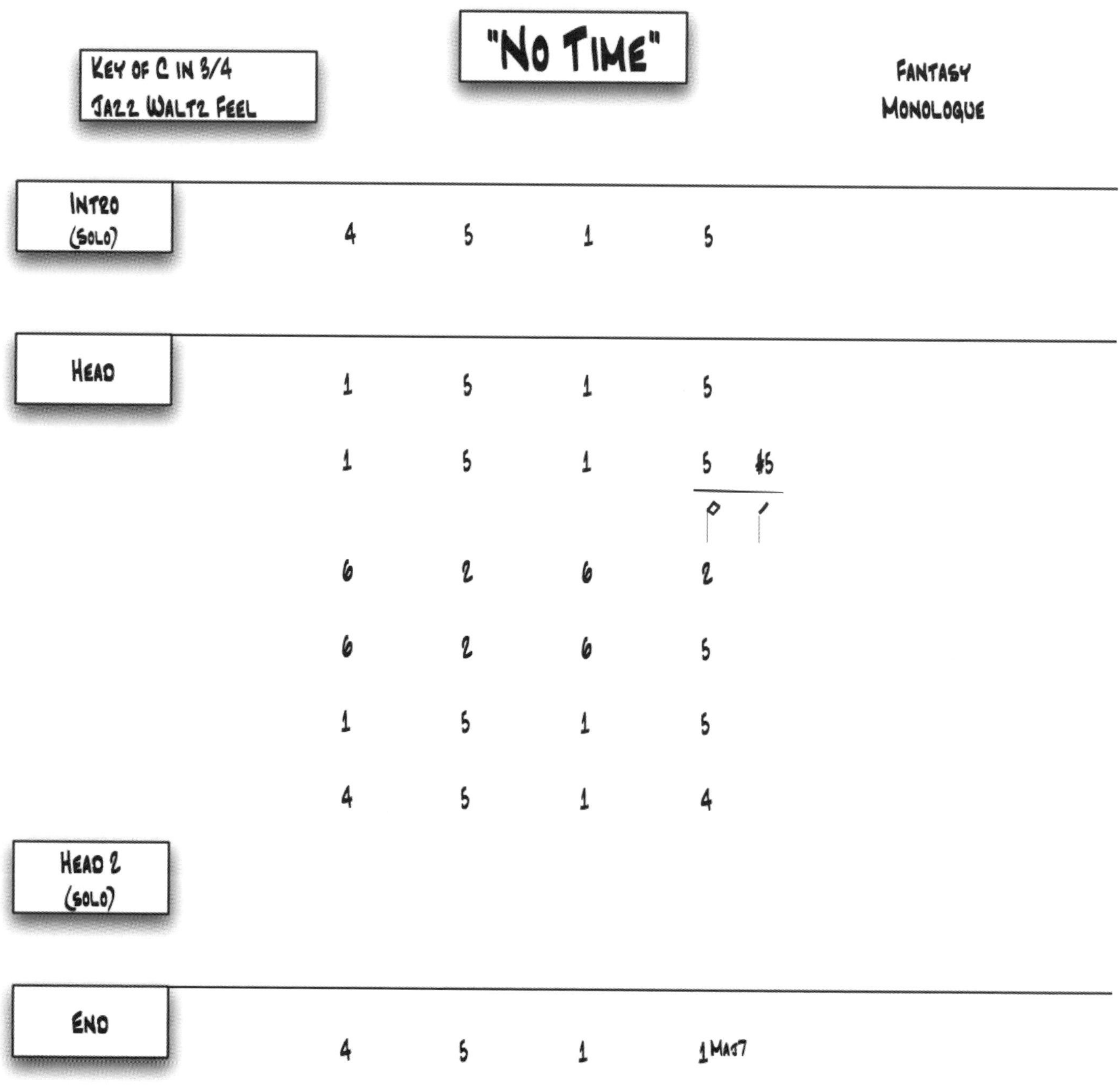

FIG. 4.11. Nashville Chord Chart for "No Time"

Other Chord Abbreviation Systems

There are two other chord notation systems to consider.

1. Minor chords set in lowercase, major chords in uppercase. While you see this in published materials, and there is a logic to it, it is fairly uncommon in contemporary practice. I recommend avoiding the practice as one with relatively few proponents. Diminished chords are similarly set lowercase; augmented chords are uppercase.

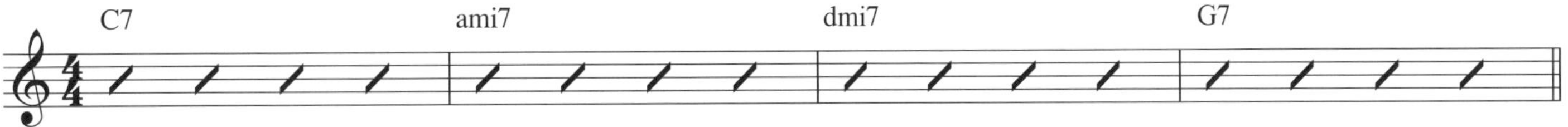

FIG. 4.12. Lowercase for Minor

2. Roman numerals. Roman numerals have been used to describe chord functions for many centuries, and they are still commonly used in harmonic analysis. However, they are not commonly used in lead sheets. In some systems, minor chords are set in lowercase Roman numerals, while major chords are set in uppercase. At Berklee, most teachers use uppercase for all the letters. In pedagogical materials, it is common to set both regular chord symbols and Roman numerals on a chart to help illustrate functional harmony.

FIG. 4.13. Roman Numerals. All uppercase and using lowercase for minor.

SLASH NOTATION

Rhythm slashes are common in lead sheet notation, and they can have either of two meanings.

1. Improvise. The player solos, creating his or her own part where the slashes are shown. This might be for an extended solo section or just a few beats of "fill." We also use it in musical examples to mean essentially "any melody," which is particularly useful and clean when demonstrating other aspects of the notation, such as chord symbols or barlines. There is one rhythm slash per beat of the measure.

   A "chord chart" is a type of lead sheet notation where there is no lead line, just chords. While there might not be any notation on a chord chart, they are often set on staves that have just regular rhythm slashes instead of notes.

2. Repeat the previous beat. This is a shorthand that can greatly simplify notation—more commonly in parts than in lead sheets. It is analogous to measure repeat symbols, discussed in chapter 7.

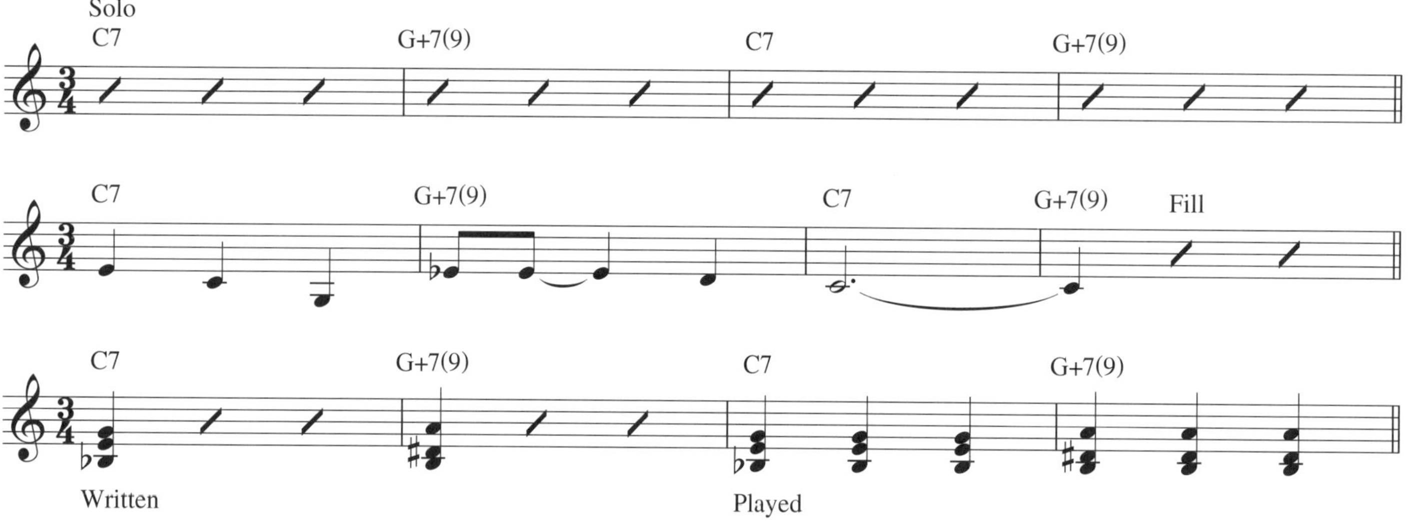

FIG. 4.14. Rhythm Slashes

CUE NOTATION, STOP TIME, AND KICKS OVER TIME

Lead sheets sometimes also specify a bass line, background line, or general rhythm for the rhythm section to play. This notation is set apart from the melody line as smaller notes, often on an auxilliary staff above the melody staff. If the notation occurs while the composed melody is not playing, it could just be set in the primary staff, though often marked with the instrument that performs it, and in smaller noteheads.

Here's an example of a tenor saxophone figure during an intro section, set as cue notes within the staff. The instrument is labeled and the notes are set at 75 percent of their normal size.

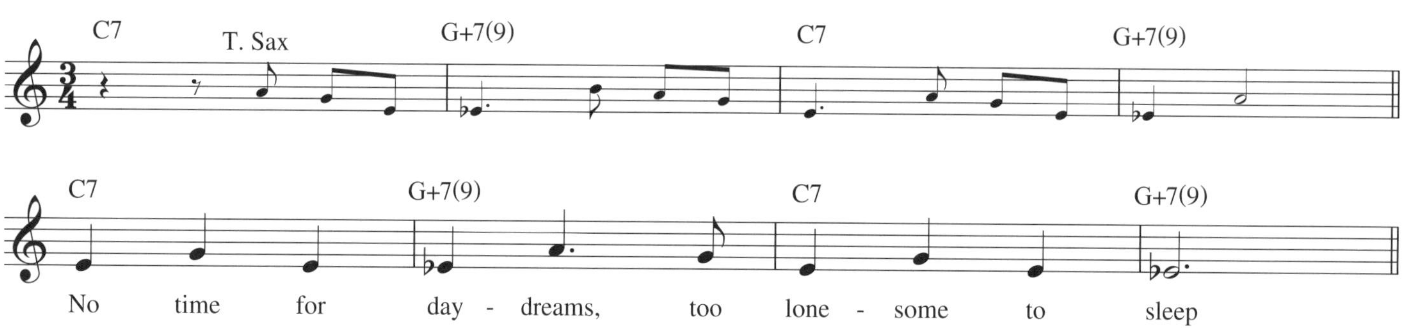

FIG. 4.15. Cue Notes in the Staff

In *stop time*, rhythm notation is used to indicate a stop-time rhythm, played by the rhythm section while the soloist swaps noises over an intermittent groove, which periodically "stops" during the rests, creating a question/answer dynamic. Individual players choose the notes for those rhythms; the pianist will most likely play a chord voicing and the bass may play roots, for example.

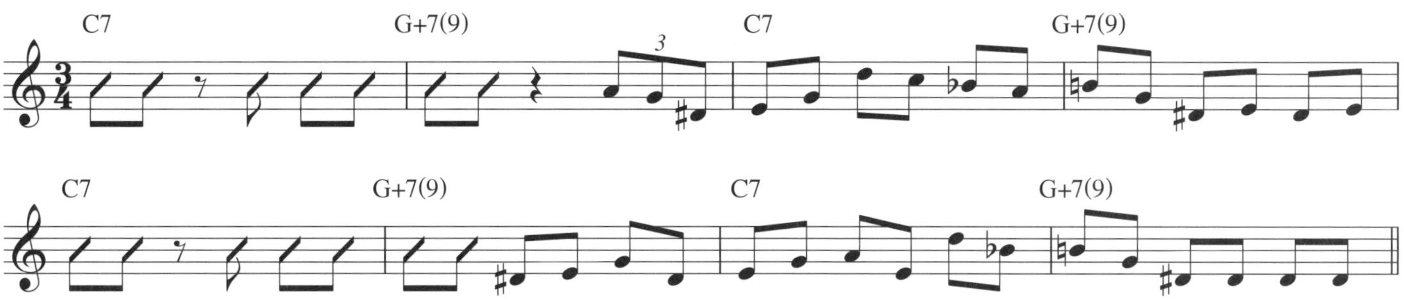

FIG. 4.16. Stop Time

Kicks over time notation is a type of cue note that shows an important pattern in the rhythm section. It is similar to stop time, but the groove continues throughout.

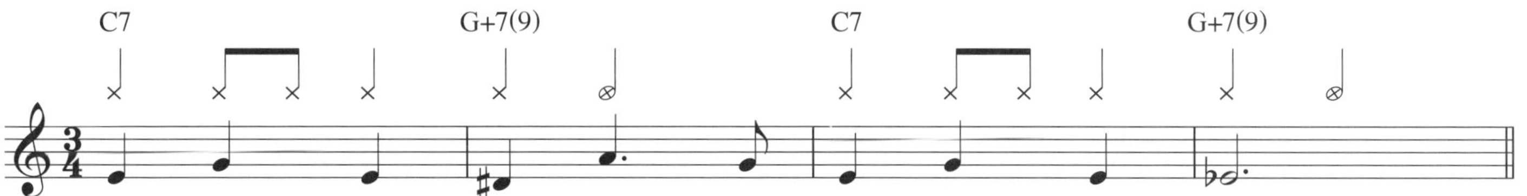

FIG. 4.17. Kicks Over Time

OBSOLETE LEAD SHEET PRACTICES

Lead sheet notation was born out of relatively informal notation styles, rather than the practices used in formally engraved publishing. Like many American musical genres, such as blues, jazz, rock, punk, hip-hop, etc., lead sheets come from an oral-tradition based perspective, and the unnecessary formal trappings of formal notation/polite society were set aside for deeper feeling, more efficient production, and a hardscrabble, real-world perspective on how to make music work—the most efficient route towards setting a groove on fire.

On the bandstand or in the pit orchestra, certain conventions were adopted for reasons of efficiency of communication and part creation rather than consistency, which is what we stuffy publishers hold so dear. Then, as fake books and most importantly the *Real Book* became published, there came to be various practices and expectations regarding the "right" way to render lead sheet notation. Some of these practices were helpful, but there are a handful that we might do better to leave behind, these days when software-generated notation makes copying parts extremely fast and many of these shortcuts unnecessary—or even more time-consuming than the more formal approaches.

Here are some common lead sheet conventions that many are currently moving away from at Berklee.

1. Omitting the clef from systems after the first one. This was common practice particularly in the "pit" orchestras of Broadway, but the balance of conciseness vs. clarity seems off, particularly because lead sheets get

shared by multiple players who normally read varying clefs (e.g., guitar vs. bass). Setting the clef symbol on every staff can alleviate potential momentary confusion.

2. Omitting the "begin repeat" symbol at bar 1. When a whole form is repeated, some writers leave out the initial repeat sign, at bar 1. However, the begin repeat is an early signal that the form will repeat. It seems kinder to include it than to surprise the reader at the very end, just when they thought they were done.
3. The dash (–) for minor. This symbol is said to have been born at Berklee, and it has the benefit of being dramatically unlike the various symbols for major. However, many render this as a hyphen, and particularly paired with an A, as in A-, it can be difficult to spot, especially in computer-generated scores. It's easier to decipher Amin7 than A-7. Similarly, as mentioned earlier, the lowercase m for minor can be problematic in certain fonts, which render it as a "small cap" and thus nearly identical to M. So, let's use mi or min for minor.
4. Handwritten notation fonts. This is a contentious issue, but the notation fonts with a handwritten feel are busier and more difficult to read than the cleaner, more elegant engraver fonts—especially for text. Reading comprehension research in other areas of graphic design show conclusively that simpler fonts are easiest to read: serif fonts for print and sans serif fonts for screens. Decorative fonts act against reading comprehension. This means you, Jazz, Broadway Copyist, Inkpen, and your ilk. Some hold that handwriting fonts are easier to read in low light, such as in an orchestra pit, but that seems more an old wives' tale than a conclusion arrived at through methodical study. Until I see some solid, empirical research showing that handwriting notation fonts do not inhibit reading comprehension, similarly to the good studies done for text fonts, I will recommend avoiding these typefaces for notation intended to be read by musicians. They are fine for notation destined to appear on t-shirts and coffee mugs, but for actual music, stick to the cleaner engraver fonts, such as Maestro and Opus—even though the sacred *Real Book* was originally handwritten.

I realize that these are local or personal preferences, and perhaps fighting words, running counter to long-practiced traditions. Many jazz musicians have become accustomed to seeing the handwritten fonts, probably because it reminds them of the *Real Book*. To me, it's a nostalgic preference that comes at the expense of readability. Sorry. Hopefully, we can still be friends.

CHAPTER 5

Lyrics

Lyrics are words that are set to music. They are usually set under the staff, centered against their corresponding notes. The first syllable of a multisyllable lyric is typically left-justified against its note, though subsequent syllables of the word are centered. If there are multiple verses, the longest syllable is centered under the first note of the song section; all verses' numerals are decimal-aligned against each other.

Figure 5.1 is a phrase with two verses of lyrics. Each verse begins with a numeral with a period after it. Notice that there is a little space between the verses (i.e., "leading"). As a general rule, use about 20 to 40 percent of the lyrics' font size as leading between verses.

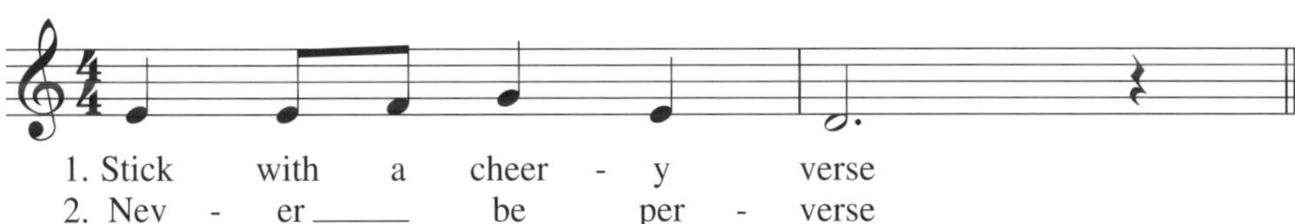

FIG. 5.1. Verse Numerals

There is often a one-to-many relationship between words and notes, and three types of symbols are used to clarify the boundaries of words. See figure 5.2 for examples.

1. Hyphens are used to connect syllables of a multisyllable word. Use a dictionary to determine where a word's syllable breaks are, rather than trying to parse out the different sounds. Singers learn to hold vowels and tuck in consonants as part of their craft, and breaking the words in nonstandard ways just leads to confusion. If there is a long melisma on a syllable within a word, multiple hyphens separate the syllables, but not too many—say, one for every couple beats. These hyphens may be omitted if the lyrics are so close together that the hyphen would make the notation look cluttered.

2. Word extensions (or "lyric extensions" or "extender lines") are used when a single-syllable word or the last syllable of a multisyllable word lasts for multiple notes. Its start follows any punctuation on that syllable (such as the period in "sometimes," in figure 5.2). The end point of the word extension is either centered or right-justified with the last notehead in the melisma, rather than extending through that note's duration.
3. Slurs further clarify all notes covered in a multisyllable word. While the slur is arguably redundant with the hyphens, it can help clarify the boundaries of an extended group of syllables. The slur connects the first note in the series to the last note of the melisma—the right-hand note of a tied pair, if the last note is tied. Not all publishers use slurs for this context.

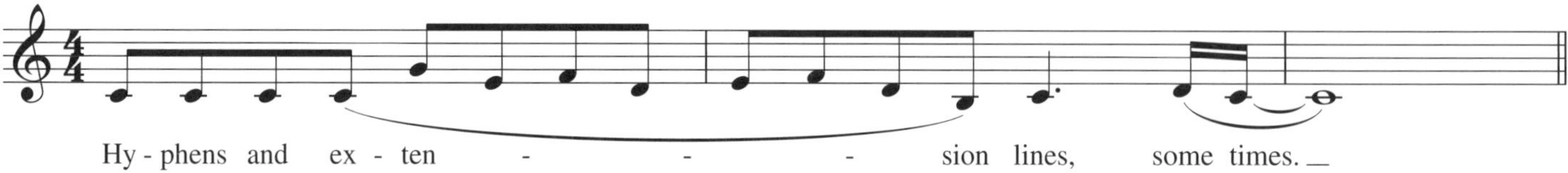

FIG. 5.2. Hyphens, Word Extensions, Slurs

When lyrics are broken across systems, a hyphen or extender line should begin the next system.

FIG. 5.3. Lyrics across System Breaks

If multiple verses are set under the notes, each verse begins with a verse number, followed by a period. If there's just one verse, there shouldn't be a numeral.

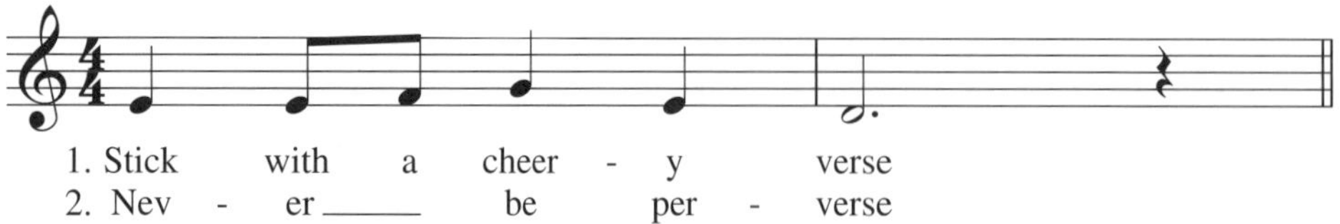

FIG. 5.4. Verse Numerals

A *brace* is sometimes used to separate multiple verses from a single-line chorus or refrain. If there's just one verse under the notes, no brace is needed.

FIG. 5.5. Verses Braced

Lyrics in some verses may require slightly different rhythms than others. In such a case, use a "broken tie" to connect the note durations of the busiest lyric. If there is a lot of rhythmic variation between verses, it may be better to write out each verse separately.

FIG. 5.6. Broken Tie

You might see three or four verses written under a staff. At a point, too many verses get cumbersome. An alternative is to just write the first verse with the notes and then set the remaining verses in a block of text, after all the notation. You might include verse 1 in this block or just omit it.

In figure 5.7, note that in the block of lyrics, indents are used to separate verses, choruses, and the prechorus.

FIG. 5.7. Notation with Block Lyrics

Particularly in hymns, when every part is singing similar rhythms, a common practice is to set the lyrics just once between a grand staff. The top staff is for soprano and alto; the bottom staff is for tenor and bass.

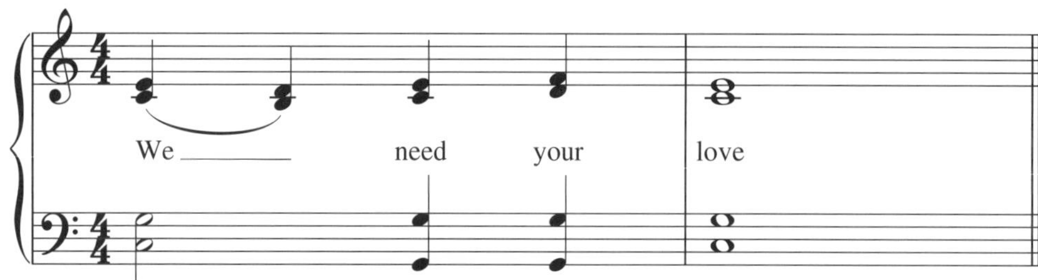

FIG. 5.8. Hymn

However, if the rhythms between parts vary considerably, it is usually better to render the music in separate staves for each voice type (four, in this case).

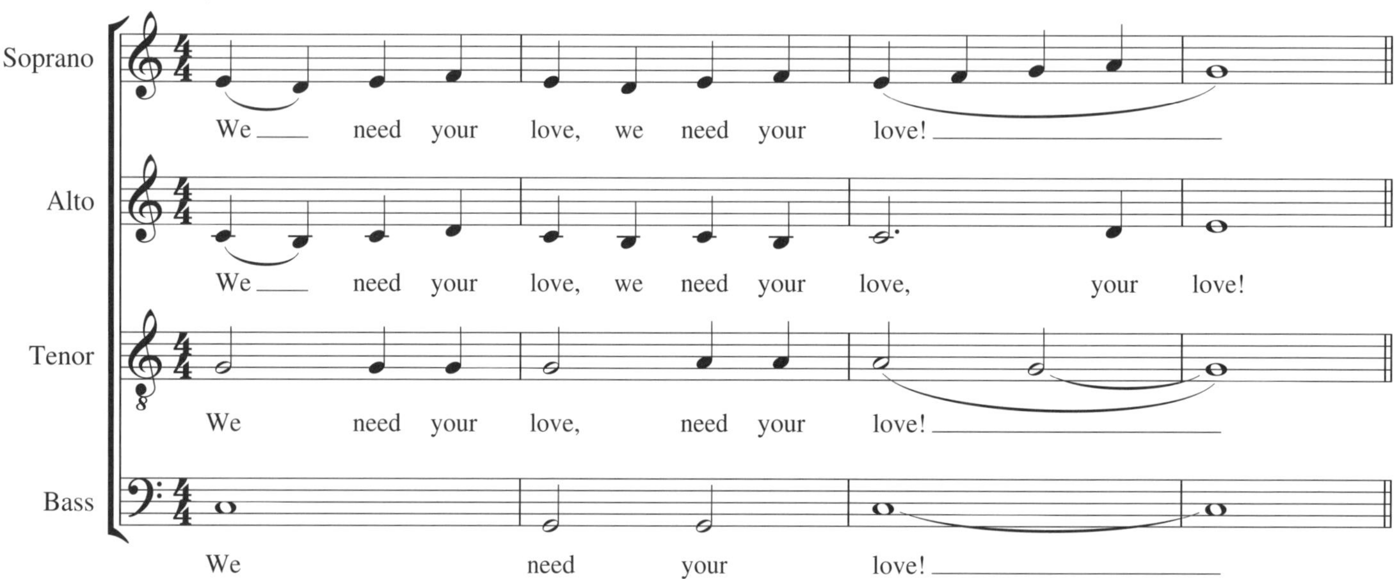

FIG. 5.9. Four Parts

VOCAL DYNAMICS

We will explore how to implement dynamics in the next chapter, but a bee to put in your bonnet for now is that it is common to set vocal dynamics above the staff rather than below it. This can take some clutter away from the lyrics, and it can alleviate some congestion in a score. However, it is not a universal practice.

FIG. 5.10. Dynamics

LYRIC PRACTICES TO AVOID

Some common practices in vocal music notation have questionable merit, and it's time that they were shed. We've been moving away from these at Berklee, even though some are fairly widely published.

1. All capital letters. Some engravers set all lyrics in ALL CAPS. There are empirical studies that show that text in all caps is more difficult to read and comprehend than text that mixes upper- and lowercase letters. Text in all caps also suggests shouting and will be interpreted as such by anyone who is marginally computer literate.

   Some engravers set just the title line/hook in all caps. Again, because it suggests shouting—and thus, a different way of performing the text that is likely unintentional—instead use mixed capitalization. As a compromise, you can use title case for song titles, setting just the first letter of each word (except prepositions) as capitals. There's some logic to that, and it doesn't hurt anything, but it's not really necessary. Another compromise is to set the title line in small caps. This appeases both the worlds of the old-school uppercase people and the more contemporary mixed-case constituency. It's rare, though, and shouldn't be considered a universal practice, though it's a fine choice for a distinctive style.

   Another capitalization practice that's considered obsolete is to capitalize the first word of every line or phrase, as you might with a poem. For normal song lyrics, this isn't necessary or currently considered standard practice. However, if the song is a setting of a previously published stand-alone poem, it's important to respect the original poet's capitalization choices.

FIG. 5.11. Title Capitalization Variations

2. No punctuation. Some engravers leave punctuation out of lyrics. I don't recommend this. Punctuation is a great clarifier of language, and omitting it can cloud meaning. Consider "I have time to kill, Mark." vs. "I have time to kill Mark." Each tells a different story....

3. All flags, no beams. Using all flags and no beams was a vocal music convention that is finally, thankfully, becoming considered obsolete. I've never heard a good argument for using all flags, other than because "that's how it's done" or because "vocal music is special." Beams greatly clarify rhythms and their relationship to meter, as discussed in chapter 1. Try hard to talk clients into using beams, if they were raised on flags. It's a battle worth picking.

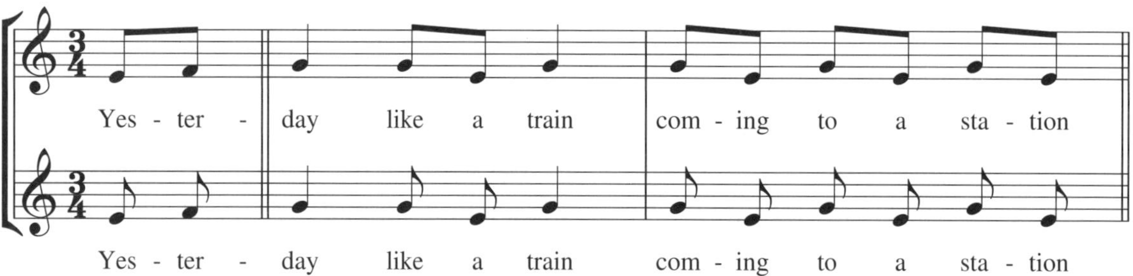

FIG. 5.12. Beams vs. All Flags

4. Hyphenation based on sound. Though some vocalists instinctively want to hyphenate lyrics based on how they sound, it is generally clearest to hyphenate them in accordance with standard dictionary hyphenation practices: yes-ter-day, not ye-ster-day. Normal hyphenation keeps the meaning of the word intact. Part of good vocal training is about how to hold onto vowels and tuck in consonants, and it is a safe bet to trust singers to render the words musically.

To clarify, these preferences for lyrics relate to the lyrics that are engraved as part of the notation. For extra verses set after the score, capitalizing the first letter of each line, as in poetry, makes sense. Also, leave out hyphenation in those text blocks, per figure 5.7.

CHAPTER 6

Expressive Markings

Various symbols and textual markings are used to specify how music should sound or be executed. Accents, slurs, dynamics, and other symbols add nuance that make music come alive.

Before the late nineteenth century, composers were relatively conservative in their use of these markings. As a result, musicians today argue fiercely about what the "correct" way to play Beethoven and Bach should be. Today, we tend to mark formal scores more specifically.

We'll break this down very broadly into two categories.

1. Expressions: Directions for regions of notes.
2. Articulations: Directions for individual notes.

We'll start with expressions, which apply to *regions*—passages of music that are all governed by the same direction.

TEMPO/STYLE/FEEL MARKINGS

At the beginning of a piece of music, it is common to have an indication for the music's tempo, style, or feel. This can evolve throughout the piece. Tempo directions tend to be relatively big and bold, with an initial capital letter. These serve well as section headers. Ideally, they are left-aligned with the time signature, but in busier scores they can appear in other places, such as left-aligned with the key signature.

Moderato (♩ = c. 108)

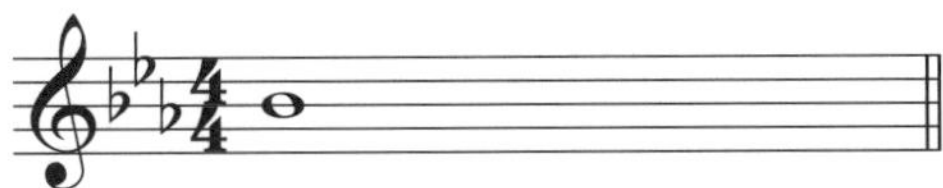

FIG. 6.1. Tempo Marking

Particularly in classical-derived music, it is traditional for English-speaking composers to use certain Italian words for these tempo/feel markings in scores; German is occasionally used as well. Some of these words indicate ranges of tempos, some indicate mood, and some indicate both. English (or the language of your choice) can be used instead of Italian, if you prefer.

In addition to words like "Moderato," or "Adagio," or "Slowly," a specific tempo might be indicated, measured in beats per minute (bpm). Traditionally, these numbers were always divisible by four (e.g., 128, 144, etc.), as the older wind-up metronomes were only changeable in 4-bpm increments. (This is a simplification; some were divisible by two at the slower end of the scale, then by three from 60 to 72, and then by four faster than that.) Today, though, this is no longer an absolute rule, as modern electronic metronomes can be set in fractions of a bpm.

Here's a very subjective chart of some common Italian tempo markings, their English meanings, and their approximate tempo ranges. Similar guidelines are sometimes printed on metronomes, and they vary between manufacturers and publishers. So, use it as a rough guide. Also, note that there are sometimes multiple terms to mean the same tempo. For example, "Andante" and "Moderato" both mean a moderate, medium tempo. "Andante" has a more nuanced meaning, though, often interpreted as "at a walking tempo" (literally in Italian, "going"), rather than the less evocative "moderate."

Italian	**English**	**Tempo Range**
Presto	Very Fast	168–208
Vivace	Very Fast	140–160
Allegro	Fast (Cheerfully)	120–168
Allegretto	Moderately Fast	112–120
Moderato	Moderate	90–110
Andante	Moderate (Walking Tempo)	76–108
Adagio	Slow	66–76
Largo, Grave	Very Slow (Broadly)	40–66
Grave	Very Slow (Seriously)	40–66

FIG. 6.2. Common Italian Markings Used Worldwide

Rather than indicating tempo, some terms indicate style, mood, or feel, often paired with a numeric tempo marking. Some common examples:

- *cantabile* (singing)
- *dolce* (sweetly)
- *misterioso* (mysteriously)

These terms often apply only to individual instruments or passages, rather than defining the character of a musical section. In this more localized case, the text is typically set in all lowercase and italics, aligned with the beat where it takes effect, and set close to the notehead. Figure 6.3 shows a Grave movement, with a dolce melody within it.

FIG. 6.3. Section Header (Grave) vs. Local Nuance (Dolce)

Some style indications have rhythmic interpretation meanings, beyond just style. For example, a "Bossa" or "Funk" indication means, among other nuances of performance approach, that the beat subdivision should be interpreted as straight/even rather than with a swing feel. "Swing" means that eighth notes are played with a triplet feel, an emphasis on beats 2 and 4, as well as other nuances of the style. Alternatively, the notation for "straight = triplet" can be set above the staff. This is considered redundant with the "Swing" indication; just use one or the other.

FIG. 6.4. Interpret Eighth Notes as Swing Feel

For some reason, the "Swing" style indication often ends with an exclamation point, as in "Swing!" No other style indication similarly does this. You never see "Grave!" That said, swing is awfully delightful, so we give it a pass. Perhaps, we will soon start seeing emoticons with style indications (Grave ☹), but as of this writing, we are not there, yet.

To get more specific about tempo, there are two common ways to indicate bpm numerically: with the abbreviation "M.M." (which originally stood for "Maelzel's metronome," after its inventor, but now is often interpreted as "metronome marking") or more commonly in contemporary scores, with a note value that is usually the beat, such as a quarter note in 4/4 time. If M.M. is used, the "click" is assumed to be on the note duration indicated in the bottom number of the time signature. Metronome markings are often set in parentheses. They may appear alone or as part of a larger overall direction. The abbreviation "bpm" might appear after the numeral, but it is not necessary.

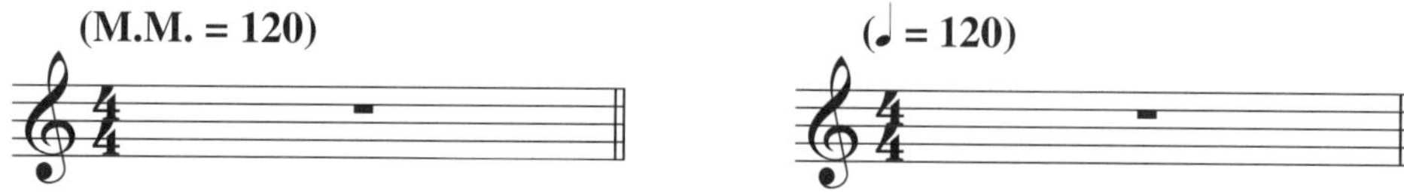

FIG. 6.5. M.M. vs. Notes

The first measure of a piece or the start of a section should have a relatively grand and formal statement of a tempo/style direction, if such markings are used at all. In figure 6.6, we use Times 10 point bold.

Tempo variations can occur within sections. In this case, they are usually set in italics, often in bold italics, and in a smaller type size than the section headers. When new sections have tempo indications, the font should match the initial one in the first measure. Tempo indications are ideally set above the staff.

FIG. 6.6. Tempo Variations

Here are some common Italian terms used to indicate tempo changes. Again, there are often multiple terms in use that essentially mean the same thing. *Stringendo* translates to "tightening," for example—a more evocative term than *accelerando,* meaning "accelerate."

accel.	*accelerando, stringendo*	gradually increase tempo
rit., ritard.; rall.	*ritardando, rallentando*	gradually decrease tempo
rubato	*rubato*	at an expressive, varying tempo of the performer's choosing, with rhythmic flexibility

FIG. 6.7. Tempo Changes

To review, we have three similar types of expressive text markings with functional nuances: section headers and two localized types of directions for tempo and for mood. They should receive distinct type treatments. All should be set above the staff, but the local nuances can go below if necessary. Unlike expressive terms that define sections, the more localized texts are set in all lowercase italics, but not bold, and often abbreviated. In figure 6.8, Grave and Allegro are grandly announcing formal sections, while little "accel." and "espress." are giving more localized nuances of expressive directions. In an ensemble, some directions such as "espress." or "dolce" might apply to only a single instrument, whereas section headers (and all tempo indications) would apply to all instruments. In most cases, tempo directions are shared by all instruments, but expressive markings can vary between parts or voices.

FIG. 6.8. Types of Expressive Markings

The term "a tempo" or the header "Tempo I" indicate a return to the original tempo—that is, at the most recent formally declared tempo/style in Roman type/bold, before an accelerando or ritardando changed it. Place it on the beat where the tempo change occurs. It can function as a section header or within a section, such as after an "accelerando." It can be set as a section header or as a tempo variation within a section. In this instance, the accelerando is paired with a dashed line showing that the music gradually increases in tempo over those bars. So, we start slow, then in bar 3 we begin gradually increasing speed, but then at the "A Tempo," we suddenly return to the slow Grave tempo. "Tempo 1" similarly means, "return to the first tempo marking in the score."

FIG. 6.9. A Tempo

DYNAMICS

Dynamics indicate relative loudness levels.

There are essentially three ways they are communicated.

- Symbols: ***ppp*** to ***fff***
- Text: Crescendo (*cresc.*) and Decrescendo (*decresc.*) or diminuendo (*dim.*)
- Hairpins/Wedges

Dynamics go below the staff (except sometimes in vocal music), aligned with the beat where they take effect, either centered or just slightly to the left, preceding it. As with all notation, make sure that they don't overlap with barlines and that there is a little white space between the dynamic symbol and a hairpin.

Lettered Dynamics Symbols

Lettered symbols indicate loudness levels, and they take effect immediately. They are relative, rather than absolute: ***ppp*** means "as quiet as possible" rather than a specific, measurable level of decibels. A recorder blasting at ***fff*** will be softer than a trumpet blasting at ***fff***. Here are the most common dynamics symbols, their names, and what they mean.

ppp	pianississimo	as quiet as possible
pp	pianissimo	very quiet
p	piano	quiet
mp	mezzo piano	medium, but on the quiet side
mf	mezzo forte	medium, but on the loud side
f	forte	loud
ff	fortissimo	very loud
fff	fortississimo	as loud as possible

FIG. 6.10. Lettered Dynamics Symbols

You may see up to five iterations of a ***p*** or ***f*** (***ppppp***/***fffff***); these extras further expand the spectrum. Doing so is helpful in serialism, as the extra symbols bring the total number of dynamics symbols to twelve, so they can be set in a row similar to the twelve pitches. They are rarely used in other styles.

In addition, some hybrid and related symbols are also common.

sfz	sforzando	an exaggerated accent
fp	forte/piano	attack loud, but then immediately drop down to quiet
subito ***p***/*subito* ***f***	subito piano/subito forte	suddenly quiet/suddenly loud
poco ***p***/*poco* ***f***	poco piano/poco forte	a little bit softer/louder
meno ***p***/*meno* ***f***	meno piano/meno forte	less soft, less loud
(hairpin) *niente*	niente	nothing; fade to silence

FIG. 6.11. Sudden Dynamic Changes

While dynamics symbols are usually set below the staff in instrumental music, they are sometimes set above the staff in vocal music so as to avoid colliding with lyrics. Instruments that read a grand staff (e.g., piano, harp, marimba) set the dynamics symbols just once between the staves, unless the hands are playing different dynamics in each, in which case the symbols are set below each staff.

Horizontally, dynamics are set aligned with the beat in which they take effect: either centered with the note or slightly left of it, but never to the right (after the horse has left the barn). The symbols are always set on notes, never on rests.

If there are any dynamics in the score, one should be set where the instrument starts to play. Whenever an instrument enters a multi-instrument score for a piece or a movement, it should get a "starting dynamic." These are set right on the note where they begin playing, not always on the first measure or first beat, if it begins on a rest.

Increasing/Decreasing Dynamics

Gradual increases and decreases of dynamics are indicated in two ways: with the words (crescendo, decrescendo/diminuendo), and with hairpin (also called "wedge") shapes. If the effect lasts a few measures, and particularly if it spans multiple systems, use the words, set in lowercase italics, usually below the staff. If it lasts under a couple measures or so, use the hairpin shapes. Use one type of symbol or the other, not both.

cresc.	crescendo	gradually get louder (literally, "swell")
decresc.	decrescendo	gradually get softer (wane)
dim.	diminuendo	gradually get softer (literally, "smaller")

FIG. 6.12. Symbols for Increasing/Decreasing Dynamics

Hairpins should vertically align with lettered symbols and open up vertically to a height no bigger than the forte symbol. In this way, the various symbols relate to each other, creating their own narrative. (See figure 6.13.)

Longer hairpins should have target dynamics—an indication of how loud or soft the music should get. Smaller ones (say, a beat or two wide) indicate a temporary swell rather than an overall dynamic change, so they don't need the target.

FIG. 6.13. Hairpins

Don't let the hairpin open too wide! It is like an alligator. He opens his mouth just wide enough to catch the flamingo. Too wide and the flamingo will fly away. Too narrow and it will peck his snout shut, and he won't be able to grab it.

Again, all these symbols should align and seem as related parts of the same story.

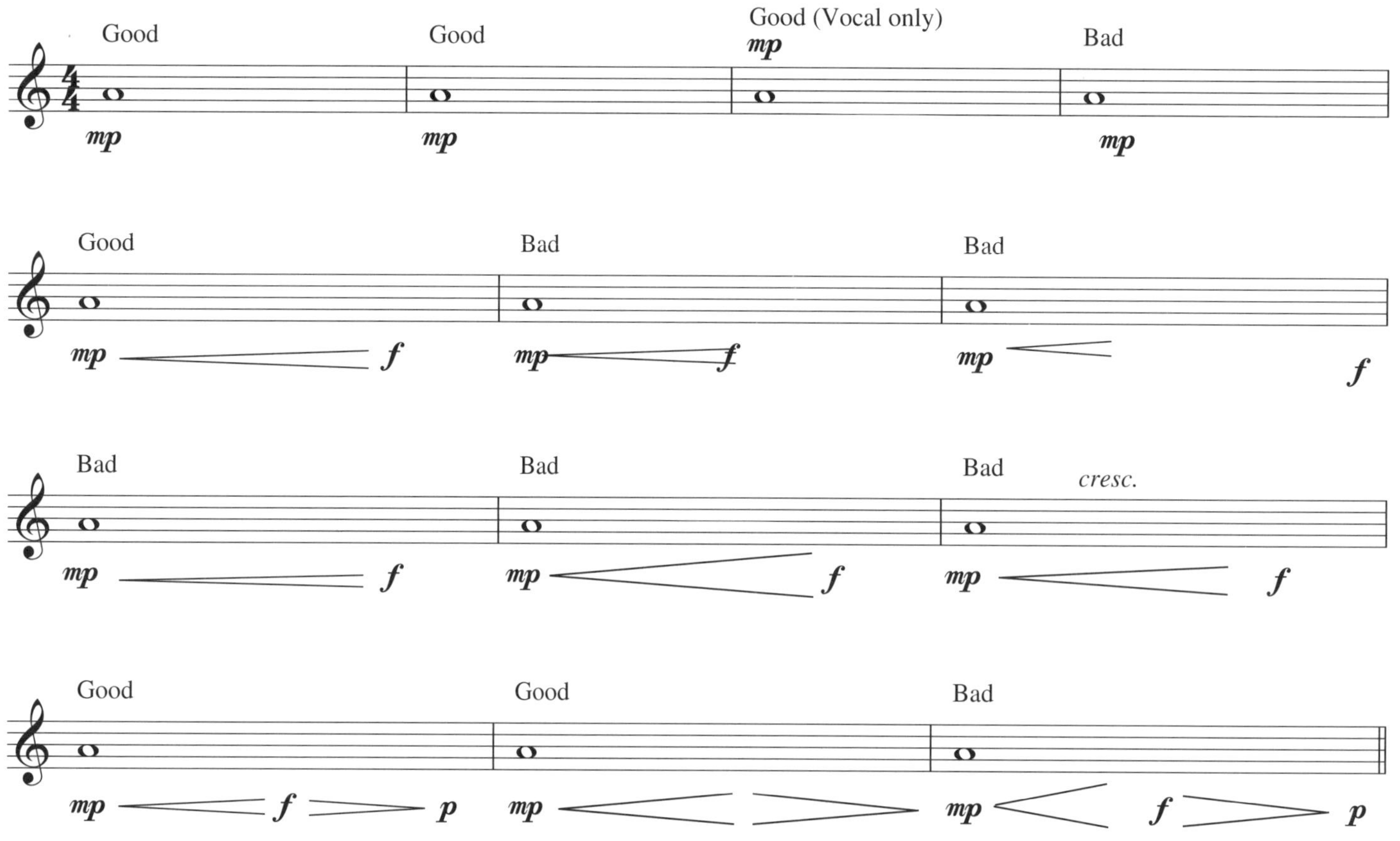

FIG. 6.14. Good and Bad Dynamic Markings

Other Text

Many expressive terms are considered common knowledge among musicians, and are as standard in music notation as any other symbol. It is to be assumed that every literate musician understands words such as "crescendo" or "ritardando." Composers frequently go outside the standard terms, however. Most contemporary composers tend to describe relatively unusual ideas in their own language, as opposed to the "traditional" Italian. This leads to some inconsistency in many scores, where one formal section might be marked with an Italian word such as "Grave" and then another section could be labeled in English, such as "Furtively." Let's acknowledge this inconsistency of language as an accepted point of awkwardness. Sure, an American composer could look up the Italian word for "furtively," such as "furtivamente," but there's something pretentious about this. So, either be inconsistent and clear, or be pretentious and obtuse. Take your pick. (You could also say "Gravely" instead of "Grave," to match the English "Furtively," and thus be seen as contrarian and clear, rather than inconsistent and clear.)

Sometimes, you need more elaborate directions than a single word or short phrase, as a section header. This could include directions for special ways to set up an instrument, choreography, or notation regarding stage directions, such as what you might find in musical theater. Some guidelines for handling this:

- Set the direction to align with the beat where it takes effect.
- If necessary, it is better to precede the beat where it takes effect than to set it after the horses have left the barn.
- If it is a very long direction, consider setting a footnote or setup direction at the very beginning of the score, so as not to disrupt the notation too much.

TYPEFACES AND FONTS

The most important goal of notation is clarity, and typeface selection should promote clarity over decoration. While dynamics symbols are generally in a font that is part of the notation itself, other text has some leeway in what typeface can be used.

A personal and professional preference: I strongly prefer simple, engraved typefaces, and I loathe handwritten typefaces, for text as well as for music. As I ranted in chapter 4, there is clear, empirical evidence that serif fonts (with small finishing shapes on the main strokes, such as this very font you are reading right now) facilitate better reading comprehension than sans serif fonts do, particularly on the printed page (as opposed to a computer screen). For expressions, as with lyrics, stick with unornamented, serifed typefaces such as Times, Garamond, and so on. It should be classy and consonant with the shapes of your notation font.

Whatever typeface you choose, keep its usage concise and logical. Use the same font treatment for analogous information types: section headers, tempo markings, fingerings, and so on.

Let's clarify terms: a *typeface* is a family of related lettering designs; a *font* is a specific iteration or form within the typeface. So, the typeface Times has specific fonts for styles (regular/Roman, bold, italics) as well as sizes. "Times" is a typeface, and "Times 12-point bold" is a font.

Most professional scores have just one or two text typefaces, and then a few font variations within them. Different fonts can help clarify different classifications of symbols. For example, it's a good idea to have fingerings in a different font than triplets (say, italics for triplets and Roman for fingerings), so that they are easily distinguished when they are close together. As illustrated previously, section headers can be in a larger, bolder font than more localized expressive markings. Capitalization is another tool for distinguishing types of meaning: an initial capital letter for a section header that applies to the whole ensemble, but lowercase (and italics) for temporary directions within a section, applying to a single instrument.

A good general rule for italics: use them for tempo changes (*accel.*) and local mood indications (*espress.*). Almost nothing else should be italicized (con sord, arco, etc.).

Consider each type of expression you are using, and then organize each strain as a narrative that leads throughout the score: dynamics, tempos, nuances, instrument-specific technical directions, footnotes, chord symbols, lyrics, fingerings, and so on. Like elements should look alike. Use as few different fonts and capitalization schemes as you can get away with while facilitating the greatest clarity possible in distinguishing between different types of information.

A jumble of fonts lends an obnoxious, chaotic, and amateurish feel to a score—what we used to call a "kid with a new Macintosh" vibe, in the 1990s, trying out every font for its own sake, rather than as a way to organize information. Consistency and logical precision in graphical design do your readers a great service.

PHRASE MARKINGS AND OTHER SLURS

The slur shape has many functions. Most generally, it means that whatever is within the slur is part of a coherent phrase, with the notes within it played legato, connected to each other, as a logical unit. Then, there are nuances in technical meaning that vary from instrument to instrument. We have already seen slurs clarify the relationship between lyrics and notes. To a wind player, a slur means to play a section legato, in one breath. To a fiddler, it means within a single bow stroke. To a pianist, it means legato, and perhaps with a slight break at the end, between the phrase and the next note.

Slur ends ideally point to the center of their anchoring noteheads, though they must sometimes point instead to the left or right edge of the note. The curve should be as gradual and elegant as possible. If a phrase ends with a tied note, the slur should end at the target note (not the first note) of the tie.

FIG. 6.15. Slur

When a phrase spans over a system break, the shape should stop and then begin again in mid-arch.

FIG. 6.16. Slur across System Break

ARTICULATIONS

An *articulation* is a symbol associated with a single note to clarify how it is to be performed. Generally, articulations are set centered against the notehead. They may be set on the notehead side of the notes, or all above the staff aligned vertically, depending on which is less awkward.

FIG. 6.17. Articulation Staff Placement Options

When a staff has multiple voices, each voice must have independent articulations above and below the staff. Most articulations are vertically symmetrical, though some (such as a fermata) have an upside-down variation, for when they are to be set under the staff.

FIG. 6.18. Articulations with Multiple Voices

Some common articulations are listed below. Some have different meanings depending on the instrument that plays them. Letters and numerals are also sometimes used similarly to articulations for fingerings and similar technical directions, and we will explore those in chapter 8.

Symbol	Name	Effect
·	Staccato	Short
>	Accent	Loud (or, sharp attack)
–	Tenuto	Long/Legato
^	Marcato	Slight accent, slightly short
^	Short/Jazz Staccato/Housetop/Hat	Short, but not as short as a staccato
𝄐	Fermata	Hold the pulse (and also the note)
,	Breath	Breathe
//	Caesura	Stop
Ped.	Pedal down	Depress/release piano pedal
❋	Pedal up	Release the pedal
	Arpeggio	Roll notes sequentially, rather than play simultaneously
tr	Trill	Alternate between two notes a step apart
∿∿∿∿∿	Trill extension	Shows how long the trill lasts
	Tremolo	Repeat a note or alternate between two notes farther than a step apart (eighth, sixteenth, as fast as possible)
	Glissando	Play from one note to the next, including all notes in between
/	Bend	Smooth transition between two notes
𝆝	Mordent	See figure 6.24
∾	Turn	See figure 6.24

FIG. 6.19. Articulations

Articulations can be combined. For example, the staccato and accent together simply mean to play the note short and loud.

FIG. 6.20. Combining Articulations

If there is a slur, the articulations should go between the slur and the notehead, following the general notation guideline that specific items go closer to the note and more general items go farther away. This is an example of *louré* (or "portato") *bowing*, common in violin playing, where the notes within a single bow stroke are slightly separated.

FIG. 6.21. Articulations with Slurs

That said, watch out for illogical articulation use, such as a staccato on a half note (or longer), or an accent on a rest. These creep in particularly when engravers use notation software copy/paste shortcuts. A fermata can go on a rest, though, as it actually controls the pulse/time of the music as well as sustaining the note.

Most articulations apply to individual notes, but some span several notes. A trill extender, for example, might include a wavy extender line that shows that it lasts through several beats. The trill symbol can appear with or without that line; it means that two notes are rapidly and continually alternated, as fast as possible, for the indicated duration of the notes shown. The assumed auxiliary note of a trill is the one a diatonic step above the notated pitch. If this is not the case, the second note can be indicated in parentheses. A flat or sharp symbol with the trill can also clarify the specific auxiliary note.

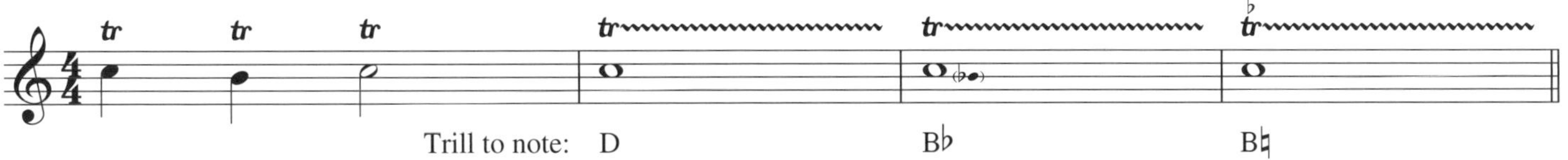

FIG. 6.22. Trills

The word *tremolo* is Italian for "tremble," and it has two different meanings. Most commonly, it refers to two notes alternating quickly. A trill is a tremolo whose notes are a half step or full step apart. A tremolo on a single note means that it repeats.

- A unison tremolo is marked with slashes on its stem or centered over a whole note.
- A tremolo a whole step or half step apart is notated as a trill, as shown previously.
- A tremolo greater than a second is notated with slashes between the two notes, which are each of the rhythmic value of the tremolo itself. Half-note tremolos are often beamed together.

One slash indicates eighth notes, two indicate sixteenth notes, and three indicate that the notes should be as fast as you can play them (i.e., unmeasured). There are two different notation conventions for them: short slash marks, or multiple beams between two notes. When the beaming convention is used, the total duration of the tremolo lasts for just one of the beamed note values.

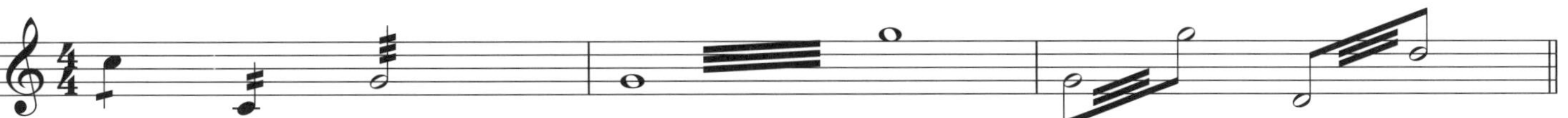

FIG. 6.23. Tremolos

Ornaments are decorations of primary notes, and their exact interpretation is a matter of some debate, as accepted practice varies between styles and eras. Here are two ornaments and their common (but not ubiquitous) interpretations: the mordent (in two forms, upper and lower/inverted) and the turn.

FIG. 6.24. Ornaments

A *glissando* (gliss.) indicates that the initial note and target note are connected by every note in between. Its symbol looks like an angled trill. Some distinguish between a glissando and a bend, where a glissando (wavy line) articulates every individual note, while a bend (straight line) smears them all together. Some instruments can only play glissandos (piano, harp), some can pretty much only play bends (trombone, fretless strings), and some can play either (trumpet, guitar with a whammy bar, electronic keyboard). The word "glissando" and its wavy line symbol are used for either, in common parlance. The word "gliss." sometimes appears with the line. Similarly, the *doit* is a short glissando, upwards, usually to infinity, and is notated with a slur (or sometimes, the word "doit"). While other instruments are perhaps capable of playing a doit, only trumpeters usually care to.

FIG. 6.25. Glissando, Bend, Doit

Some articulations, such as a staccato or accent, are purely expressive markings, indicating the length, loudness, or timbre of a note. Others are explicit technical directions, more akin to fingerings. For example, a ° symbol is often classified as an articulation, but a string player will interpret it to mean "harmonics" and thus specific fingerings, while a drum set player would see it as an indication to open the hi-hat.

So, the meaning of some common articulations will vary across instruments, and even across styles. The ^ symbol, for instance, to a classically trained musician, means "marcato" (short and slightly accented). To a jazz musician, it means "short" or "jazz staccato," which is longer in duration than a regular staccato, but has no accent or dynamic increase. However, a jazz horn player educated in school band programs might see it either way—with an accent or not. As musicians become more eclectic in what styles they perform and where they learn, and as ensembles include players from different backgrounds, misunderstandings such as this increasingly creep in, so it's important to make sure everyone is clear on meaning, and to understand the diversity of ways our language is used in the world. (Note: Some jazz engravers make the "housetop" a bit bigger to distinguish it from a marcato symbol.)

FIG. 6.26. Marcato, Short, or Jazz Staccato? You decide!

The terms *simile* (similarly) or *sempre* (always) can be used to mean that a pattern (such as articulations, bowings, drum stickings, fingerings, etc.) should continue, though individual notes are not marked. This is a way to simplify the page. In figure 6.27, we have a repeated rhythmic figure with an accent followed by two staccato markings every time. First, it is notated with every articulation showing, and then stated just once (or twice), with the word "simile" indicating that it is to continue. Either way is acceptable; simile is just a way to declutter the page. Both systems, below, are performed in exactly the same manner.

FIG. 6.27. Simile

MAKING UP YOUR OWN ARTICULATIONS

It is "legal" to make up your own symbology, if necessary, when you are asking for something that is truly novel. If you are inventing new effects or are using existing symbols to indicate unusual usage, add a notation key to the beginning of the score to clarify exactly what you intend. Keep your invented symbols simple and unique, and consider whether something standard will actually get the job done. For example, you might have a piece where a clarinetist performs a special effect involving a goldfish bowl. Sometimes, notes are played with the bell of the instrument underwater, and sometimes, notes are played normally, above water. On the page preceding the score (or at the end, if you must), you might have a key like this:

Clarinet is used in conjunction with a small goldfish bowl filled with water.

U Bell is submerged underwater.

A Bell is above water, played normally.

FIG. 6.28. Special Notation Key

While you might use a **U** and an **A** to indicate these directions, the more standard + and ◦ symbols might get the job done equally well. However, if the ◦ was also used for clarinet harmonics in the score, it might be best to find a unique symbol.

CHAPTER 7

Repeats and Roadmaps

Repeats are directions such as repeat barlines and multiple endings. *Roadmaps* are rehearsal letters, codas, segnos, and their supporting directions. Together, these symbols comprise a shorthand that helps us avoid having to present the same exact music more than once and generally to keep our bearings. They help us to minimize unnecessary redundancy, clarify the form, streamline scores, keep our places, and save paper.

REPEAT BARLINES

Repeat barlines designate a selection of measures to be played a second time verbatim, unless otherwise marked. They are comprised of a thick barline, a thin barline, and two dots surrounding the staff's middle line. Some publishers set wings at the top, which makes them easier to spot. In figure 7.1, the repeat barlines show that we play for eight measures, total.

The "path" of these measures to be performed in figure 7.1:

1 to 4

1 to 4

FIG. 7.1. Repeat Barlines

In bar 1 of figure 7.1, the left barline's *forward repeat* symbol (or *beginning repeat*) shows the starting boundary of the repeating section, with its two dots around the middle staff line and the wings facing to the right into the music of the repeated material. At bar 4's right bar line, the *backward repeat* (or *end repeat*) marks the end of the repeated section, with the dots and wings facing left. Generally, repeat barlines are only used when formal sections or phrases repeat, rather than when just one or two measures within a section repeat.

An unadvised but common shortcut is to leave out the beginning repeat when it is at measure 1; this is particularly common in theater music and jazz charts, and started as a handwriting convention. Whether or not to do this now is a matter of house style. I recommend always stating the forward repeat, though, as it serves as a "heads up" to the performer that an end repeat is coming, and it will save them from having to scan the whole chart later on, in search of where the repeated section begins. They will know right off the bat that the section is going to repeat and will not be surprised, just when they thought that they were done.

Figure 7.1 showed repeat barlines with those fancy wings. That style stands out well and is easy to see, and the wing direction further clarifies what music is "inside" the repeat system. On the other hand, there is also this simpler style, which might work better for particularly busy scores. It means the same thing.

FIG. 7.2. Repeat Barlines: Straight

When two repeating sections are adjacent within a system, they share a common thick barline in the middle. That said, it's often better to start a repeated section in a new system, rather than midway, particularly if the second section begins a new major component of the musical form (such as a chorus). Starting the repeat section on a new system is not always possible or desirable, depending on the score, but doing so sometimes helps to clarify the music's form/narrative.

FIG. 7.3. Adjacent Repeats

Additional Directions

Repeated sections are often accompanied by text that provides additional directions, either for how many times the repeat should be played or for special instructions about how the repeated measures might be varied, such as with different dynamics or other nuances on different iterations. These directions are usually set above the staff, either left-aligned with the first measure's beat 1 or right-aligned just before the last measure's right-hand barline. In the first bar, it will come across more like a section label. At the right, it will seem more like a technical direction.

(Usually, you wouldn't number every measure like I do below, but I'll do it for some of these examples to clarify the meaning of the symbols.)

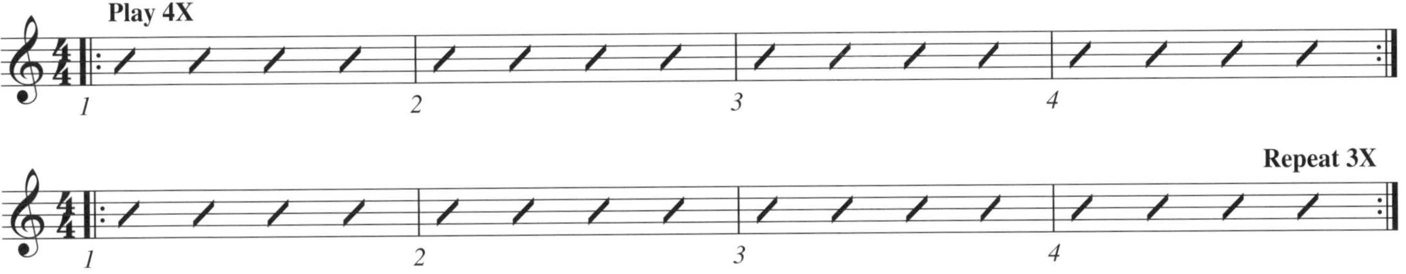

FIG. 7.4. Play and Repeat. Note: Use one or the other, not both!

Watch out for the distinctions "Repeat 4X" vs. "Play 4X." Some writers use the word "Repeat" to actually mean "Play," so if you are a musician trying to make sense of your chart, get clarification on how many iterations are intended, if there's ever any question. Sticking with "Play" will help you avoid this ambiguity—with the added benefit that it is fewer letters than "Repeat," but you see it both ways, and people may mean "Repeat" with either interpretation. Play is usually used at the beginning of the section; Repeat is generally used at the end of the section.

The path in both these examples of figure 7.4 is:

1 to 4

1 to 4

1 to 4

1 to 4

Vamps

A *vamp* is a section of music that is repeated an undetermined number of times, at the performer's discretion. A vamp might occur at the beginning of a score, in a solo section, or at the end. The word "tag" is also used to mean a vamp at the end. You might also see this written as "Tag Ending" or "Vamp Out."

FIG. 7.5. Vamp

The term "ad lib" means that the repetitions need not be played verbatim. They are to be performed "at the liberty" of the performer, who should feel free to stretch creatively, adding notes or other modifications, and generally improvising or embellishing a part as they see fit.

To indicate variations in how each repetition is performed, use "1st time," "2nd time," "last time," etc. For instance, a part might play background lines only on the second time through, or the dynamics might be different each time.

FIG. 7.6. Second Time Only

All these text clarifications are ideally set above the staff, not below.

MULTIPLE REPEAT ENDINGS

When a repeated section has different endings on different iterations, these different endings can be set in measures identified by numbered brackets, called "repeat endings." A repeat ending is a multipart symbol.

- Repeat barlines show the repeated areas, as usual, with backward repeats in the endings that jump back to an initial forward repeat.
- A bracket stretches over all the measures included in that ending. The bracket will have a "hook" on either one or both of its boundaries.
- Numerals show the sequence of the endings. The numeral should be set equidistant from the left and top boundary of the bracket. Each numeral ends with a period, and multiple numerals within the same bracket are separated by commas.

Bracketed repeat endings are useful for relatively extended structures where significant space will be saved (say, a page). For short examples (like the following ones used to illustrate the different symbols), it is usually better to write out the repeated measures.

Most commonly, there are just two endings. In figure 7.7, the sequence of measures played is:

1-2

1-3-4

There should be daylight visible between the right bracket of the first ending and left bracket of the second ending. No touching!

FIG. 7.7. Repeat Endings

You could also have three or more endings. The sequence in figure 7.8 is:

1-2

1-3

1-4-5

FIG. 7.8. Three Repeat Endings

You can also use the same ending brackets for multiple "passes" through them. Just have one period, at the end of the series of passes. In this case, we are playing the section four times: the first ending is repeated twice (played three times), and then it goes through again with the fourth ending:

1-2

1-2

1-2

1-3-4

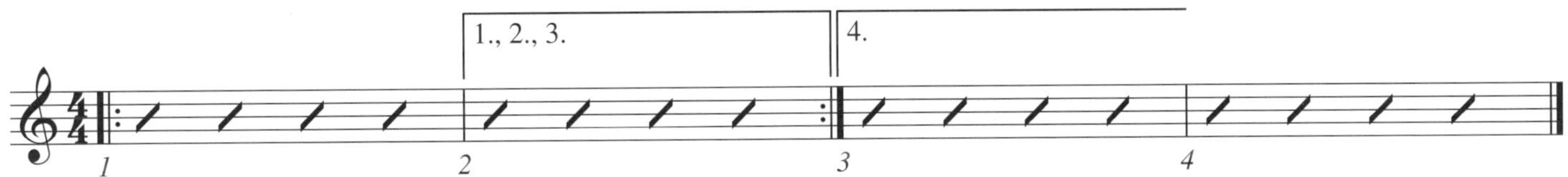

FIG. 7.9. Multiple Passes

There are various conventions for the brackets regarding their beginning and ending left/right boundaries. Some publishers use a hook on both ends that extends only to the base line of the ending numeral, as we have been doing.

Other publishers extend the line to connect with the barline, to be more of a barrier, leaving the left side of a first ending open and inviting for the musician to enter, then forming a hard barrier at the end that connects to the staff. For a second/last ending, the connecting line is on the left, with no vertical line at the end of the second ending, which makes for a clear getaway. However, if the end of the second ending is also the end of the piece, it should have a hook on the right (see figure 7.13).

FIG. 7.10. Open Second Ending

There are also two common ways to handle the length of the second ending. Some publishers limit it to a single measure, as above. Others extend it through the end of the section. In either case, the end of the bracket should align with the right-hand barline of the terminal measure of the repeat ending.

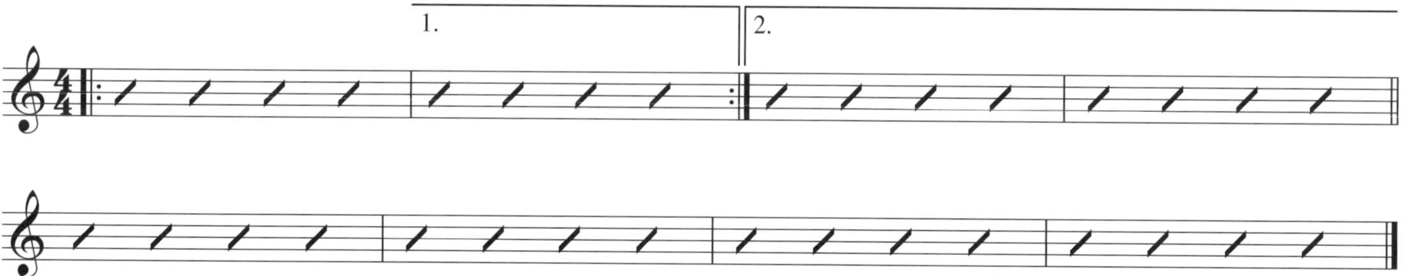

FIG. 7.11. Bracket over Complete Second Ending

There are two common conventions for how to handle a first ending that spans multiple systems. First, you could just set the bracket over the first measure and the last measure of the first ending, with no hook on the right of the first part or the left of the second part.

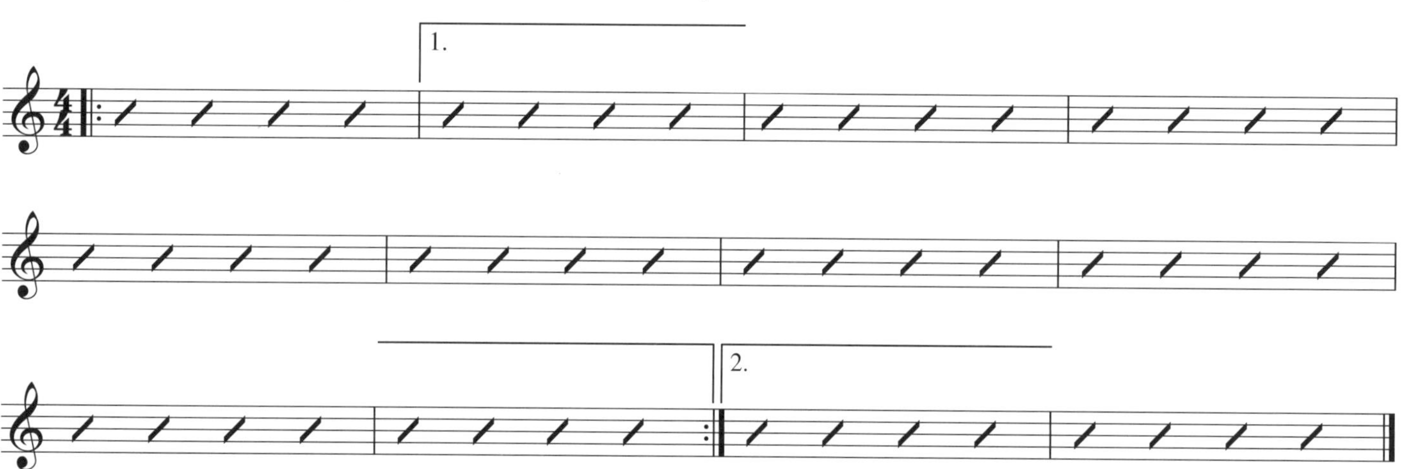

FIG. 7.12. Broken First Ending

Alternatively, extend the line across all the systems, including an extra line on the system(s) between them, if applicable. This way is easier for a musician to follow, but it can add clutter. Note that in the last measure, we have a hook at the end of the second ending bracket, clarifying that this is the end of the piece.

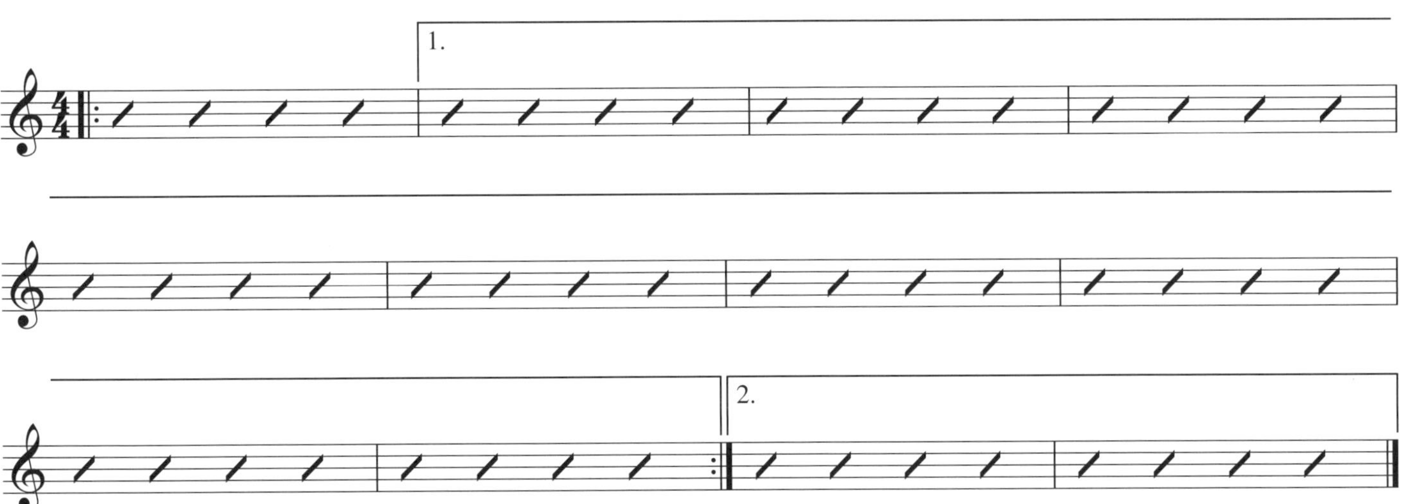

FIG. 7.13. Extended First Ending Bracket

If chord symbols are present, set them between the repeat ending bracket and the notation, not above the brackets. This follows the general convention that symbols more locally relevant to the notes are closer to them. Repeats are more general than chords, so they are farther away.

FIG. 7.14. Repeat Endings with Chord Symbols

While you can use all these symbols in your scores, keep in mind that many musicians are utterly baffled by them. If they haven't had significant musical education, there is a high likelihood that train wrecks will occur. These performers may get lost in the repeat endings, so go over their use in rehearsals. Also, particularly for music with lyrics, different verses require different rhythms or note variations. You can use dashed ties and lyrics in parentheses to make these retrofits work, but it is often clearer to just present the measures multiple times, rather than give into the temptation to use multiple repeat endings. Donate to a conservation organization, if the extra paper required bothers you.

ROADMAPS

Major formal sections are often marked by capital letters enclosed in boxes. Set them above the staff, either left of or centered with the left barline of the measure starting the section. Hide the measure number for that measure if there would ordinarily be one. In extended works such as operas or symphonies that use up the whole alphabet, double letters (AA, BB, etc.) can be used after you arrive at Z. Generally, a double barline accompanies rehearsal letters, particularly if it also marks a significant formal section.

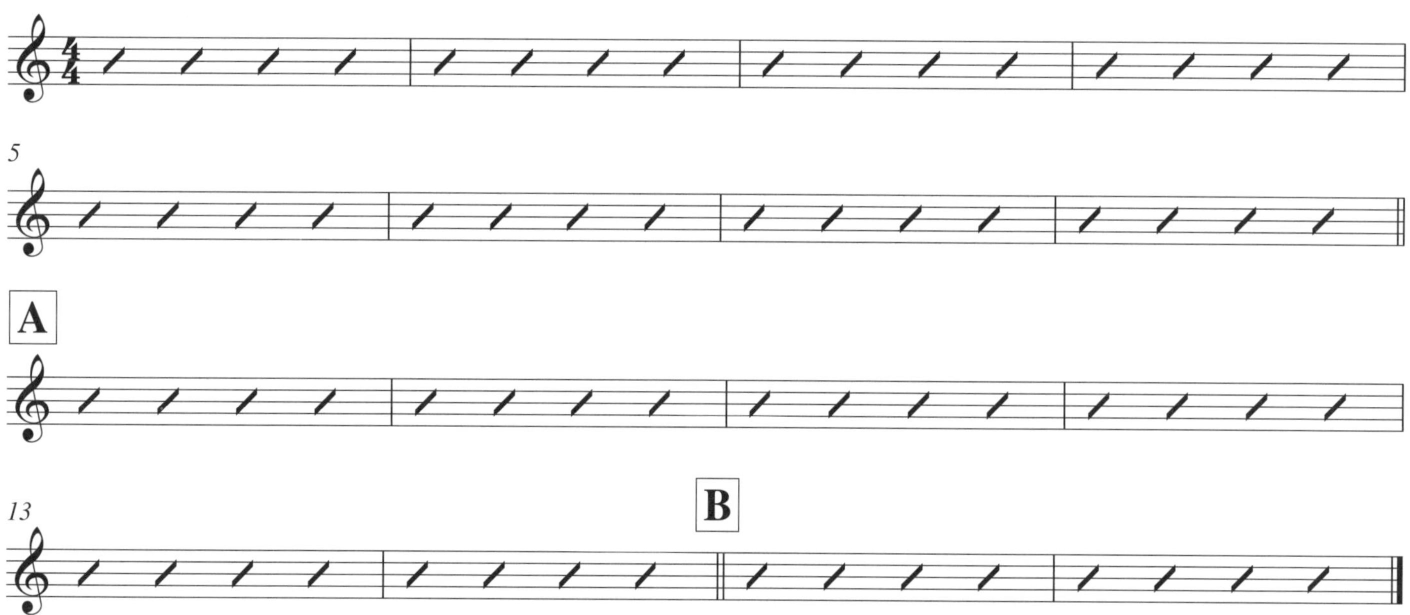

FIG. 7.15. Rehearsal Letters

There are a few noteworthy alternatives or accompaniments to using rehearsal letters. You might instead use:

- Measure numbers instead of letters at the start of sections.

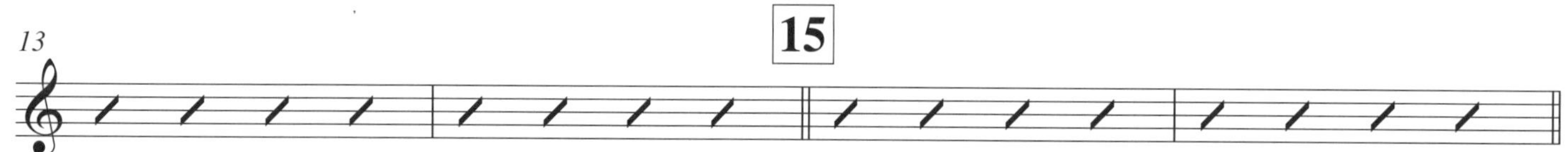

FIG. 7.16. Measure Number as a Roadmap

- Words that describe song sections, such as Intro, End, Verse, Chorus, etc. These are often used in conjunction with measure numbers or other rehearsal markings, serving as further clarification.

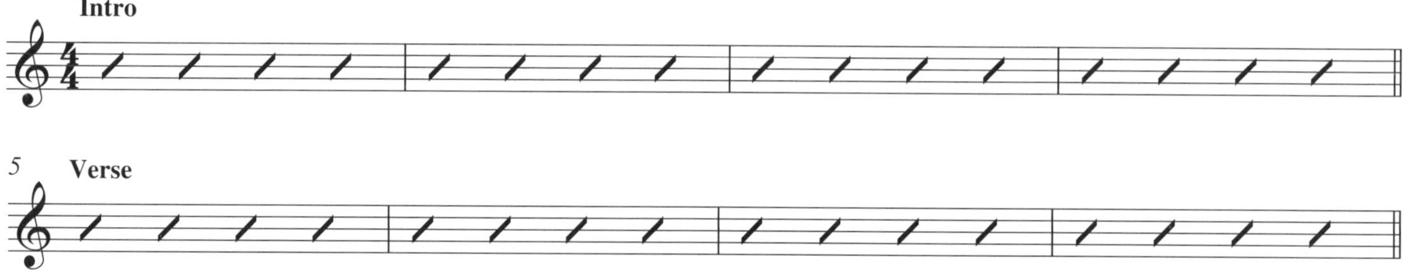

FIG. 7.17. Words

Handwriting-style scores, particularly for jazz, often will set text like this with a three-quarter frame around it, cuddling it close to the staff. This clarifies which system the text references and separates it from other notation symbols.

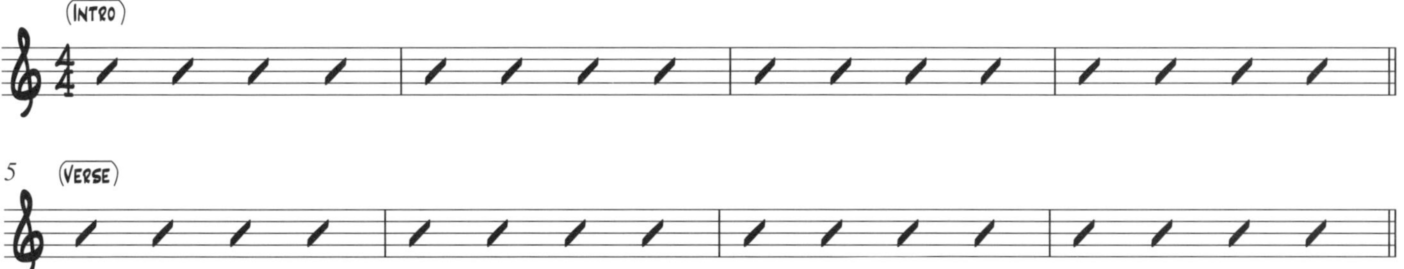

FIG. 7.18. Words with Bracket

- A combination of letters and measure numbers within the section, where the letters indicate an iteration of a verse/chorus or other recurring multipart formal construction, and the numbers show subsections within that iteration. This is an instance where a single barline might well precede the rehearsal marking, rather than a double barline separating the verse/chorus pair. Note the potential confusion between the ninth bar of the whole piece and the ninth bar of the A section. A9 can also be called measure 13. It might be better to choose one numbering scheme or the other.

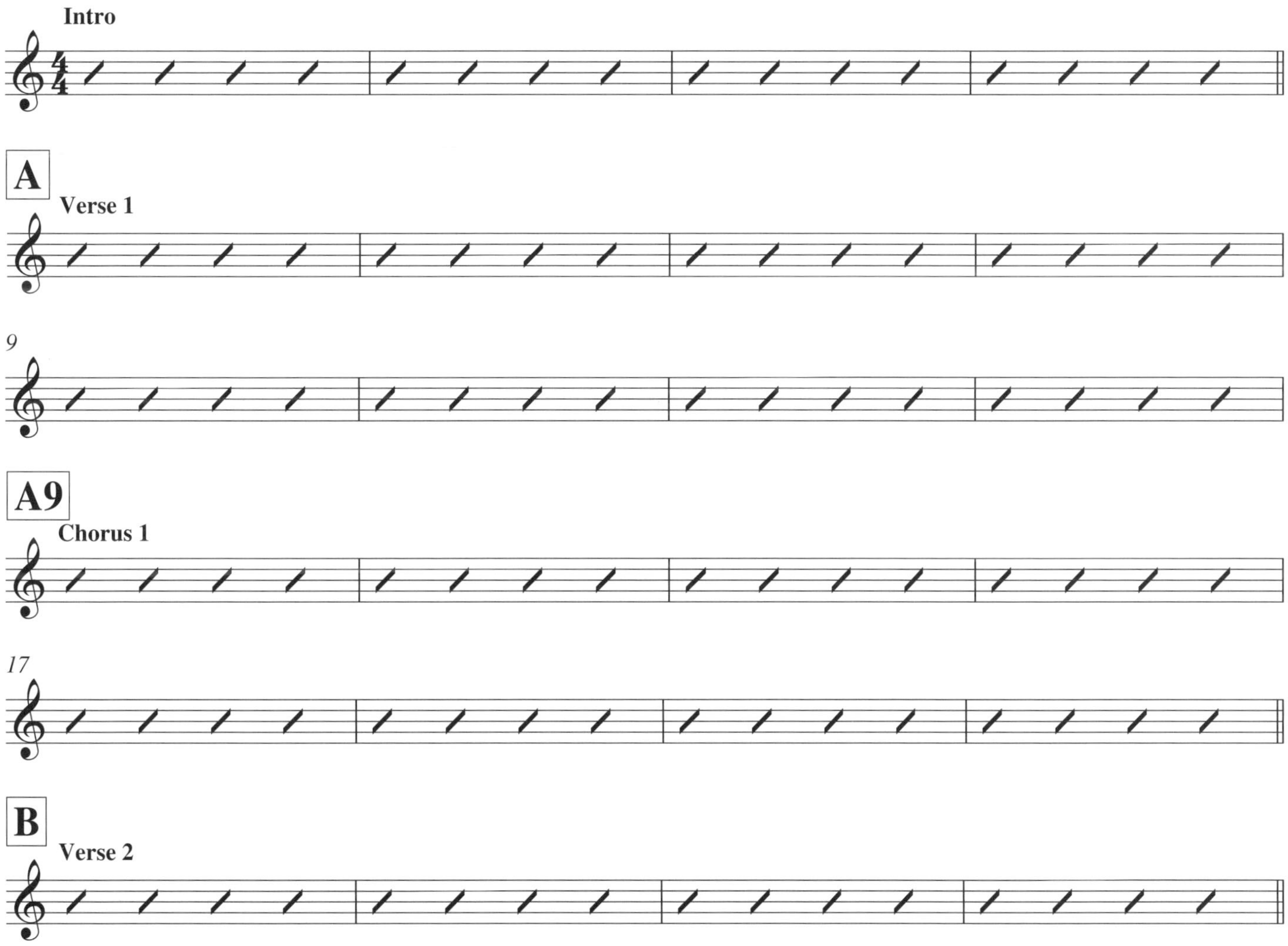

Intro

A

Verse 1

9

A9

Chorus 1

17

B

Verse 2

FIG. 7.19. Letters with Numerals

CODAS AND SEGNOS

Coda

"Coda" translates literally to "tail." Musicians use it to mean "ending." The coda symbol indicates the start of the coda measure or measures, which might simply be a final measure or two of ending, or more of a substantial section of the form.

FIG. 7.20. Coda

Most often, the coda symbol at the end is used as a destination point that we jump to from a "To Coda" direction that is set at an earlier measure.

The path in figure 7.21:

1 to 20

1 to 10

21 to 22

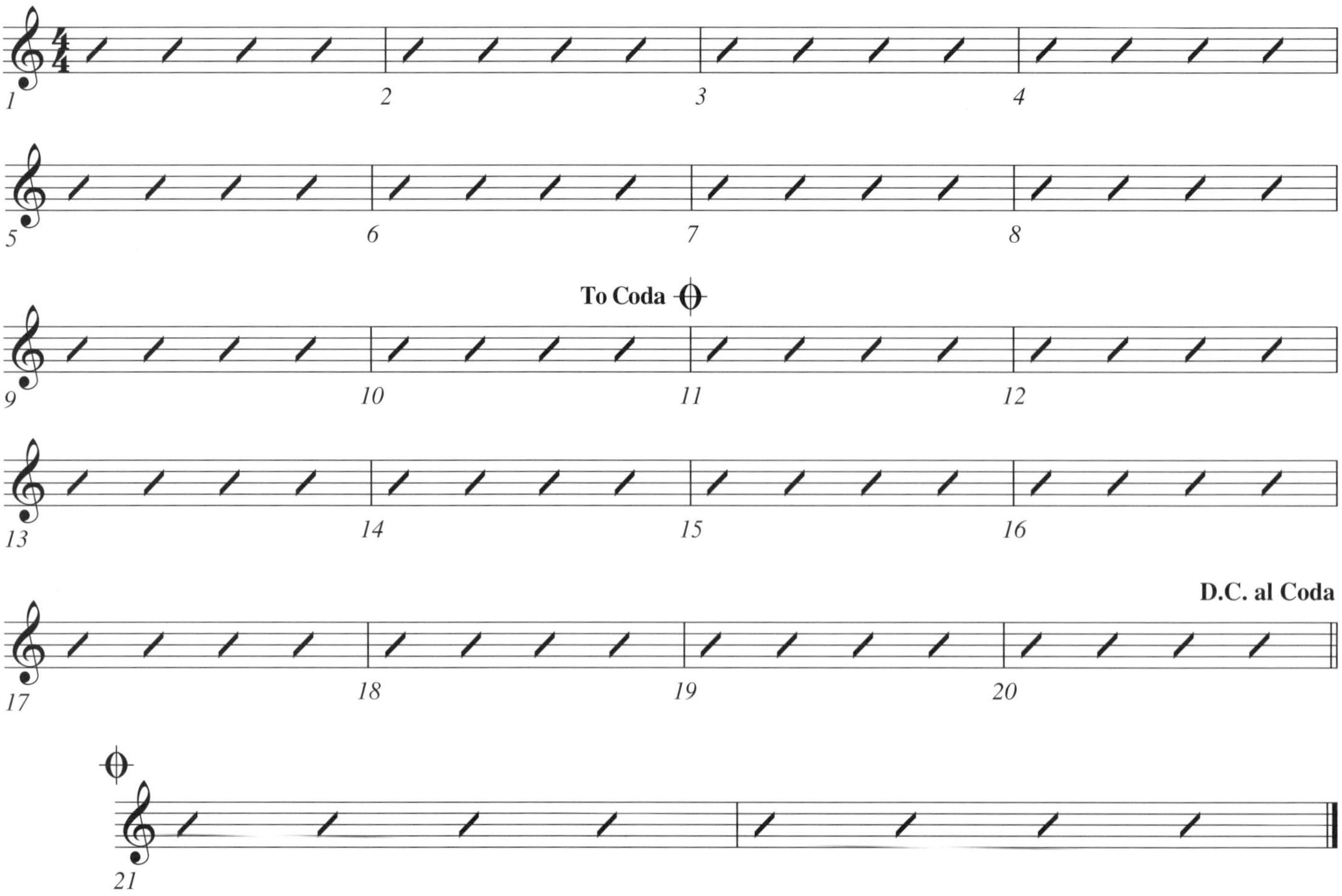

FIG. 7.21. Coda System

In figure 7.21, we have a form that repeats, and then the last time only, halfway through, we go to the coda, rather than continuing on to bar 10. In bar 20, we see the direction "D.C. al Coda," meaning, "take it from the top (i.e., da capo) and then play the coda." In this way, the coda performs much like a second ending, but it can be a simpler, more elegant way to achieve the same result than the bracket system. Just remember the three components, in the order that they appear:

1. Direction to jump to the coda symbol, such as To Coda, or To Coda 𝄌, or To 𝄌, or just the 𝄌. This is right-aligned with the end of the measure where it occurs.
2. D.C. al Coda (or variant). This is also right-aligned with the measure in which it takes effect.
3. Coda. This is the ending itself. A common convention is to indent the coda, but only do that if it doesn't otherwise complicate your life. The coda symbol should be to the far left of the measure, or possibly aligned with the indented staff.

Codas can also start mid system to alleviate page turns or clarify the form. When they do, add some white space between the preceding measure and the start of the coda, and begin the coda measure with a double barline.

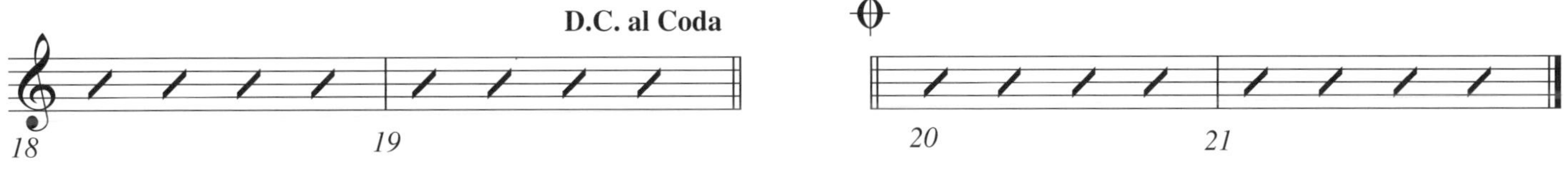

FIG. 7.22. Coda Starting Mid System

Segnos

A *segno*, or sign, is like the opposite of a coda. While a coda is a point in the future that we jump to, a segno is a point in the past, where we go back in time and play some material again. This is useful when we are not repeating from the beginning of a chart, but rather, from a point partway in, such as the beginning of a verse after an introduction. It is also used when there is a pickup measure. Instead of a D.C. al Coda, we now use a D.S. al Coda: del segno (from the sign) and then to the coda.

Here's the path through this score with a segno system:

1 to 20

5 to 10

21 to 22

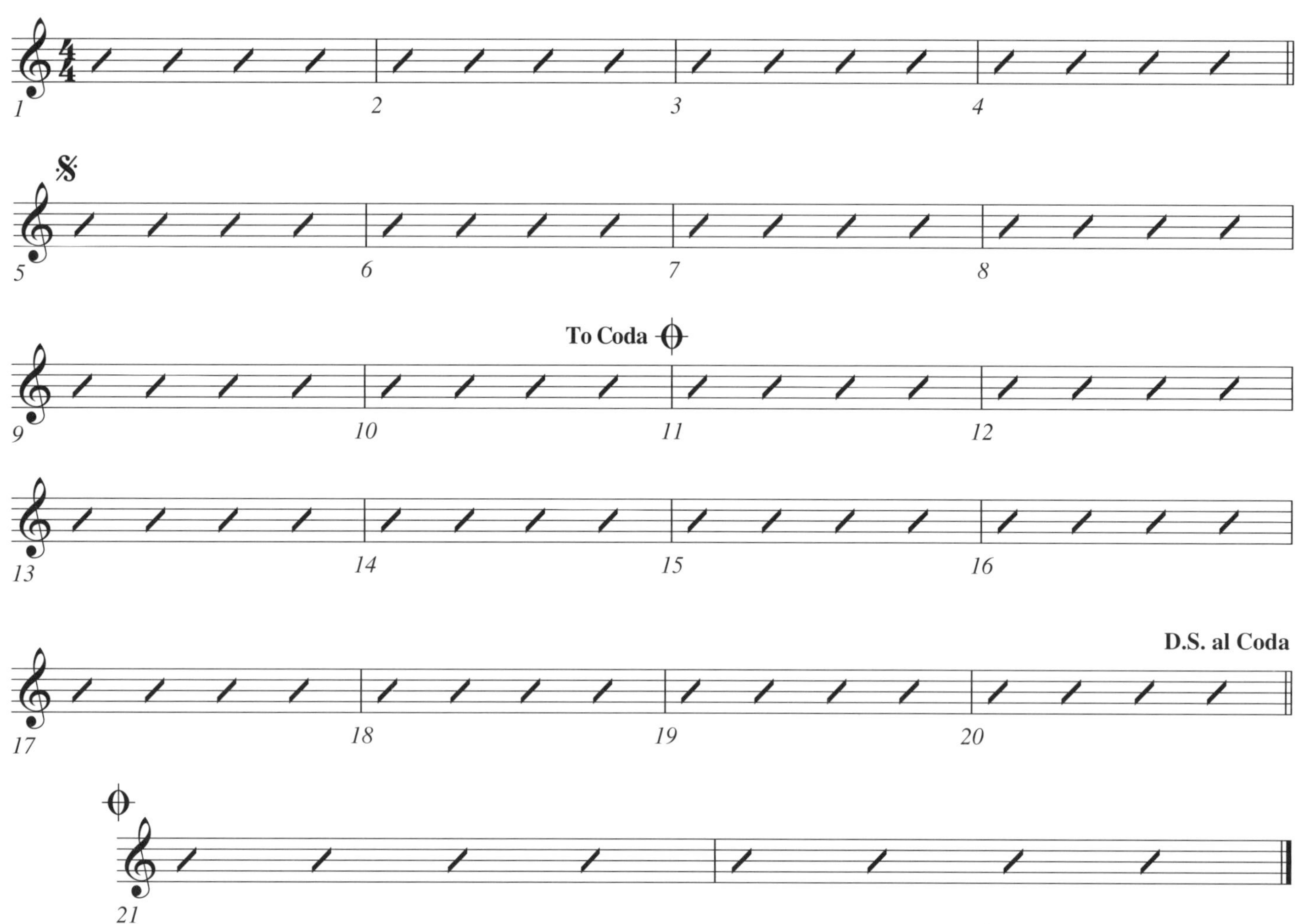

FIG. 7.23. Segno System

Very long scores (symphonies, operas, etc.) might have multiple coda or segno systems, marked with two adjacent symbols. You have a coda within a coda. Here is a very compressed example, just so that you can follow the logic.

The path through figure 7.24:

1 to 12

5 to 10

13 to 20

13 to 18

21 to 22

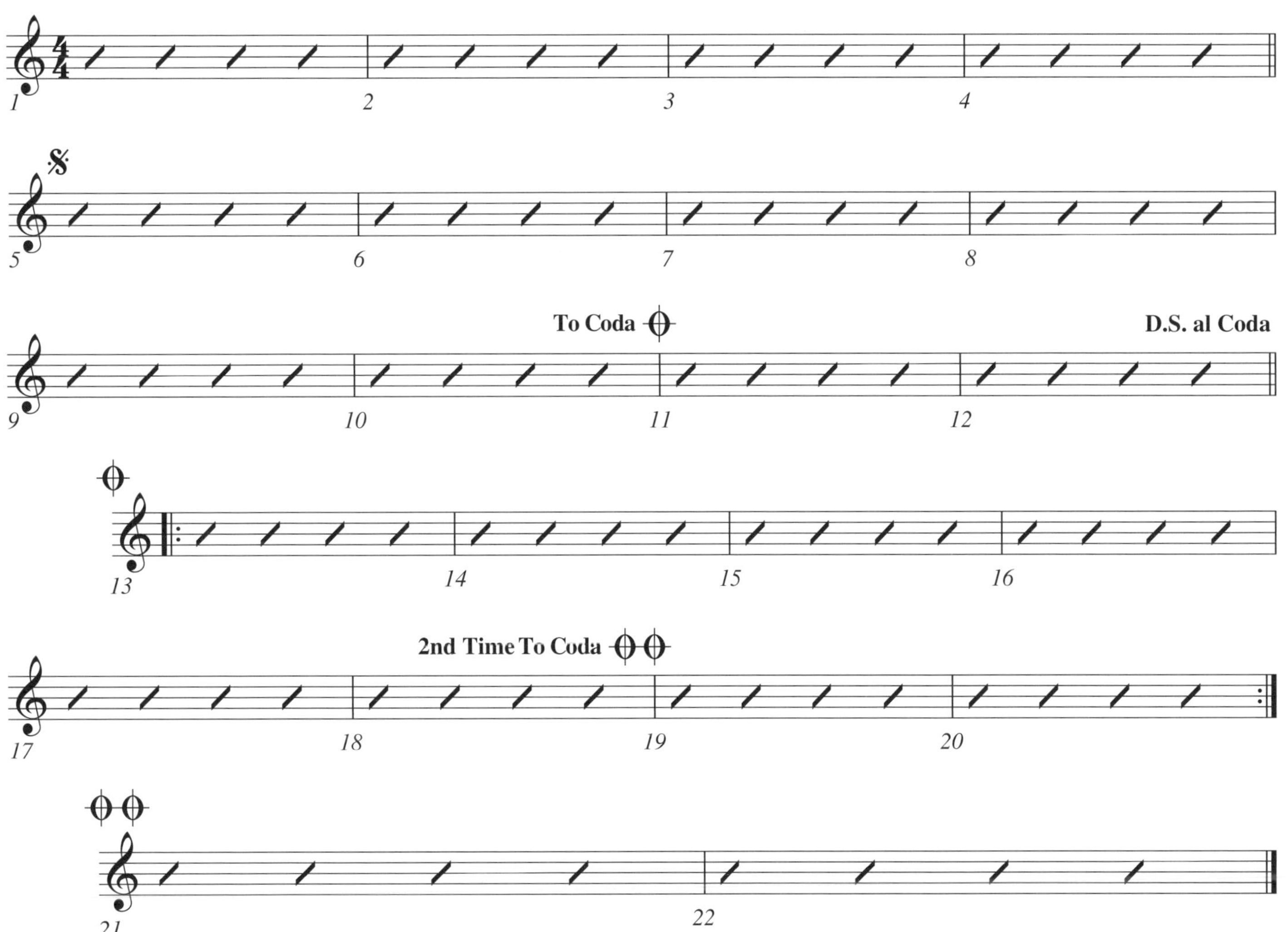

FIG. 7.24. Double Coda System

Anticipate confusion. . . .

Fine

Similar to "al coda" is "Fine." *Fine* (fee-nay) means "the end." In this case, rather than jumping to a coda, we end at the word "fine." Whereas a coda is an ending section of a piece, a fine is a specific point of ending.

The path in figure 7.25 is:

1 to 20

5 to 12

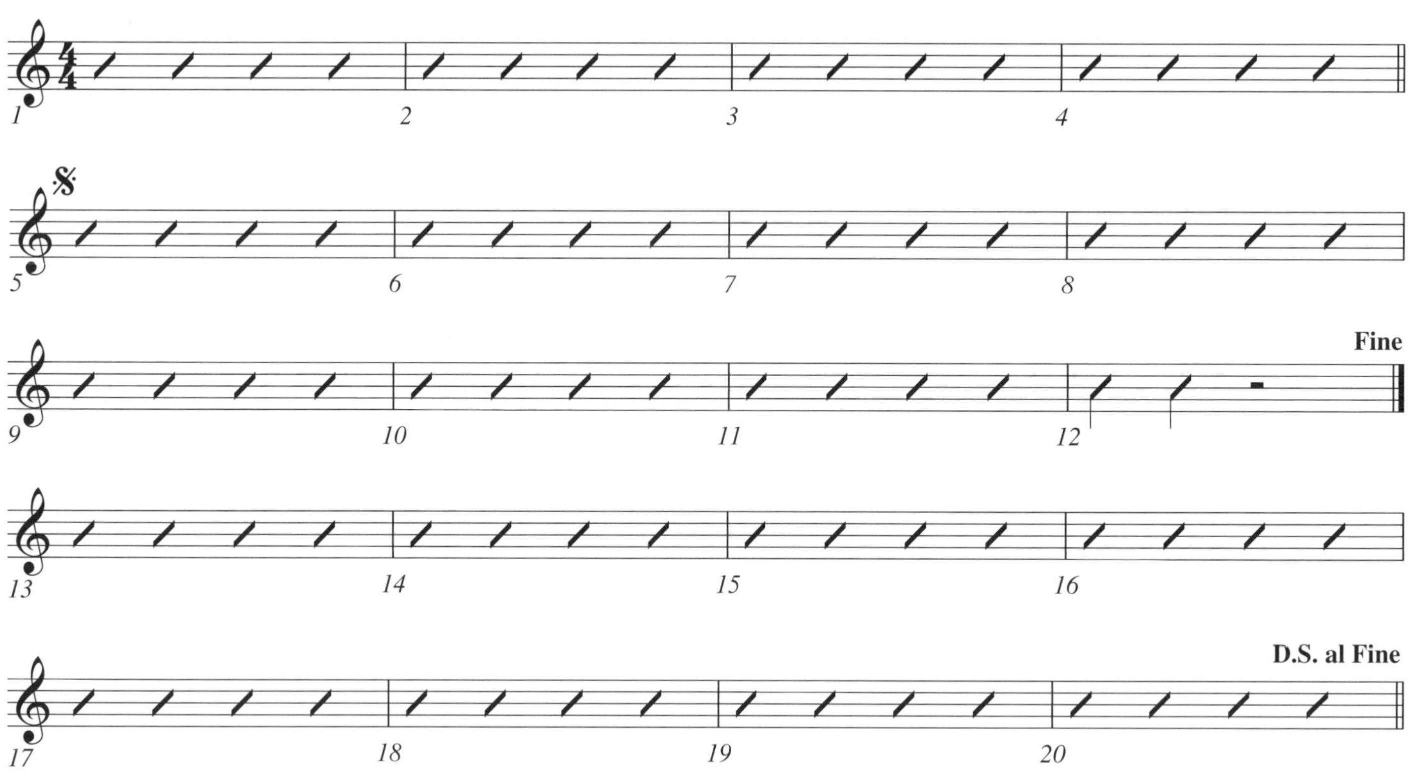

FIG. 7.25. Fine

Make sure the "fine" measure shows a clear way to end. Again, align the **Fine** in the measure with where it takes effect.

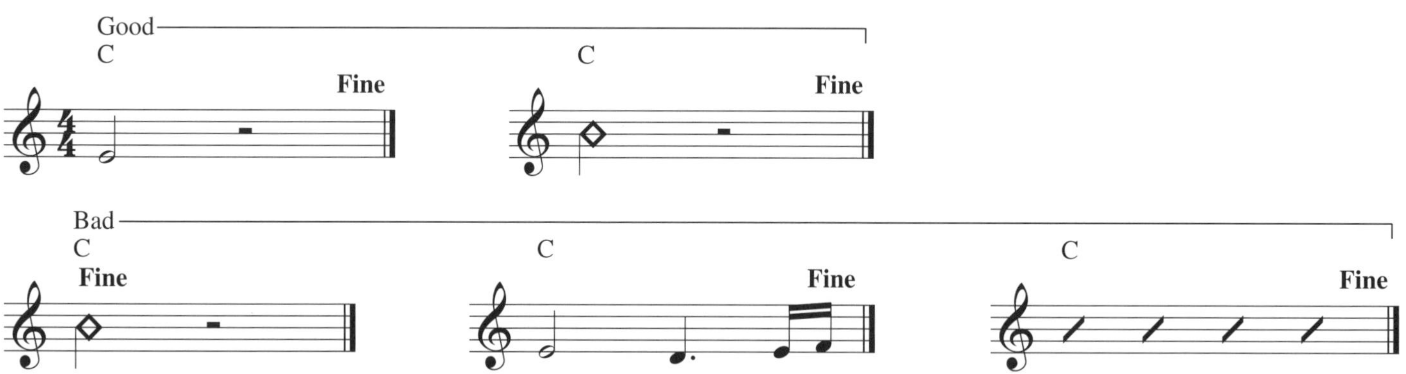

FIG. 7.26. Good and Bad Fines

That's all, folks!

CHAPTER 8

Instrument-Specific Notation

Most instruments have specific notation conventions. Fingerings are common in many instruments, from violins to pianos. They show which fingers play which notes. Drum notation may include R or L to indicate the right or left hand. Trombones have position numbers, with the addition of a flat or sharp showing that the slide should be a little farther out or in. Guitar notation uses circled numerals to differentiate the string numbers from the finger numbers. And guitars and other stringed instruments sometimes use tablature, which shows strings and frets, rather than (or in addition to) the traditional staff.

This chapter explores how to use many kinds of instrument-specific notation. Most techniques are adaptable for several related instruments.

GENERAL TECHNICAL NOTATION PRINCIPLES

Common Fingering Standards

Every instrument has its own conventions for fingerings or other markings to assist the player with technique. Many share the use of numerals to correspond to fingers. Piano fingerings label the thumb through pinky as 1 to 5. Guitar, though, numbers the thumb as T, the index finger through pinky as 1 to 4—or alternatively, as *p-i-m-a* (and rarely, *c*) for thumb through pinky. A trombone chart will use the numbers 1 to 7 to mean slide positions, rather than fingerings.

RH and LH (or r.h. and l.h.) universally mean "right hand" and "left hand." That said, it is a long-held notation convention for guitar and other strings to discriminate against left-handed players. For these cases, the "right hand" more specifically means the "strumming hand," "bowing hand," etc., and the "left hand" is the "fingerboard hand." A player who uses an instrument strung or designed for lefties will likely be accustomed to making this mental shift and suffering the marginalizing assault to their egos with as much dignity as they can muster. For the record, I believe that lefties are people too, despite my perpetuation here in sharing standards that are not in support of their plight. Lefties: you're always right.

At any rate, the point is, there are similarities between instruments in that many use numerals, though what these numerals mean varies considerably. In this section, we will look at special practices for many instruments. First, let's consider some general fingering practices for all instruments. I'll use the term "fingerings" in the most general sense, to mean actual fingerings, slide positions, drum stickings, etc.

Placement

The ideal place for most fingering numerals is centered above the note. That's where it's easiest to see—unassailed by staff lines and altogether in clear relationship to their fellow fingerings. However, depending on what else is happening on the page, this may not be possible, so let's consider the pros and cons of various fingering placement options.

- Above the staff, centered horizontally with the note. Ideal for visibility and logic, particularly for individual notes (as opposed to chords). This placement makes them easier to see as a whole, in relationship to all other fingerings, and so they become an independent narrative. This placement also ensures that the fingering numerals are not in conflict with the staff lines. An alternative standard is to set them opposite the stem direction, like articulations.

  For keyboards or other instruments that read two staves, the top staff fingerings go above the staff and the bottom staff fingerings go below the staff.
- Off the staff, but to the left side of the note. Another good choice, if articulations make this necessary, though it may add a little busyness to the page, and the independent narrative of fingerings is disrupted.
- On the staff, left of the note. Often, the best choice for chords, with multiple fingerings corresponding to different notes. Avoid confusing overlaps between staff lines and the fingering numerals, such as the horizontal lines of a 2 or 5, and try not to cross the numeral with more than one staff line. It's better set left of the note than right, so that the player has some warning about what fingering to use before the note sounds.
- On the staff, right of the note. Only when necessary, such as when a chord is on beat 1, thus forcing a battle between the left barline and perhaps some accidentals. It's not ideal, though, as the player sees the fingering only after the note sounds—after the horse has left the barn. However, it is sometimes the best option. Frown when you do it; it is an ugly business.

FIG. 8.1. Fingering Placement

When to Use Fingerings

Some fingerings are actually expressive markings with timbre implications, while others are purely technical suggestions, included for pedagogical purposes rather than musical ones. The ones that have a musical effect, such as slap bass articulations, should appear on both an individual part and on an arrangement. Fingerings that are present for more pedagogical purposes, such as trumpet valve positions, need only be present on the individual instrumentalist's part, rather than the full conductor's score.

The level of fingering detail depends on the level of the reader and the pedagogical goal of the material. Music for early players tends to have more fingerings. An etude for a beginning-level musician might have fingerings on every note. Some edited scores for more advanced players will only show fingerings when there is something non-obvious to illustrate, such as a specific string that will result in a specific tone color.

Songbooks, lead sheets, and conductors' scores usually do not have fingerings.

To simplify the page, it is common to use "*simile*" or "*sim.*" to mean that a fingering technique continues.

Special Notation

Many notation conventions for prepared piano—plucking the strings, smashing the instrument with sledgehammers, and such—are not standardized. However, there are a few useful common conventions that generally apply.

×	Generally used to indicate a non-pitched note.
○ +	Two different states of something, such as a hi-hat open and closed, or a mute removed or inserted. By itself, the ° indicates a special state of a note, such as a harmonic or a special preparation.
○ ◇	Natural and fingered harmonic.
-----┐ ———┐	Something continues for the line's duration, ending at the hook.
vib., *non vib.*	Use vibrato; don't use vibrato.
⌇	Rolled/broken/arpeggiated chords.
∿∿∿	Techniques such as trills or flutter-tongues are indicated as continuing through beats and/or notes by use of a horizontal wavy line. There should be a text clarification of exactly what technique is being specified.
/	Pitch bend.
⌒	Different technical meanings for different instruments, but they generally mean to play legato, and to group the notes as a coherent idea.
1–1; 1–2	Finger shifts, with portamento (an audible slide). If the numbers are the same, the first finger slides to another note. If the numbers are different, the fingers change while still holding the note, without rearticulating it. Without the dash, 1 1 is a finger shift without portamento.
simile (sim.) or *sempre*	Continue the previously described technique.
ord. or *nat.* or *normale*	Ordinario, naturale, normale. Stop doing the special technique.

FIG. 8.2. Common Technical Symbols

Text directions clarify any points of ambiguity. Make sure that they either align with the beat or precede it, giving the player a chance to prepare. Whenever you use nonconventional notation, include a key at the beginning of the score to clarify exactly what you mean.

PIANO

Piano and other keyboard instruments are normally notated on a grand staff—treble and bass clef braced together—though synth parts might be on a single staff (such as for a synth bass part). Fingers are numbered 1 to 5, thumb to pinky. Typically, the right hand plays the treble clef and the left hand plays the bass clef, but the hands can cross over and share a clef. LH and RH are used to disambiguate what they are doing, particularly if the left hand must play higher than the right, or vice versa.

FIG. 8.3. Piano Notation

Tempo and mood directions are set above the top staff. Dynamic symbols are set between the staves, unless the hands are playing at different levels, in which case the symbols are set under each individual staff. Pedal markings are set below the bottom staff.

Here are some piano-specific markings.

Ped.	Damper pedal (rightmost) engaged.
❋	Damper or sostenuto pedal released.
______⌋	Pedal engaged and released.
_/_/_	Damper pedal depressed halfway at each dip.
sos. or *sostenuto*	Sostenuto pedal engaged.
una corda	Una corda (leftmost) pedal engaged.
tre corde	Una corda pedal released.
High Stick, Med. Stick, Low Stick, Open	Stick height for grand piano. "Open" generally means to open the top of whatever piano you have as wide as possible.
◇	Notes depressed without hammers striking strings. Also used to indicate notes to be held while pedalled by sostenuto pedal.

FIG. 8.4. Piano-Specific Notation

Pedals

A grand piano has three pedals: una corda, sostenuto (only on grand pianos), and damper, also called the "sustain" pedal (easily confused with sostenuto). The most commonly used pedal is the damper, which raises the hammers off the strings so that the notes continue ringing, rather than releasing when the keys are released. The damper pedal is sometimes set only halfway down.

There are three common systems for indicating pedal engagement. All may be used with the damper pedal; the other two pedals do not use the Ped. and ❋ markings. Though just one staff is shown here to save space, usually piano music would be on a grand staff.

FIG. 8.5. Pedal Notation

Rolled Chords

Notes of a *rolled chord* (or "arpeggio" or "broken chord") are attacked in fast succession, as if strumming the strings of a harp, rather than struck simultaneously. They are notated with a wavy vertical line, left of the noteheads, connecting through the staves, with the end points aligned with the top and bottom notes of the chord. Arrows sometimes indicate whether the chord is rolled from bottom to top (low to high) or top to bottom (high to low). If there is no arrow, it is assumed that it rolls from bottom to top.

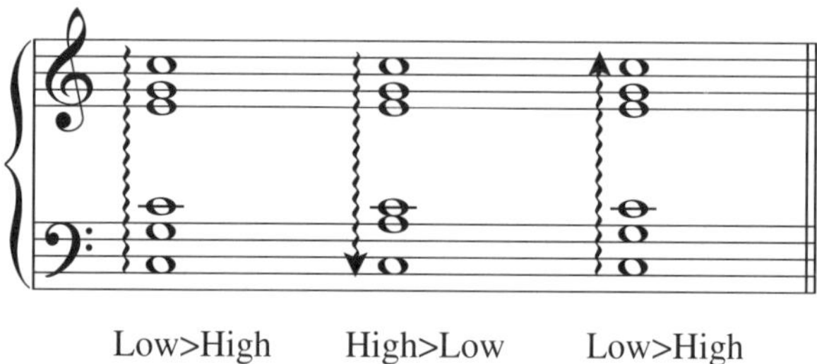

FIG. 8.6. Rolled Chords

GUITAR/PLUCKED STRINGS

Guitar notation may be rendered in three styles: traditional notation, tablature, and fretboard diagrams. Other string instruments, such as ukulele, banjo, mandolin, and bass guitar, also use forms of these conventions, though modified for their specific number of strings and transpositions.

When more than one is present, the fretboard diagrams are set on top, above the traditional staff. The tablature staff is set below the traditional staff.

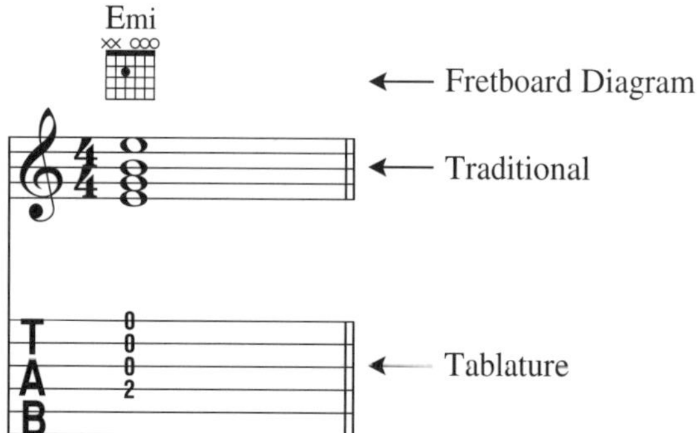

FIG. 8.7. Three Types of Guitar Notation

Guitar Notation Symbols

Here are some common guitar notation symbols.

T or *p*	thumb (*pulgar*)
1 or *i*	index finger (*indice*)
2 or *m*	middle finger (*medio*)
3 or *a*	ring finger (*anular*)
4 or *c*	pinky (*chiquito*)
o	open string (no fretting-hand fingers)
◦	harmonic
①②③④⑤⑥	strings, high to low, usually E B G D A E for guitar
Roman numerals	fretboard positions
sul (string letter name)	on the string specified
C (often paired with a Roman numeral to indicate fret)	capo—that is, your index finger barred across all strings at the indicated fret
⊓ or ↓	down-stroke
V or ↑	up-stroke
H or HO	hammer-on
P or PO	pull-off
S with a line	slide (or scoop)
B or ⤴	bend (unspecified distance)
1/4 ⤴ 1/2 ⤴ 1 ⤴	bend: a quarter, half, and whole step
⌒	A slur connecting two notes indicates that the second is articulated with the fretboard hand, rather than plucked with the strumming hand.
R	release
L	lift
∿∿∿	vibrato
× notehead	muted string

FIG. 8.8. Guitar Notation

Traditional Staff Notation

In traditional notation for guitar, the notes sound an octave lower than written. Guitar is thus considered a transposing instrument. Notes and rhythms are indicated on a treble clef staff. Strings are indicated in circled numerals from 1 to 6, with 1 being the high E string, and 6 being the low E string. Numerals without circles indicate fretboard-hand fingerings, usually the left hand. The letters *p i m a c* (often called "the PIMA system") indicate plucking/strumming-hand fingers, usually the right hand; the PIMA system is particularly common in the classical guitar world. Numerals plus T for thumb are also often used for fingerings.

A line might be used to show how long the string specification should stay in effect. If there are extensive fingerings and string indications, the strings can go below the staff and the fingerings above. Otherwise, it is permissible to have both above the staff, or to follow the noteheads. If the string and fingering numerals are near each other, the strings go above and to the left of the fingering, which should be centered on the notehead.

Fretboard position numerals are specified with Roman numerals, indicating the fret number to which the index finger is oriented. Guitarists can stretch outside this to grab an occasional note, but the markings show where they should orient their hand.

A C followed by a Roman numeral (e.g., CV) indicates a *barre*; the index finger holds down the strings at the indicated fret (5th fret, in this case). C means all strings, but you can also indicate fractions of the strings (out of 6): 1/2C for three strings, 2/3C for four strings, 5/6C for five strings, etc.

There are multiple approaches to traditional guitar notation, using all these symbols. Some writers prefer to indicate string numbers and fingerings for every note, while others prefer simply to indicate positions. Both yield the same effect.

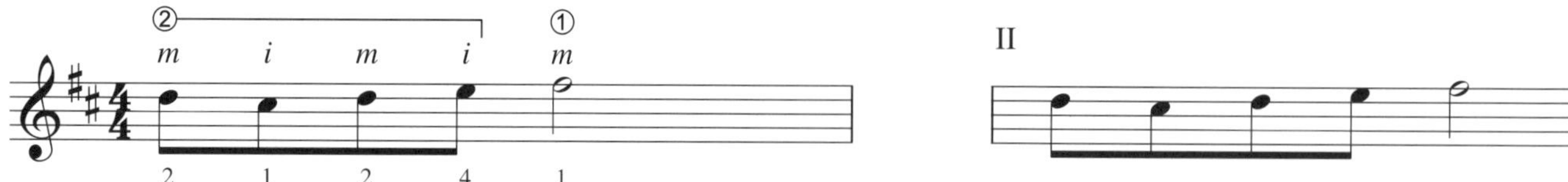

FIG. 8.9. Detailed vs. Sparse Fingering Directions

Harmonics

Harmonics are isolated overtones of a vibrating string; using them expands the range of the guitar. They are played by lightly touching a vibrating string at various points (nodes) along its length, and different notes can be achieved depending on where the string is stopped. Electric guitars have more possibilities for which harmonics can be used effectively, as their amplification capabilities can boost the volume of harmonics that would barely speak on an acoustic instrument. There are two types of harmonics:

1. *Natural* harmonics are on an open string.

2. *Artificial* harmonics are on a string that is stopped at one of the frets.

Guitar notation for harmonics varies considerably. What seems to be the most widely accepted approach is that either diamond noteheads or regular noteheads with the harmonic symbol ° are set at the sounding pitches. Some writers instead set the diamond at the fingered pitch; you can tell the approach being used by the range of the note (high notes are harmonics, low notes are fingered notes). Text clarifications are also common: they may specify that harmonics are in use, a position/string/fret indication, or a combination of any of these.

Figure 8.10 presents a roundup of harmonic indication styles for guitar. All notes sound the harmonic A on the first ledger line above the staff. In addition to being different notation conventions, they also reveal different philosophical approaches for how prescriptive to be about fingerings and timbre. Different guitarists may use different strings and node points to produce these sounds, with some of the more general approaches, and the nature of the resulting sound will vary. A writer may or may not want to encourage such flexibility.

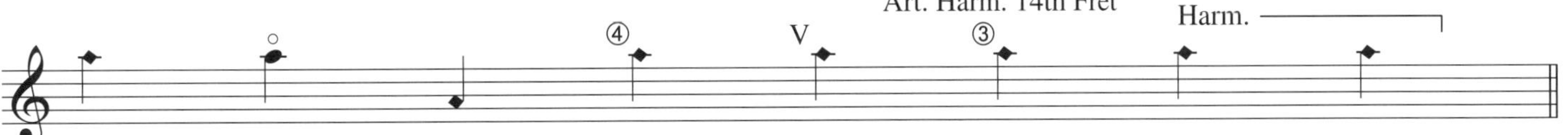

FIG. 8.10. Guitar Harmonics

Finger Shifts

A *finger shift* is a technique in which the same finger is used on the same string for two or more consecutive notes. Finger shifts are indicated with lines connecting the fingerings, generally following the melodic contour and centered between fingering numerals. When a shift occurs across a system break, the initial fingering has the line and the target fingering has just the numeral.

FIG. 8.11. Finger Shifts

Alternate Tunings

Generally, the guitar is tuned (high to low) E B G D A E. However, alternate tunings of the strings are also common. If this is the case, it should be specified in the first bar.

You might specify that a single string is tuned to a specific note or that multiple strings (e.g., DADDAD, DADGAD, etc.) are retuned; it is assumed that they are listed low to high, in the latter case.

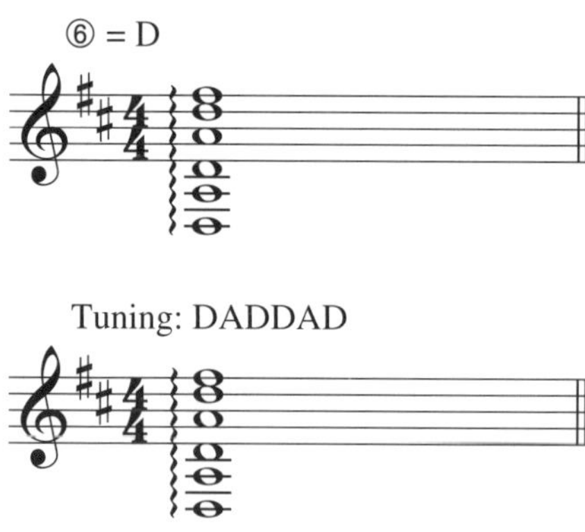

FIG. 8.12. Alternate Tuning Indications

Articulations

Guitar strings are generally plucked with a finger or plectrum by the "strumming hand." They can also be sounded by the "fretboard hand," through various techniques such as pull-offs, hammer-ons, releases, bends, and slides. The articulation is set above the notes, centered between them. A *slur* connecting two notes indicates that the second is articulated with the fretting hand, not the strumming hand. Some articulations, such as slides, might appear with or without the slur, depending on the intended attack of the target note. Other articulations, such as hammer-ons or pull-offs, wouldn't make sense without the slur, as articulating the string with the strumming hand would negate the effect. Articulations might appear in either the traditional staff or the tablature staff.

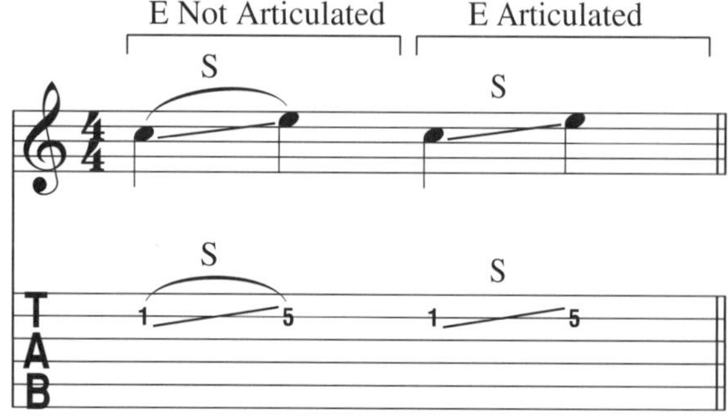

FIG. 8.13. Slide Articulations. With and without slur.

A *bend* is when the pitch of the string is altered not just by pressing the string at the fret, but by applying additional pressure on the string (up or down) to further raise the pitch, releasing the bend to lower the pitch. A numeral indicates the distance of the bend: ¼ step, ½ step, 2 steps, etc. In traditional notation, the bend's target note might be indicated on the staff. In tablature, and for quarter-pitch bends, fractions or numerals are included to clarify the distance of the bend.

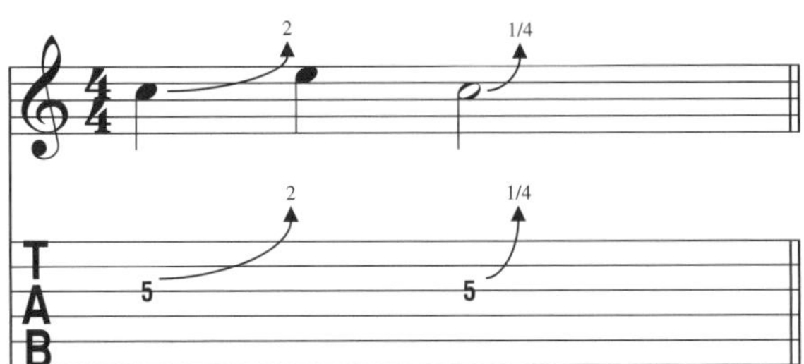

FIG. 8.14. Bends

Tablature

Many guitarists, bassists, banjo players, and so on prefer to read tablature rather than standard notation. Tablature looks like a staff, but the lines represent strings, not notes. Instead of noteheads, tablature shows numbers that indicate frets. Generally, rhythm is not represented. The assumption is that the musician knows the tune by ear and just needs the pitches/frets to be able to play it.

The use of tablature is a topic of debate. Teachers argue that it prevents beginning students from learning to read standard notation and that it fosters a narrow view of music, as they can only read music for their own instrument.

At Berklee Press, we sometimes include tablature in our guitar and bass books, but we always, always pair it with standard notation. Our position is that there is much to learn about music, besides reading. Some of our books do teach reading, and those do not include tablature. But some of our books teach listening, or developing time, or ensemble techniques, and for these, we think that tablature may help some people focus on the topic at hand, rather than spend their time frustrated as they puzzle out notes.

Bass guitar tab is like guitar or banjo tab, except that there are four lines (four strings), rather than six for guitar or five for banjo.

The bass strings, from bottom to top, are E, A, D, and G. An 0 on a tab line indicates an open string (non-fretted notes), so 0 on the E-string line would be the note E.

Each fret is a half step, so the number also indicates the number of half steps above the open string note. For example, a number 1 (first fret) on the E string would be the note F: one half step (also one fret) above E. The number 5 on the E string would be the note A (count out five half steps above E).

Here is a traditional staff with a notation figure played by a number of tablature-reading instruments. Ranges have been adjusted to suit the different instruments.

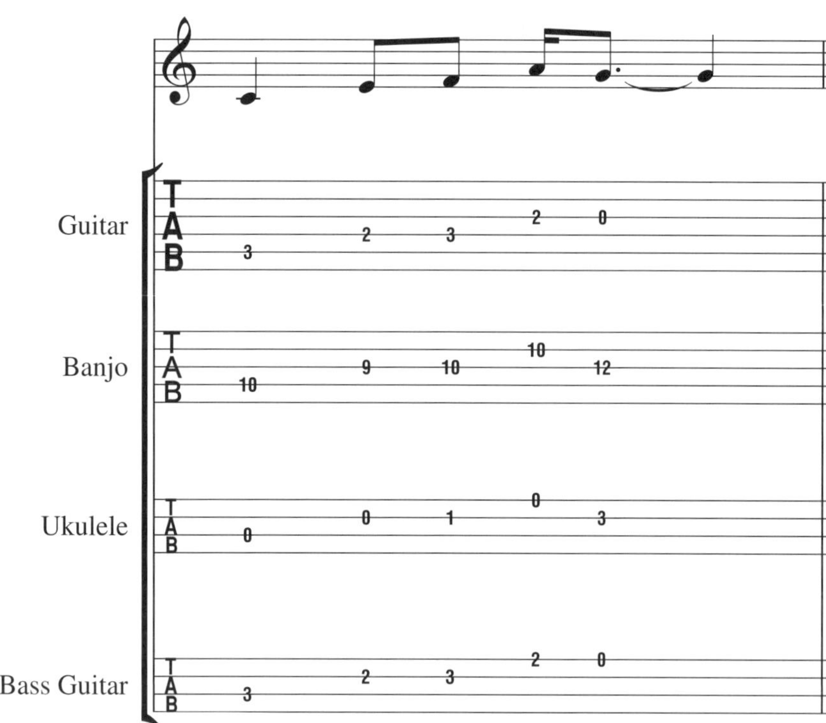

FIG. 8.15. Tablature

Harmonics in tablature are notated either with the circle above the numeral (above the staff) or with the fret number in brackets, such as <12> to mean that the string indicated should be played as a harmonic at the node located on the 12th fret.

ASCII Tab

ASCII tab is a low-tech way to communicate guitar techniques, common in online discussion forums and in some magazines. A typeface is selected where every character is the same width, such as Courier.

```
--------------
--------------
-----20-------
---23---------
-3------------
--------------
```

FIG. 8.16. ASCII Tab

Fretboard Diagrams

Fretboard diagrams (or *chord frames*, or *chord diagrams*), usually paired with standard chord symbols, are grids that indicate specific voicings for that chord, and how to play it. Back to figure 8.7, vertical lines represent the guitar's six strings, with the low E string on the left and the high E string on the right. Horizontal lines represent frets, and a number on the top right indicates the position, or the fret number of the highest row. Solid dots indicate which frets are held, open dots above the grid indicate open strings, and x's indicate strings that don't sound. The assumption is generally that guitarists will develop their own comping parts (rhythm, voicings, embellishments, etc.) based on these diagrams.

Most commonly, guitar fretboard diagrams are used to illustrate chords, as in figure 8.7. However, they can also be used for scales or other groupings of notes. Figure 8.17 shows a fretboard diagram indicating the frets for a major scale—this time, with horizontal lines indicating strings and vertical lines indicating frets. This potential application for scales is why I prefer the term "fretboard diagram" to "chord diagram," though both are in common use.

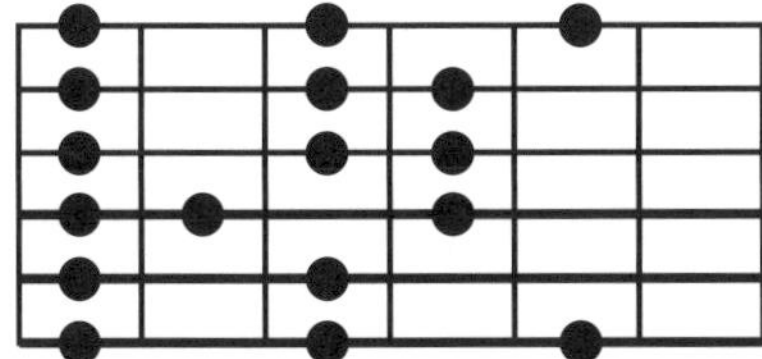

FIG. 8.17. Fretboard Diagram for Movable Major Scale Shape

Figure 8.17 is a movable diagram; it works on any fret. Fretboard diagrams can get a lot more specific, though. Figure 8.18 shows two different voicings for an A minor chord. The chord symbol is the same for each voicing, but the notation and tablature indicate what the different notes and positions are, and how the fretboard diagrams translate. There are many other options for this chord, as well.

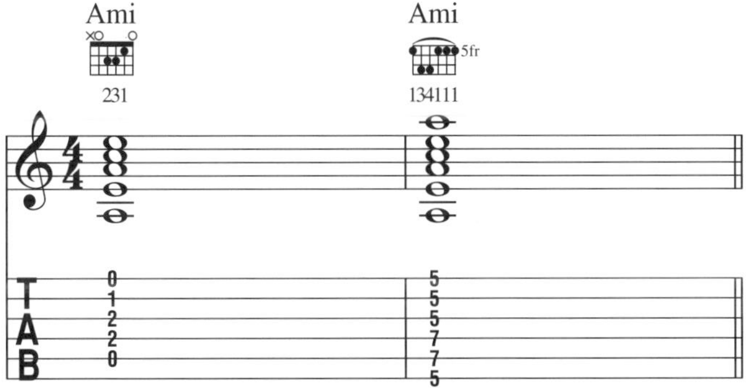

FIG. 8.18. A Minor Chord in Two Voicings

Fretboard diagrams contain the following elements.

Symbol	Name	Description
●	Solid dot	String depressed at fret.
○	Open dot	Set above the grid, it indicates an open (non-fretted) string.
×	Muted/Unsounded	On a fret, it means a muted string at the fret shown. Above the grid, it indicates a string that isn't sounded (by avoiding striking it or by muting it).
	Barre	Index finger barres multiple frets.
5fr	Fret number	Set as a numeral with "fr." (as in, 2 fr., for second fret) to the top-right of the grid, aligned with the first fret.
	Nut	Nut at the top of the fingerboard (first position).
134111	Numerals under grid	Fretboard-hand fingerings.

FIG. 8.19. Fretboard Diagram Notation Elements

A few style variations for guitar fretboard diagrams:

1. Some fretboard diagram systems always show four frets, whether or not they are used in a chord. In figure 8.18, we used only the required number of frets.
2. Barres are sometimes indicated with a thick black line across the frets rather than a slur.
3. Fingering numerals sometimes appear inside the dots. More often than either system, fingerings are left out of the diagrams entirely.
4. Omitted strings don't always have the x; they are sometimes left blank.
5. In alternate tunings, the string letters may appear above the grid.
6. Fret numbers may be indicated as Roman numerals.

DRUMS AND PERCUSSION

Drum notation is different than notation for other instruments in a number of ways. Most instruments interpret the lines and spaces of a staff to indicate pitches. On drum set, they indicate specific instruments. Drum notation also utilizes different noteheads. Solid noteheads indicate drums, such as bass drum, snare drum, and tom toms. X noteheads indicate cymbals, such as hi-hat, ride, and crash. Other noteheads are used to indicate additional percussion or special techniques, such as ▲ for cowbell and ◒ for cross-stick on a snare.

FIG. 8.20. Drum Set Notation

As you can see in figure 8.20, drum set notation is often written with two "voices" on a single staff. The top voice (stems up) is for instruments played with the hands, such as hi-hat and snare drum. The bottom voice (stems down) is for instruments played with the feet, such as bass drum and hi-hat foot. However, this convention is not universal. Instead, a cymbal pattern might be isolated in the top voice, or a close union between snare and bass drum might be stemmed together to show their camaraderie, or all the notes might share stems to illustrate linearity. How voices are organized varies not only between publishers or writers, but depending on musical intent.

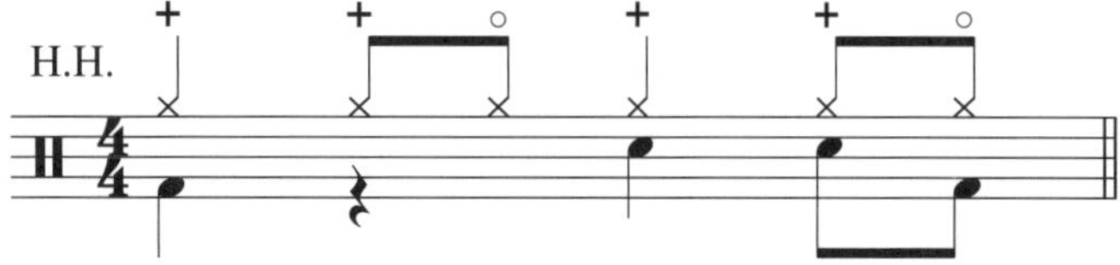

FIG. 8.21. Isolated Hi-Hat Pattern

Certain aspects of drum notation are practiced among nearly all drummers, and others are not. This makes drum notation a relatively fraught undertaking—and drum set, especially so. When you consider that a typical drum set has six to ten or so different drums and cymbals, plus potentially dozens of other percussion instruments (cowbell, claves, gongs, etc.), you can see that it gets complex fast. It would be lovely if every drummer on the planet used the same exact notation to indicate the same instruments, but this is far from the case. An individual drummer might switch between practices based on the musical situation.

Another unique aspect of notation from drums and percussion is that often, the durations of the drum sounds aren't particularly controllable. This means that notes usually indicate *attacks* rather than duration. So, for a wood block part, notating something as a quarter note or sixteenth note yields the same musical result. The note's best rhythmic value often depends on clarity, rather than actual duration or the usual drive to express an idea in as few notes and rests as possible. On the other hand, a gong has an extended decay, and it might need to be "choked" (silenced) at a specific point.

Some general principles for notating drums and percussion with short decays:

1. Minimize the number of notes and rests.
2. Avoid ties and dots (except for rolls).
3. Use half notes and longer only for rolls.
4. If two instruments are playing simultaneously, try to keep the duration the same if the effect is essentially the same. Consider whether they can/should share a stem.

All these principles may be broken for the sake of clarifying a beat or the interrelationship between voices.

Here are some abbreviations and symbols for drum and percussion notation.

	Unpitched percussion clef
	Drum, played using hands/sticks (snare, tom-tom)
	Drum, played using pedal (bass drum)
	Cymbal, played using hands/sticks (hi-hat, ride, crash, china)
	Cymbal, played using pedal (hi-hat)
	Additional percussion, such as cowbell or woodblock (Stem up, played with sticks; stem down, played with pedal)
○	Open, usually for hi-hat
+	Closed, usually for hi-hat
	Cross-stick
	Rim shot
	Flam
	Ruff
	Let ring/Let vibrate. This is a short tie, unconnected to a target note.
	Ghost note, feathered note
⌖	Choke (stop ringing/decay immediately)
Hard, Med., Soft, Wood, Brushes	Mallet/stick types
HH	Hi-hat
SD	Snare drum
BD	Bass drum
Kick	Bass drum (also called "kick drum")
	Eighth notes for the indicated duration
	Sixteenth notes for the indicated duration
	Roll for the indicated duration
16	Play drumbeat for indicated number of measures. (Informal, not for arrangements.)
R, RH	Right Hand
L, LH	Left Hand
RF	Right Foot
LF	Left Foot

FIG. 8.22. Drum Notation

Drum Set Notation Standards

The Percussive Arts Society (PAS) did a heroic job of defining a specific set of standards for drum notation, and many publishers and notation product developers adhere to their recommendations—or at least some of them! PAS has an excellent publication (*PAS Guide to Standardized Drumset Notation* by Norman Weinberg, 2002) showing many nuances of their preferences; it is a helpful resource. Here are a few of the basic rules they suggest.

1. Drums (snare, tom-tom, bass drum) are written using regular noteheads, unless they use special effects such as cross-sticks or rim shots.
2. Cymbals (ride, crash, hi-hat) are written using X noteheads.
3. Particularly for repetitive drumbeats, instruments played using drumsticks or brushes (snare, tom-tom, regular hi-hat) have stems pointing upward. Instruments played using pedals (bass drum, hi-hat foot) have stems pointing downward. Among the benefits of this are isolating steady parts such as steady eighth-note ride cymbal patterns, away from parts that are more varied.
4. Melodic parts, such as solos or fills, might have all stems up and have all simultaneously sounding notes share the same stems. Some music is more clearly rendered with the stems all going down, particularly in cases where there are multiple bass drums.
5. Each instrument of the set is assigned to a specific line or space.

Again, these aren't universal practices, but they have found some resonance with many players and writers, and I applaud the effort.

Drum Set Keys

Notation keys are particularly common and necessary for drum notation, due to the lack of standardization. These are often set at the beginning or end of a score, without a time signature.

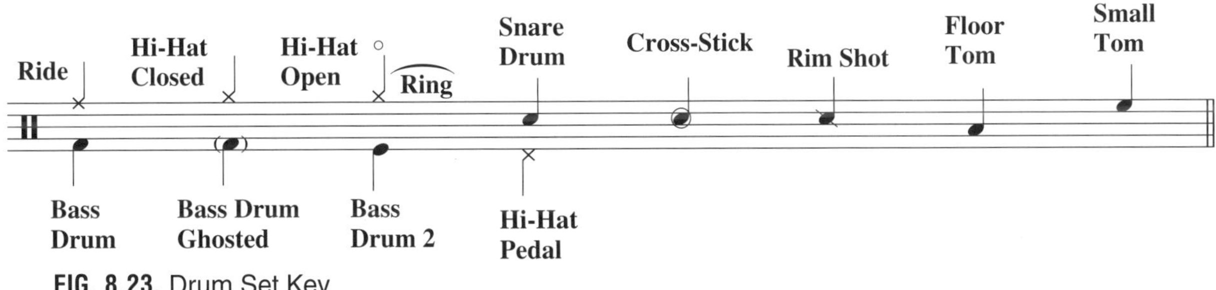

FIG. 8.23. Drum Set Key

Keys like this are often included where drum set notation is provided, such as in books, websites, and scores. Since the practices aren't standard, keys help communicate the specific practices in use to the drummer/reader.

At Berklee, we also use other common conventions for drum notation, in addition to those recommended by PAS. For example, here, the top space is used for the hi-hat, and the space above the staff is interpreted more flexibly and generically, possibly used for the ride, crash, or other cymbals, as labeled.

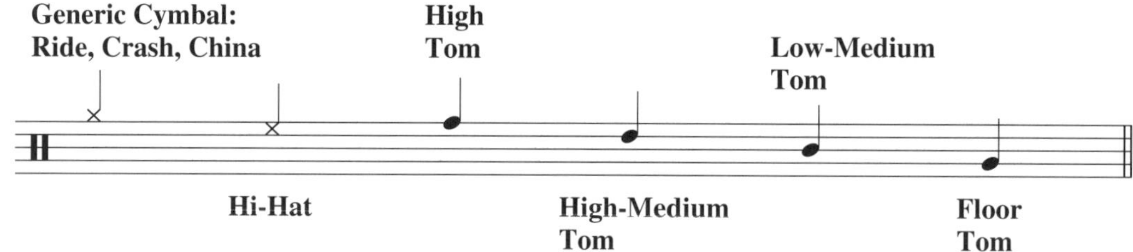

FIG. 8.24. Alternatives

Instrument clarifications, such as for specific cymbal types, are also commonly indicated throughout the notation itself, particularly for the more generic notation styles. Center the instrument name above the first note or slightly left to precede it.

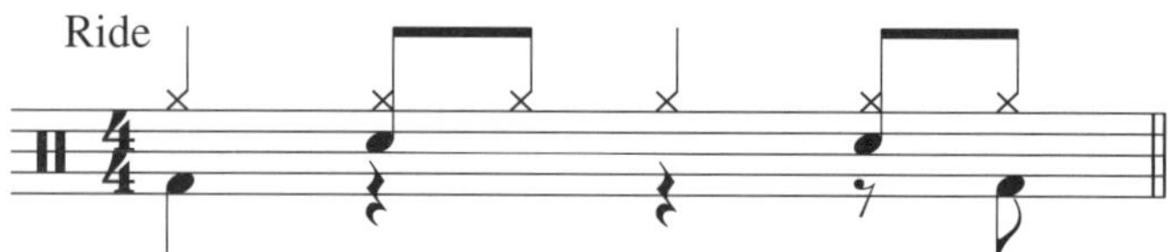

FIG. 8.25. Labelled Cymbals

Repeated Drumbeat Practices

The drum set tends to play repeating patterns, and the notation makes common use of all the repeats discussed in previous chapters. In addition to the repeats for individual beats, single-measure patterns, and two-measure patterns, a wavy line may be used in informal charts to mean "continue the specified beat for the specified number of measures." This wavy line is really only used informally, generally handwritten on the fly during a session, though sometimes indicated also in pedagogical drum-only materials; avoid it in formal scores. When it is used, there may be an initial notated drumbeat or simply a style indication.

Drum notation also commonly numbers every measure (or every two or four measures), particularly when there is a long string of repeat symbols. Rhythm notation is also used in drum notation to indicate a specific rhythm while leaving the exact instrument choice up to the discretion of the player.

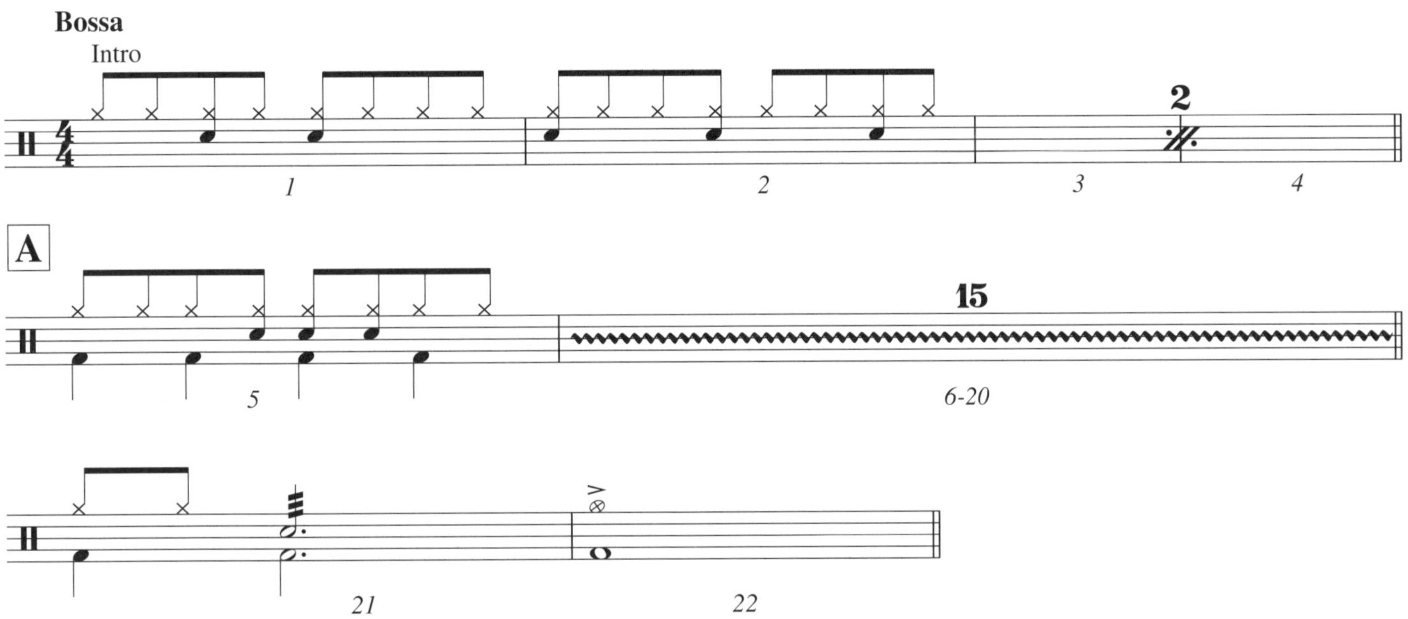

FIG. 8.26. Drumbeat Repeat Symbols

Percussion

Individual percussion parts are either set on a five-line staff with notes on the middle line, or sometimes, on a single-line staff with the noteheads all on the line. When it's just one unpitched instrument, a single-line staff is often used, though you may see either one or five lines. If two different instruments share a staff, or if a multipitched instrument is in use (such as certain kinds of bells), most publishers use a five-line staff (grand staff, for marimba).

Multipitched percussion, such as timpani, glockenspiel, marimba, etc., use whatever clef suits their range: bass clef for timpani, treble for glockenspiel, grand staff for marimba, etc. Unpitched or single-pitched percussion (snare drum, triangle, cymbals) are set on a percussion-clef staff, with either one or five lines. In a score, pitched percussion instruments are generally set above unpitched percussion.

FIG. 8.27. Various Percussion Staves

Notation for two instruments played by a single player might also share a single-line staff with stems pointing in opposite directions.

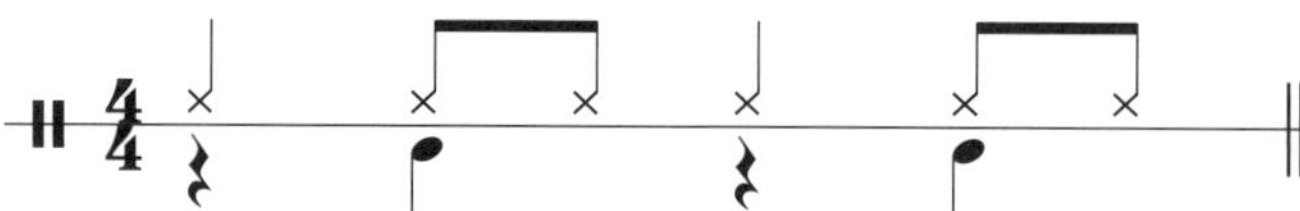

FIG. 8.28. Single-Line Notation

Snare drum exercises are core studies for percussionists of all types, and they are traditionally indicated on a five-line staff. The notehead is indicated on the second space from the top. It is standard for all the stems to point up.

FIG. 8.29. Snare Drum Sticking Exercise (Paradiddle)

Timpani

Timpani notation is set in bass clef. Often, the key signature is omitted and every note is marked with an explicit accidental, particularly if only two notes are used throughout the piece. However, for more complex timpani parts, setting a key signature can be helpful and simplify the score. Timpani parts only include the timpani, not any other percussion instruments.

There are usually either two or four timpani played by a single musician—sometimes three or five drums, but rarely more than five.

At the beginning of a score, the initial tunings of the drums is indicated, either above the staff or (only if they are not going to be retuned) as part of the staff name.

These note indications are listed from low to high, left to right. They may be either arranged in a line or as more of a diagram that mimics the physical arrangement of the drums (which may vary, depending on playing style).

Retuning indications are ideally set as early as possible, during rests, so that the player has time to alter the pedals. The word "Retune" might introduce the change: Retune B♭ to C. Alternatively, diagonal lines might show the change, with the ascent or descent of the line showing the new octave, and parentheses clarifying which note is the original one being modified. A third way: lines are drawn from the actual note, leading to a letter indication of the new note. A fresh complete layout diagram can be helpful after a series of individual drum changes.

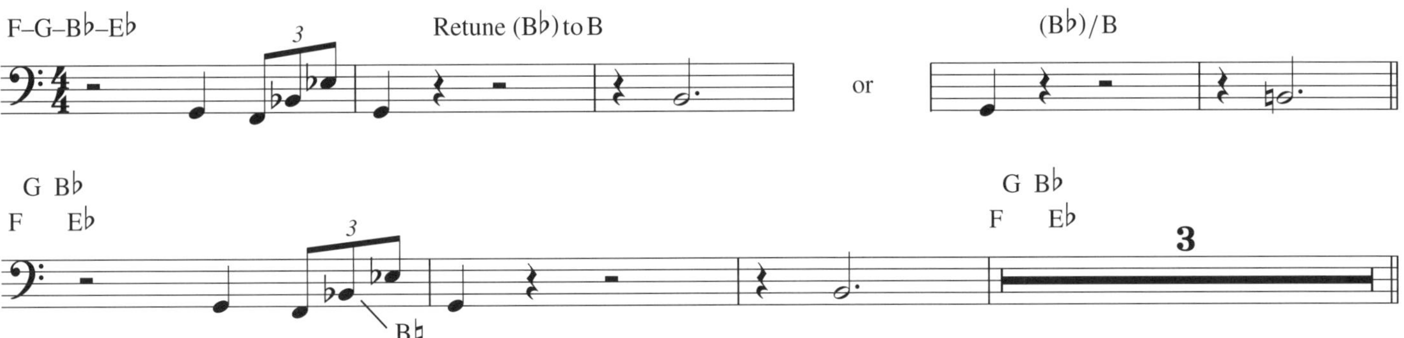

FIG. 8.30. Various Timpani Tuning and Retuning Standards

Percussion Grid Notation

Grid notation is sometimes used for hand percussion, particularly for percussion ensembles or relatively informal notation shared only by fellow practitioners of that instrument. It is the drum equivalent of guitar tablature.

Here's an example of a percussion duo that uses such a grid. The djembe and dundunba are African drums, here playing a "sofa" rhythm. The dundunba is played in conjunction with a bell, so the top row indicates the bell and the bottom row is for the drum. The traditional notation equivalent is shown underneath.

Djembe

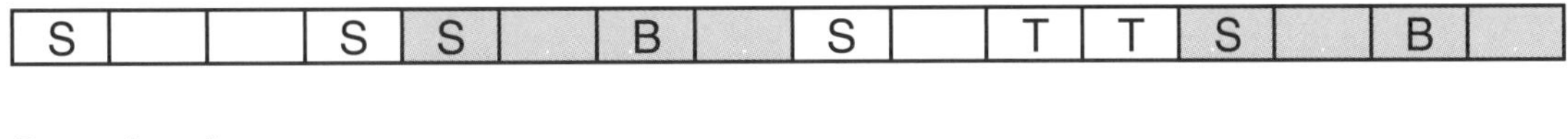

S			S	S		B		S		T	T	S		B	

Dundunba

X	X		X	X		X		X		X		X		X	
						O		O		O		O		O	

FIG. 8.31. Percussion Grid Notation

In the grid notation, each square represents a subdivision of a beat, and each shaded group of squares indicates a beat. Heavy lines separate the measures. An X means that the instrument is struck at that point of the measure. Nuances of articulation can be indicated through different letters. Some common ones in hand percussion:

X	Play (generic strike)
O	Open
C	Closed
B	Bass
T	Tone
S	Slap
–	Rest
TT	Flam (small letter preceding larger letters)

FIG. 8.32. Percussion Articulations

BRASS

Brass fingerings are typically written above the notes. More common than actual fingerings are valve indications for trumpet, horn, tuba, etc., and slide positions for trombone. There are multiple ways to perform most notes of a brass instrument, and indicating specific fingerings can clarify both facility and timbre options that might not be immediately evident otherwise. Valves are numbered usually from 0 (open) to 3 (or more), ordered from closest to farthest away from the mouthpiece. If multiple valves are depressed, the numbers are stacked in increasing order, top to bottom. Trombone slide positions are numbered 1 to 7 and sometimes modified with a sharp or flat to indicate "closer in" or "farther out."

FIG. 8.33. Trumpet Fingerings, Trombone Slide Positions

Figure 8.34 indicates the clefs and transpositions used by the more common brass instruments. Related instruments are listed as well. In this and the following similar charts, clefs are listed in their preferred order, with the most common clef stated and then other possibilities listed in parentheses, based on their order of preference. Readability is the goal, and clefs are only generally changed when there is an extended use of notes that require, say, four ledger lines or so. Stick with the primary clef listed, if you can.

Some of these instruments are established members of the orchestra, such as the bass trombone. Some are specific to marching bands, such as the sousaphone and baritone horn. Some are commonly doubled instruments, such as the piccolo trumpet or mellophone. And others are monstrosities that should never have been created, such as the valve trombone, but they still somehow find their ways into specific situations, such as jazz bands. A few historical precedents are included, just for fun. I have separated the baritone horn from the euphonium because their practitioners get offended when you lump them together. But nobody else can tell the difference.

Most Common	Clef	Transposition	Similar
Trumpet	Treble	B♭	C trumpet, piccolo trumpet, flugelhorn, mellophone, cornet, bugle, shofar
French Horn	Treble	F	Natural horn
Trombone (Tenor)	Bass (tenor, rarely alto or treble)	Concert (rarely, B♭, especially when in treble clef)	Bass trombone, valve trombone, tenor trombone with F and/or E♭ trigger, sackbut
Baritone Horn	Bass (treble for high notes) or all treble	If treble clef, then B♭, a ninth lower than written	Euphonium
Euphonium	Bass (treble)	Concert	Baritone horn
Tuba	Bass	Bass clef, 1 octave lower than written	Sousaphone

FIG. 8.34. Brass Family Clef and Transposition

Wind players need to plan where they breathe. Articulation markings can help guide these breath points, so as to ensure that intended phrases will be kept intact. These can be marked with slurs and with breath marks. Slurs, for brass and woodwind instruments, mean to play the enclosed notes legato, and usually, in a single breath. Depending on the instrument, it can have technical implications as well, such as whether the note is articulated with valves vs. tongue, or the precise way it is tongued. Breathing is usually left to the discretion of the player, though a breath mark might be given to protect an important phrase or added to pedagogical materials. If so, it appears after the slur, always above the staff and aligned at the end of the note's duration, though the player is likely to breathe at the end of a phrase whether or not they receive an invitation. The markings in this example help confirm that the second measure will be uninterrupted by a breath.

FIG. 8.35. Phrases and Breath Marks

Mutes

Brass instruments may employ mutes: cup, straight, wah-wah (or Harmon), plunger, hat, plus whatever other plumbing equipment or junkyard gadgetry those crazy guys come up with! The generic direction "con sordino" (or "con sord.," meaning "with a mute") typically refers to a straight mute. If you mean anything besides that, indicate the specific type. Some mutes (wah-wah, plunger, hat) have multiple positions that can be quickly altered, note by note.

,	Breath mark
Add mute, *con sord.*, or a specific mute type	Play using the mute.
No mute, *senza sord.*	Play normally, without the mute.
+	Closed (mute in, or hand over mute or bell)
o	Open (mute/hand out)
wah	Go from closed to open, making a "wah" sound, like Charlie Brown's teacher.
Flz. Fl.	Flutter tongue
	Doit
	Gliss/Bend

FIG. 8.36. Brass Notation

Effects

There are a number of idiomatic effects for brass, but their notation tends to be fairly generic, often labelled with words to describe them rather than using unique symbols. Lines, both wavy and straight, are used to indicate glissandos or pitch bends. Related are scoops, doits, and rips. Here is how brass players distinguish between these types of pitch transition.

- A *glissando* is a smooth transition between notes.
- A *bend* spans a small interval, under a whole step.
- A *scoop* is a short, upward gliss up to a specific pitch.
- A *doit* is a short, upward glissando stab away from a specific pitch.
- A *rip* is like a scoop or a doit with a clear beginning and target note. It tends to be louder and more aggressive than a glissando, roughly catching individual harmonics, rather than aiming for a smooth transition. It typically spans large intervals, and moves from low to high.

The effect names may or may not appear on these three iconic brass sounds.

FIG. 8.37. Types of Brass Glissando

An x-notehead can be used to mean that generally, something is amuck. It might indicate a half valve, or a slap tongue, or other percussive effects. The name of the desired effect accompanies the symbol, as it might for effects that go with pitches, such as growls. Flutter tonguing is articulated with three lines (like a tremolo) or with a z character; "Fl." or "Flz." might or might not appear above the note. Vibrato may be indicated with "Vib." and a wavy line; no vibrato is indicated with a tenuto dash (or the text *non vib.* or *normale*).

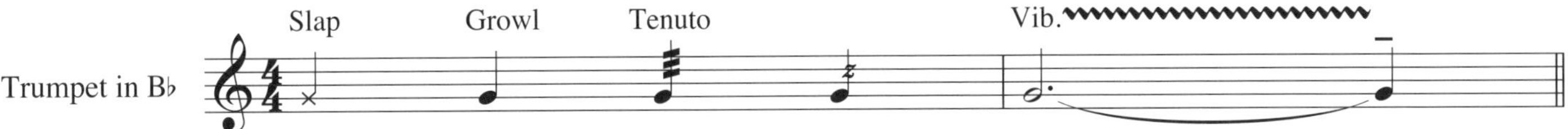

FIG. 8.38. Brass Effects

Syllables may be used to clarify the type of articulation: tu, tut, du, doo, dah, dat. These specify the gentleness or explosiveness of the attack. They can be combined with hyphens and exclamation points to further clarify the phrasing or relationships between notes. They are generally set above the staff.

FIG. 8.39. Attack Syllables

WOODWINDS

Here are the most common woodwind instruments, with their typical clefs and transpositions.

Most Common	Clef	Transposition	Similar
Flute	Treble	Concert	Piccolo
Recorders: Many ranges	Treble (some instruments read bass)	Concert	Many sizes
Clarinet	Treble	B♭	Many other keys and sizes, bass clarinet, basset horn
Oboe	Treble	Concert	English Horn
English Horn	Treble	F	Oboe
Bassoon	Bass (tenor)	Concert	Contrabassoon
Soprano Saxophone	Treble	B♭	All saxophones
Alto Saxophone	Treble	E♭	
Tenor Saxophone	Treble	B♭	
Baritone Saxophone	Treble	E♭	
EWI (Electronic Wind Instrument)	Treble (varies)	Concert	Soprano saxophone, clarinet, can be set to mimic others

FIG. 8.40. Woodwind Family Clefs and Transpositions

Fingerings

Woodwind fingerings are often provided as graphics depicting the instruments' key structures, particularly in pedagogical materials. Blackened shapes indicate depressed keys. In harmonica "tablature," arrows (↑/↓) indicate blow/draw, dashes (–) indicate that the slide is engaged, and numerals indicate hole numbers.

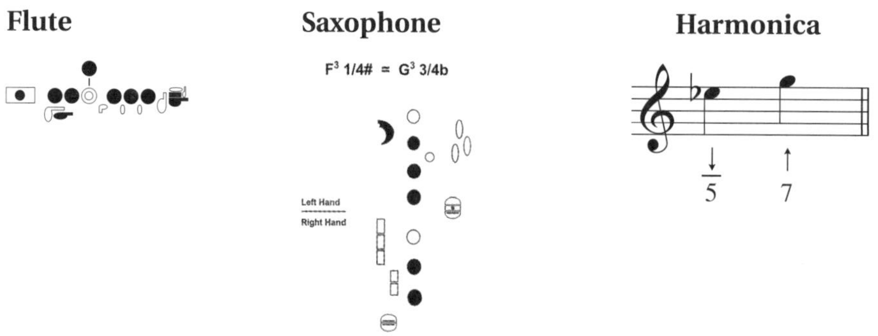

FIG. 8.41. Flute and Saxophone Fingering Diagram and Harmonica Tab

Harmonics

Woodwinds can perform harmonics by overblowing on a note. These are indicated with a diamond notehead showing the fingered fundamental pitch, a regular notehead for the sounding harmonic, and an ° above the notehead.

FIG. 8.42. Woodwind Harmonics

Multiphonics

Some woodwinds can play multiphonics—two or even three (or more) notes at once. The ability to do this varies greatly depending on the individual instrument model and the player, so the use of multiphonics is unpredictable. There is no standard notation. If you are working with an individual and know their capabilities for multiphonics, you can notate them as normal pitches. A way to cheat at multiphonics (really, it's a technique in its own right) is to have the player sing a note while they play another on their instrument. Notate this as two voices on the staff, one marked "Sing" and the other marked "Play."

FIG. 8.43. Multiphonics

Bends

Woodwinds bend pitches easily. These are subtler motions than the brass doits or scoops. Bends may approach or leave a note, or leave and then return to the same note. The direction of the bend follows the line or curve.

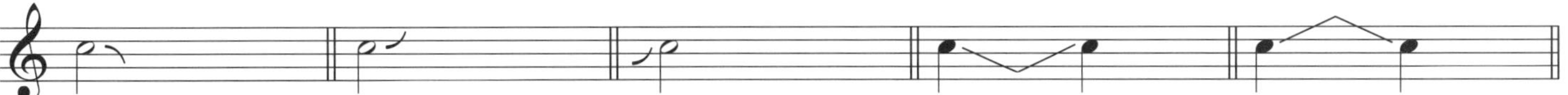

FIG. 8.44. Bends

STRINGS

The family name "strings" in this context refers to violin, viola, cello (or 'cello, if you want to be like that), and acoustic upright bass. The group is sometimes called "orchestral strings," but its members, of course, frequently appear outside of orchestras—not just chamber music, but in rock bands, as soloists, in fiddle competitions, and so on. The Berklee "String Department" includes violin (fiddle), viola, cello, mandolin, banjo, harp, etc., but not bass or guitar. Harp has more of a notation kinship to the piano than to the violin, and mandolin notation is more like that of the guitar. Perhaps "bowed strings" is a better descriptor? But these instruments can all be played pizzicato as well as bowed, and Jimmy Page sometimes bows his guitar. Hopefully, you know what I mean, by "Strings." It's hard to define, but you'll know it when you see it.

Here are the most common instruments of this chapter's "string family," which I am lumping together here out of convenience because they share some notation practices. The bass sounds an octave lower than notated, and it is the only transposing member of the family.

The individual stringed instruments have substantially different playing techniques, so arrangers and composers need to be cautious when scoring parts for string players who double. The most common string doublings involve bassists who play bass guitar, violists who play violin, acoustic players who play their electric counterparts (e.g., cello and electric cello), and fiddlers doubling on mandolin.

Name	Clef	Similar Instrument
Violin (Vl.)	Treble	Electric violin, viola
Viola (Vla.)	Alto (treble)	Violin, electric viola
'Cello (Vcl.)	Bass (tenor, treble)	Electric cello
Contrabass (Cb., Ac. Bs., Bs.)	Bass	Electric bass guitar, electric upright bass

FIG. 8.45. A String Family

It's becoming increasingly common for string instruments to have more than the standard four strings. Five-string basses have been around for a while, and particularly electric instruments of all types may now have five, six, or seven strings. The five-string violin adds the low C; six-string violins and violas add the F below that. An octave violin has the usual strings, but they are pitched an octave higher. The five-string acoustic violin is often found in the country, jazz, and folk worlds, and the six-string electric violin is starting to develop a solid repertoire of concertos and solo pieces.

While these strings might seem at a glance to be similar to guitar and other plucked string instruments, their performance and notation traditions are worlds apart. Fingering numerals (T for thumb, 1 to 4 for index to pinky, 0 for open strings) most commonly refer to the fingerboard hand (usually left). It is rare for bow-hand fingers to be specifically indicated, particularly for violin and viola. When they are, *p-i-m-a-c* (thumb to pinky) are preferred, as letters differentiate them from LH fingerings. But T-1-2-3-4 are sometimes used for the right hand, as well, often enclosed in a box or circle.

Specific strings are indicated using two systems:

1. Roman numerals, with I being the highest string. On violin, I is the E string, II is the A string, III is the D string, and IV is the G string.
2. Text indication, such as "sul G" for "on the G string."

String indications are best placed above the staff, centered above the note. A line (solid or dashed) after the string numeral may indicate how long it should stay in effect. This works best when the fingering indication is used sporadically, rather than having every string choice marked. While such a line is a great clarifier, it also adds busyness to the page.

Unlike guitar notation, strings are not circled. Fingerboard positions (not strictly analogous to frets) are usually not indicated.

Here are some other common symbols used by strings.

⊓	Down-bow
V	Up-bow
(slur over three notes)	Slur. Notes within a slur are played using the same bow stroke, unless also marked with the up-bow and down-bow indications.
(notes with one, two, three and four tremolo slashes)	Eighths, Sixteenth Notes, Thirty-Second Notes/Unmeasured Tremolo, Unmeasured Tremolo. Particularly, the single-note tremolo is idiomatic of orchestral string sections, where the notes are played as fast as possible, like a field of crickets. Sometimes, the three lines are interpreted as measured thirty-second notes and four slashes interpreted as an unmeasured tremolo, so a clarification is helpful.
○	Harmonic: sounding note
◇	Harmonic: location where string is lightly fingered. Note: this is fairly advanced, and should probably be left to writers who are also string players.
⦽	Snap pizzicato (or Bartók pizzicato)
♀	Thumb position (cello and bass)
+	Left-hand pizzicato. Always set above the notehead.

FIG. 8.46. String Notation

Bowing Techniques

A down-bow (bow moving downward, hand heading away from the instrument) is indicated with a ⊓, and an up-bow (bow moving upward, hand heading towards the instrument) is indicated with a V. Set these above the staff. They are used sparingly in professional scores—only when necessary, such as a series of down-bows. In the rare circumstance when two violin voices share a single staff and both require independent bowings, the symbols stay in their original form, rather than being flipped upside down (as are fermatas, for example).

A slur indicates that all the notes are played within the same up- or down-bow direction. If the slur is also above the staff, any initial up/down bowing for the group is set outside the phrase marking. In figure 8.47, the down-bow symbol isn't actually necessary, as it can be assumed based on the up-bow marking and the end of the slur. It is included to illustrate the relationship of the symbol to a slur. That said, the up-bow and down-bow markings can be used in conjunction with a slur to mean bowings within a legato phrase.

Whatever bowings you write, the players will likely change them. It is difficult for non-string players to get bowings right, and the players are used to altering written bowings to make them suitable and playable.

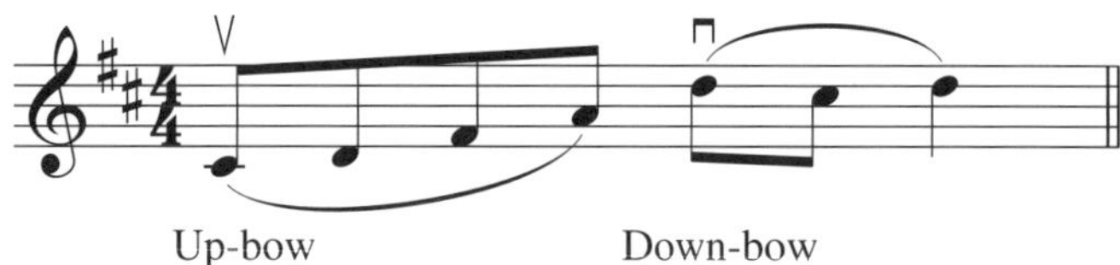

FIG. 8.47. Bowings

Many special bowing techniques are used by string players, but most are indicated with text, rather than with unique notation symbols. They tend to be set in Roman type, rather than italics. Some common ones:

pizz.	Pizzicato: plucked strings, not bowed.
arco	Arco: bowed strings, not plucked.
sul pont., sul ponticello	Bowed near the bridge.
sul tasto	Bowed over the fingerboard.
col legno	Articulated using the wood of the bow, rather than the hair.
ricochet (or jeté)	Bow bounces on the string to play a rapid series of the same pitch (in the same direction). It is notated with staccato articulations and a slur, which are also used for "flying staccato" and slurred staccato, so use the word "ricochet" as well.
spic.	Spiccato. Short, rapid, alternate, bouncing bowing. Notated as staccato.

FIG. 8.48. String Techniques

Some bowing techniques have special names but use common symbols, without further direction. *Portato* bowing (sometimes "louré"), for example, means repeating a note, legato, within a single bow stroke, without lifting the bow from the string. It is notated with tenuto articulations inside a phrase; the word "louré" doesn't appear. Similarly, *détaché* bowing, where the bow direction changes on every note, is simply notated without any special articulation markings, even though it is a named technique (and a confusing one, as the bowing changes aren't exaggerated to sound more "detached" than other techniques).

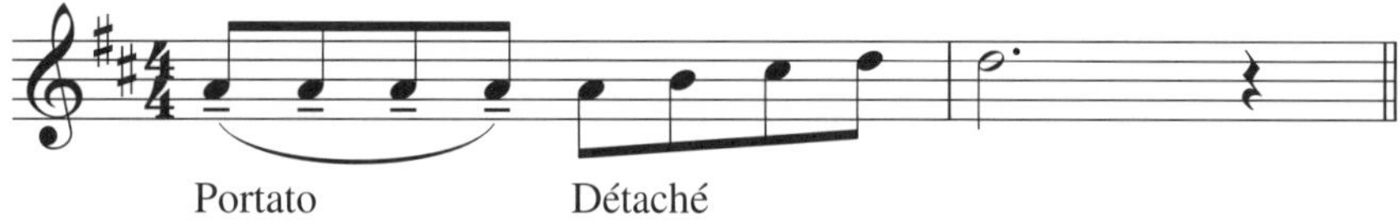

FIG. 8.49. Unique Techniques with No Special Notation

There are two types of col legno bowing: col legno *battuto* (struck with the wood) and col legno *tratto* (bowed with the wood). If neither is indicated, battuto is assumed, as it is more common and more effective. Note that players may switch to a cheaper bow for extended use of col legno, so as not to damage an expensive bow.

Harmonics

Strings harmonics are of two types. A natural (or "open") harmonic is performed on an open string, with the string lightly fingered at the point (node) where it will produce the desired sound (such as half the string length, to create an octave). A *fingered* (or "artificial," "false," or "stopped") harmonic is sounded by playing a note while lightly touching the string at a second point, usually a fourth (for two octaves above) or fifth (octave and fifth above) above the stopped note. At Berklee, we prefer the term "fingered harmonics," as it is less derogatory than the others, but particularly "artificial" and "false" are perhaps in more common use, particularly in older literature.

Natural harmonics are notated in two ways:

1. A small circle above a normal notehead indicates that the notehead is the sounding pitch. For writers who are not string players, this is the safest, most predictable method.
2. A diamond notehead indicates where the string is lightly stopped to produce the desired harmonic. It is paired with a string indication such as "III" or "sul D," for the string used to produce the note. This method is easier to sight-read.

Fingered harmonics are notated with a regular notehead showing the stopped note and a diamond notehead at the point where the harmonic note is lightly fingered, producing a third note that isn't usually actually shown on the score. Sometimes, the resulting note is indicated in parentheses.

If there's the occasional open harmonic within a run of fingered harmonics, it may be written with the open string on the bottom, in the style of fingered harmonics.

The most common fingered harmonics are fourths (two octaves) and then fifths (octave and a fifth); fifths more common for cello than for other strings. Other harmonics are possible but less common and less reliable.

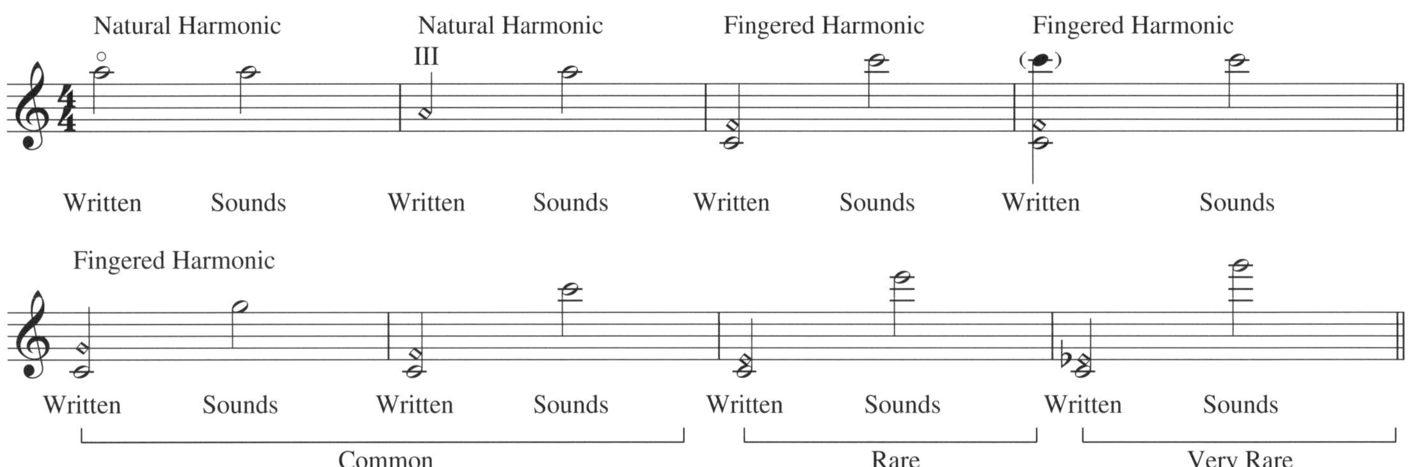

FIG. 8.50. Harmonics

Chop Techniques

Chop is a percussive fiddling technique. Chop notation is not yet universally standardized, but figure 8.51 shows what we currently recommend at Berklee. It is currently being codified by Casey Driessen, who is developing symbology originally put forth by players in the Turtle Island Quartet, particularly Darol Anger. Keep an eye on the Berklee String Department's website for the current iteration of their preferred standard.

	Hard chop. Usually set on open strings, and often, on pairs of adjacent strings. These are always played down-bow.
	Soft chop/ghost note (pitched/fingered). X notehead indicates pitch fingered in left hand.
	Soft chop (muted/not pitched) Note stem only, without a head. (Shown: quarter note, eighth note, beamed eighth notes.)
	Sounding point: (•) bow chop located on string towards the player's body. This and the other two bow placement markings (•, +, x) are used in conjuction with other symbols, most commonly bowings.
	Sounding point: away from the player's body
	Sounding point: behind the bridge
	Scrape inward (towards the player's body)
	Scrape outward (away from the player's body)
	Circular scrape: move bow clockwise
	Circular scrape: move bow counter-clockwise
3 or 3	Triple chop. Usually shown with indications for moving towards (shown)/towards the player's body, as in the scrape. Generally, just three, but could be other numbers.

FIG. 8.51. Chop Notation

HARP

Harp notation is set on a grand staff. Fingers are numbered 1 for thumb, 2 for index finger, 3 for middle finger, and 4 for ring finger. The pinky is not used.

Here are some common harp notation symbols.

	Placing brackets and connecting bracket.
	Do not connect to next group of notes.
PT, *pdlt*	Près de la table. Play close to the sounding board (table).
	Articulate using fingernails, not fingertips.
	Harmonic: This symbol may be used to indicate either the sounding note or the fingered note, which is an octave below the sounding note. Clarify which approach you are taking with a publisher's note.
	Rolled notes, as in a chord (arpeggio), bottom to top (up arrow) or top to bottom (down arrow).
	"Block" or "flat" chords; notes sound simultaneously.
L.V.	Let vibrate.
	Muffle all strings. Often used at the end of a piece or section, when you want total silence.
	Muffle specific strings only. Small noteheads show the exact pitch.
+	Muffle an individual note or octave within a series (usually LH only, for lower strings).
	Muffle a specific subset of the sounding notes.

FIG. 8.52. Harp Notation

Harp fingerings can include two types of brackets. A *placing bracket* indicates a group of notes moving in the same melodic direction. A *connecting bracket* above a pair of placing brackets indicates a change of direction, requiring a shift of hand position (crossing over or under). Brackets might be notated only on the top staff, but it is understood that both hands follow the patterns.

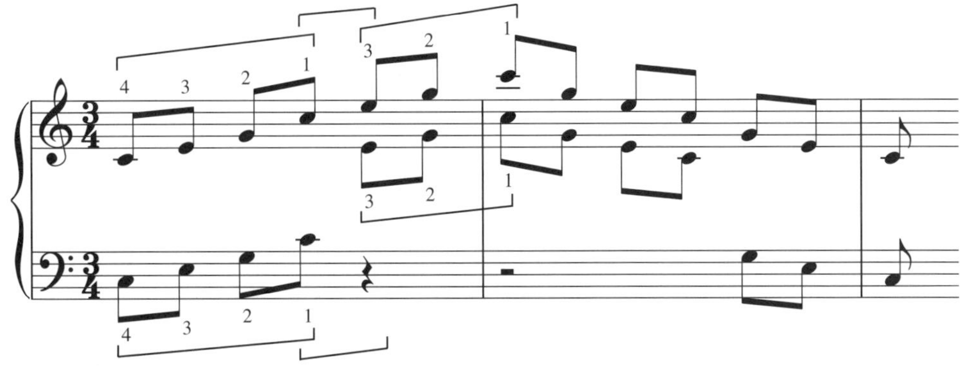

FIG. 8.53. Harp Brackets

If you've watched the Marx Brothers' *A Day at the Races*, you might know that when you smash a grand piano to bits, you will essentially find a harp inside. Unlike an intact piano, such a liberated harp has no dampers to mute the sound after its strings are plucked. Therefore, to stop their ringing, harpists use their hands to still them. They may dampen (or "muffle") all the sounding notes or just select ones, using the three following types of symbols. Here is the effect of each mute.

(a) All notes are stopped.

(b) Low C and G stopped; remaining four notes ring.

(c) Left hand notes only are stopped.

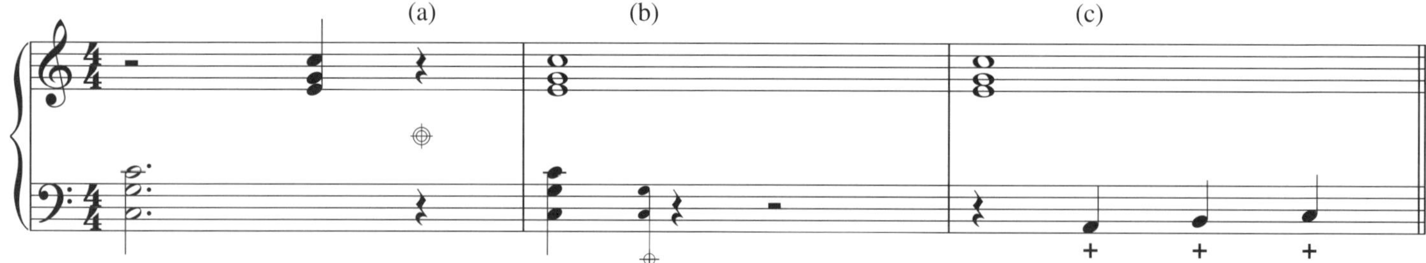

FIG. 8.54. String Dampening

Harps can play harmonics, sounding an octave above the plucked string. There are two widely accepted standards: either notating the plucked fundamental string or the sounding harmonic that results. Clarify which approach you are using.

The most common types of harps are pedal and lever harps. Pedal harps have a wider range and more versatile capabilities, and lever harps have some specific requirements regarding enharmonics. That said, the same notation is often intended to be readable by either instrument. If a note is only possible for pedal harp, it is notated in parentheses, or for extended passages, clarified in a cue notation staff.

FIG. 8.55. Cue Notation for Optional Lower Part

Pedal Indications

Harp pedals set the strings to play at the appropriate accidentals, and the initial pedalling setup is specified at the beginning of a composition by use of pedal diagrams. Pedal harps have seven pedals: one for every note letter, positioned in the order DCB | EFGA, and there are three possible positions for each note letter: flat, natural, or sharp. Contemporary harpists can read double-sharps and double-flats, and even play microtones, despite what some older notation guides advise.

There are two styles of harp diagrams: letters and graphics. Lettered systems list the accidental position of every note (i.e., pitch class), such as D♮ C♮ B♭ | E♭F♮ G♮A♭, if we were to play in the key of E♭major. Graphics systems have a horizontal line, and then short vertical lines set at three positions in relation to the pedals: above the line for flat, on the line for natural, and below the line for sharp. There would be no text on an actual pedal diagram: just the lines.

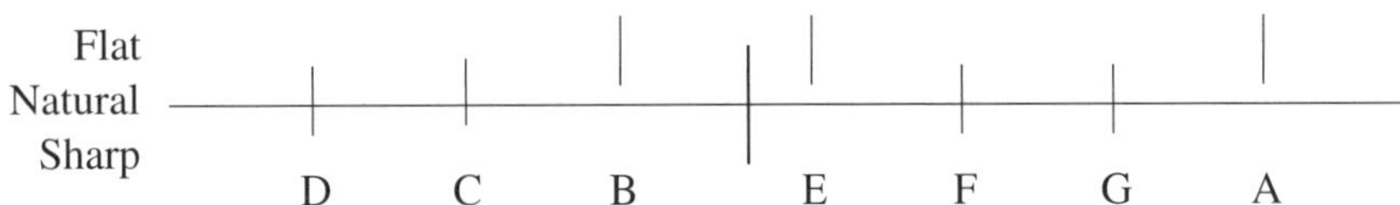

FIG. 8.56. Harp Pedals

At a key change or when a new accidental is required, harpists need direction in advance of the change to give them time to adjust the pedal. Just the letter and new accidental is shown: A♮, for example, to show that A is now natural, such as if we have moved from the key of E♭ to B♭. Harpists can usually only change two pedals at a time (one with each foot, associated with the note groupings shown). If two notes change, such as going from the key of B♭to C, those notes should be stacked vertically, right foot pedals over left foot pedals. A bottom pedal indication in a box indicates a right-side pedal change with the left foot.

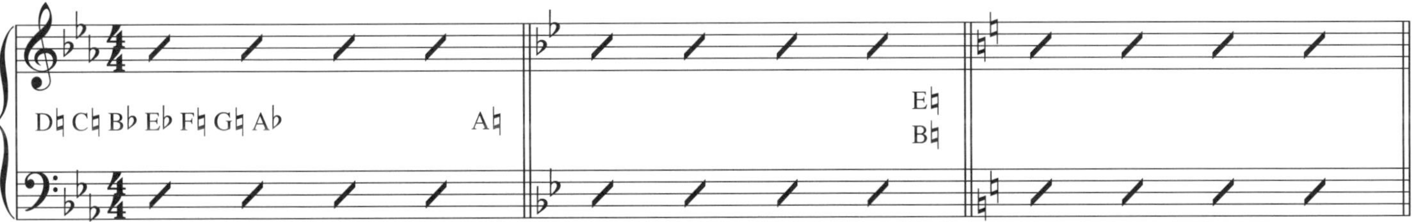

FIG. 8.57. Text Pedal Indications and Pedal Changes

Composers need not indicate pedal changes. This notation is more typically done by experienced harpists who are creating pedagogical materials, or specially annotated works for harp. Harpists are accustomed to figuring out the necessary pedalling and then writing them in themselves, without relying on the published notation.

Glissandos

Manipulating the pedals allows harpists to play two different types of glissandos: diatonic and enharmonic. A *diatonic glissando* includes all notes of a scale, such as F major (pedals set to D♮ C♮ B♭E♮ F♮G♮ A♮). An *enharmonic glissando* includes doubled notes, such as for an F pentatonic scale (pedals set to D♮ C♮ B♯ E♯ F♮G♮ A♮), which is one of the ways that the harp achieves its unique sound and effect.

A harp glissando may be written in several different ways. For precise glissandos, with scripted starting and target pitches, you can specify just the starting and ending notes, indicate the notes of one octave (usually in thirty-second notes), or notate all pitches. A glissando can be based on a single-note line, an interval, or a chord (up to four notes).

FIG. 8.58. Harp Glissandos

Glissandos can ascend or descend. They can be written in specific rhythms and notes, or they can be played more ad lib. For a continuous swirling series of glisses, you can use more graphical notation, indicating rising and falling lines on the staff rather than plotting notes. In figure 8.59, a pedal diagram specifies the notes, but the range and rhythms are up to the discretion of the harpist.

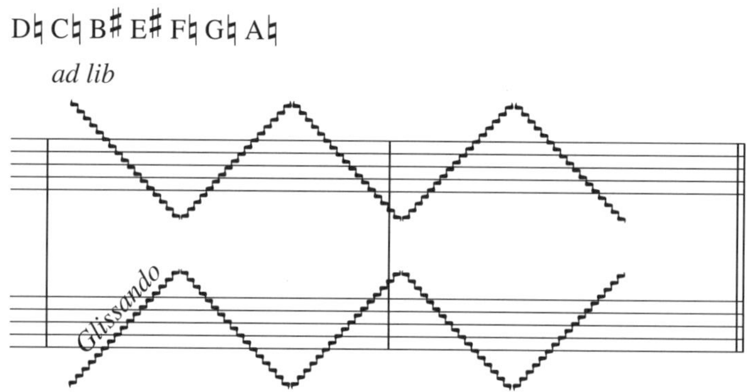

FIG. 8.59. Rising and Falling Glissando

Notation conventions come and go, for many of these instrument-specific practices. Instruments and playing techniques evolve. Method books by specific practitioners fall in and out of favor, and their preferred notation standards ebb and flow with them. Some of the great notation books from decades past suggest practices that are no longer commonly used or understood. One of our own books, written in the 1960s, featured a new notation preference, but after the author taught out of it for a few years, he ultimately decided that it was awkward, and he regretted advocating for it—after many hundreds of students were trained to consider it "correct!"

Some of the practices in this very chapter will surely suffer the same fate. So, it's important to keep an open mind, to talk to players, and try to keep up with whatever is currently considered best practice.

CHAPTER 9

Scores and Parts

A *score* is the notation showing what every instrument in an ensemble is to perform. Generally, the term implies to an ensemble score, as opposed to a *part* (a single instrument that is "part" of a larger ensemble) or a *lead sheet*. The word *score* is also used informally to mean any notation, generally. While we're at it, *book* is used primarily in musical theater circles to mean the bound collection of all notation for the show (whether full score of individual parts), and jazz musicians use *changes* (short for "chord change") and *chart* to refer to lead sheets. Gotta stay hip to the jive.

SCORES

There are various specific types of scores, and they have distinct practices based on who is likely to be reading them. Conductors have different preferences for scores than do composers or music theory students. For example, at the podium, most conductors wish to see every part notated in the transposition being read by each individual, so that they can quickly reference the same note that the player reads from their part. However, a composer might prefer instead to work on a score that is *concert*, or nontransposed, in order to more quickly see the tonal relationships between notes. Conductors use scores that are printed on larger paper so that they can easily spot the details from a distance, while waving their arms dramatically from the podium. Students, however, might prefer a reduced-size "study score" that easily fits in a backpack. There are different ways to render the same music, and various practices that will help facilitate the various purposes that music readers might have.

Achieving the most useful rendering for a score is often a process of weighing clarity vs. completeness. Notation for different instruments of the ensemble share much of the same information: tempo, measure numbers, repeat directions, and other nuances. Many of these elements only need to be stated once in the score, however, to avoid the distraction of needless "ink" (i.e., redundancy). For example, measure numbers are the same for every instrument. They certainly don't need to be stated on every staff. Just once, above the top staff (or below the bottom staff) is enough for small ensembles; once per instrument family is enough for large ensembles, such as orchestras. Setting measure numbers on every staff adds clutter to the page and doesn't clarify anything. It's an example of how being complete and correct can actually hinder communication rather than facilitate it.

Expect that every element appearing on a score will be noticed and considered. If you can avoid giving your readers unnecessary markings to decipher, you will reduce their burden and ease their path to the music. Minimize redundancy! Just make sure that the required performance information is clear.

Let's look at some of the general issues for preparing scores. Then, we will examine practices for specific types of ensembles.

Common Paper Sizes and Orientation

Notation has long been traditionally printed on paper other than the 8.5 x 11 inch paper that is standard in most desktop printers. Here are some of the common paper sizes for different types of scores—that is, standard publishing sizes for notation rendered by commercial publishers. You will find other variations of these, as well.

Most notation is printed with the page in "portrait" (vertical) orientation. There are some exceptions, such as marching band parts and some pedagogical materials. Landscape (horizontal) orientation is more awkward, particularly on a music stand, and generally considered less professional in most circumstances.

Instrument part	9 x 12, 9.5 x 12.5, 10 x 13
Marching band "flip-folder" part. Note: This is a critical measurement. Folders vary, so find out if there's a standard folder being used, if you can.	5.25 x 7, 5.5 x 7, 6.25 x 4.75, 6.5 x 9
Choral score (sometimes called "octavos")	6.75 x 10.5, 6.875 x 10.5
Hymnal	5.75 x 8.25
Conductor's score	9 x 12, 12 x 18, 13 x 19, 14 x 22
Study score (miniature score, short score, compressed score)	5.5 x 8.5, 6.2 x 8.5
Method book, songbook	9 x 12
Fake books	8.5 x 11, 9 x 12
Analytical music book	8 x 10, 9 x 12

FIG. 9.1. Paper Sizes

The proliferation of downloadable PDF scores and the ubiquity of desktop printers has resulted in more scores being published to suit standard "letter" paper sizes: 8.5 x 11 for parts, 11 x 17 (double letter sized) for conductor scores, and 5.5 x 8.5 (half letter) for choral scores. If you are a do-it-yourselfer and in the market for a printer or copying machine, there is a benefit to choosing a machine that can print larger paper.

Beyond legibility, the dual blessing and curse of paper sizes other than 8.5 x 11 or 11 x 17 is that they are relatively difficult to photocopy. It's good in that they are perhaps a slight deterrent to piracy, but bad for your own convenience and budget.

Binding

There are various types of binding, for scores, parts, and books commonly used for music publication. They each have their pros and cons. Speaking as a publisher, I can assure you that you will get complaints on whatever binding you choose.

Binding Type	Pros	Cons	Note
Folded; No Binding	Effortless, free.	Pages fall out and get lost.	Obviously, a single sheet needs no binding. Scores that involve only two sheets of paper (eight sides) can be folded together, one inside the other. It is risky, but easy, and often okay for a single-use score.
Taped	Cheap, DIY.	Can be amateurish, not durable.	A better choice than nothing for a short, single-use score. Both amateur and professional options exist for this.
Saddle stitched/ Stapled	Clean, cheap, easy to find, pro- fessional.	Staples aren't durable. Longer works won't lie flat. No spine.	Best for scores and parts, up to about 12 sheets (48 sides). If you do it yourself, keep flat side of staple on the outside of the binding.
Perfect (glued)	Cheap, ubiqui- tous, can have a printable spine.	Falls apart relatively easily, particularly for very thick scores. Doesn't lie flat.	Okay for trade books that will be read once or twice, but too fragile for anything that will be reused, because the spine will be broken in an attempt to make it lie flat.
Ota/"Lay flat" binding (glued, but with some give)	Durable, and it lies flat. Printable spine.	Hard to find a vendor that can do it. Relatively expensive.	Often the best choice for music books—particularly thicker ones.
Plastic Comb	Cheap, lies flat, ubiquitous. You can buy your own machine to do it.	Falls apart easily, looks amateurish. No printable spine.	Disposable. Avoid, particularly if the printed notation is to be used more than once. DIY/ indie feel.
Spiral Bound	Cheap, durable, lies flat.	Damages piano desks, book- shelves, clothing, and people. No printable spine (usually).	Avoid, despite its temptations. It is too dangerous. Scratching a Steinway isn't worth it.

FIG. 9.2. Score/Book Binding Types

For most practicing musicians who prepare notation, a simple two-page affair is among the most common end results. Rather than printing two 8.5 x 11 pages, if you can, print (or photocopy) them side-by-side on a single 11 x 17 page, so that they open as a spread. This will be much easier to manage, read, and keep on a music stand.

Stapling pages along the side (side-stapling) is the worst choice! It is also what's most commonly done in the amateur world. But such scores never lie flat, they fall apart, and they will cut your hands. Instead, if you are stapling your own scores, staple them down the middle of the centerfold, if you can, so that the stable ends are inside the book, not poking through the back.

Paper Weight

Heavier, firmer paper behaves better on a music stand than does flimsier paper, which is likely to curl down and fall to the floor. Heavier paper will also better survive multiple performances. Around 80 lb. (often stated #80) for scores and parts is ideal.

Margins

Ideally, on full-sized pages, keep about a one-inch margin on all sides of a page, particularly for the notation itself. Headers and footers can come closer to the margins than this. Some binding styles, such as perfect binding or side-stitched, require a greater "inside" margin along the spine, as they don't lay flat.

Page Turns

Whether you are conducting or playing an instrument, the need to turn pages is an annoyance. Measures should be laid out in order to minimize the impact of page turns. Here are some ways to facilitate page turns.

1. Organize measures and systems so that the last measure of a page is relatively simple, musically (and logistically), so that the reader doesn't really need to look at it. Ideally, the last bar preceding a page turn is a rest.
2. Set multiple systems on a page. This will be a function of the size of the notation generally, the spacing between staves, and the spacing between systems. If you've got fewer than six measures on a page, consider whether there is some way to reformat so that more measures can fit: bigger paper, smaller font, tighter spacing between staves, etc. Otherwise, readers will spend all their time flipping pages, rather than thinking about the music. The system divider symbol (⫽) separates systems, set on the left; it is generally only used for larger ensemble scores—particularly those that vary in how many staves are in a system.
3. Orient the score horizontally or vertically on the page to accommodate a greater number of systems or measures. Some musicians abhor horizontal pages, however. (Organ scores are often set horizontally.)

4. Use staff optimization, the judicious use of repeats and "roadmaps" (see chapter 7), and other notational devices for reducing redundancy.

Recto and Verso Pages

In publishing, right-hand pages are called "recto" and have odd page numbers. Left-hand pages are "verso" and have even numbers. Page 1, therefore, should always be on the right—a recto page. In books, everything before chapter 1, page 1, is "front matter": the copyright page, table of contents, acknowledgments, preface, foreword, introduction, dedication, publishers note, etc. Front matter is numbered with lowercase Roman numerals, and "page 1" is the first page of chapter 1—even though it might be preceded by many physical pages.

In sheet music publishing, the goal of facilitating easy page turns is more important than beginning the content on page 1, particularly for sheet music that is either two or four pages long. In those cases, it is common for the first page of notation to be a verso page—on the left, so that most of the pages will be together on spreads (a facing pair of verso and recto pages). Otherwise, start on a recto page.

If we do begin on a verso page, then the other (preceding) side of that page can have a reiteration of the music's cover, or perhaps an instrument list, copyright notice, performance note (such as a drum key), or some other material. Make it look like a deliberate choice.

Sheet music often dispenses with the convention of Roman numerals for front matter, and even the cover might be technically counted as a page. Page 1's numeral is generally not printed, so you will commonly see a number 2 or 4 as the page number for the first page of notation.

Page Setup

Every page of a score contains one or more staff *systems*—that is, complete sets of staves showing all the instruments playing, spanning the width of a page. The first system of a large score presents the instrument names written out fully. On subsequent systems, the names are abbreviated. Make sure that the abbreviation matches the name you are using, such as Contrabass and Cb., not Contrabass and Dbl. Bs. (for "double bass"). Abbreviated names are usually two to four letters.

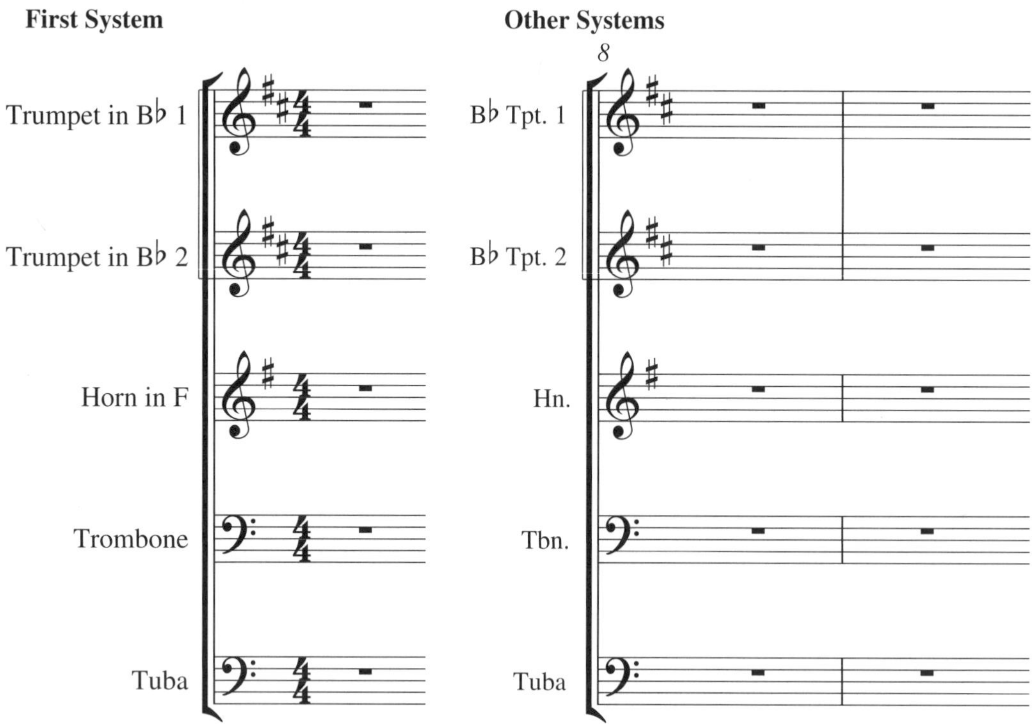

FIG. 9.3. Instrument Names. First system (full name) and others (abbreviated names).

Instrument names are only necessary on staves when they are not obvious. A score for a single instrument, for a piano with a soloist, for a string quartet, choir, or other small ensemble can instead have the name of the ensemble indicated in the page header, without individual staff names shown. If the header says it's a string quartet, and the staves are two treble clefs, an alto, and a bass, it is completely clear who is playing what. No staff name required. Alternatively, in a small ensemble (say, up to four instruments, plus keyboard), the instrument names may appear on the first system, but subsequent systems are not labeled. Lead sheets usually don't have instrument names, as they are instrument-generic—unless they are specifically transposed for an individual.

When the instrument names are shown, the first system (only) is indented. Some publishers always indent the first system, particularly in a volume with multiple similar-appearing exercises or pieces, such as a book of snare drum etudes. An exercise number may appear to the left of an indented first system. Indentation isn't really necessary, though, unless you have instrument names.

Spacing between systems should be greater than the spacing between staves, to avoid confusion between the bottom staff of one system and the top staff of another.

Page Headers

The first page of a score has various unique text elements regarding the piece, in addition to the actual notation. At the top of the page, the header includes the music's title, subtitle, dedication, composer, perhaps a lyricist and/or arranger, year/opus number, possibly an instrumentation indication, and whether or not it is a concert score. If the first page of the notation is page 1 of the product, it will not have a visible page number, but starting from page 2, it will, either at the top or bottom.

The Notation Book Tango

For Jackie

Concert Score

MUSIC BY Jonathan Feist
LYRICS BY Eloise Kelsey
ARRANGED BY Emily Jones

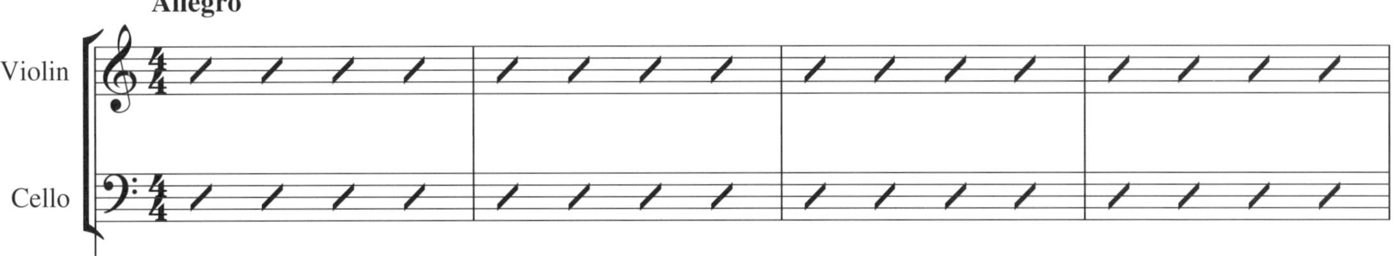

FIG. 9.4. Header

At the bottom of the first page is often the footer, which may have a copyright notice, catalog number, and perhaps a logo. Copyright notices are not legally required for a piece to be legally protected by U.S. law. However, they are helpful in letting readers know where to obtain licensing information. They also help frighten the lesser criminally inclined pirates (e.g., your average kindergarten music teacher) from performing their dark work.

A proper copyright notice includes the word copyright or copyright symbol © (not both), the year of copyright, the name of the copyright holder(s), and the words "All Rights Reserved." Many publishers like to include some frightening language as part of this, though it actually doesn't change the legal status of the work. If you write it, you own the copyright, unless you transfer the rights to someone else. Registering the copyright with the U.S. Copyright Office helps you prove ownership in a lawsuit, but you don't need that registration to officially own the work.

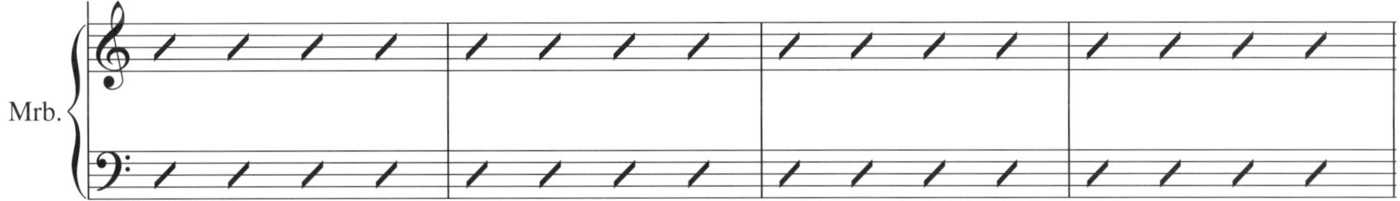

© 2017 by Berklee Press. All Rights Reserved.
No portion of this score may be reprinted or distributed without
the express written permission of the publisher.

FIG. 9.5. Page 1 Footer with Copyright Notice

Due to this extra text, there is less space for the actual music on the first page than on the other pages. To make room, the first page will usually accommodate fewer systems. The systems should be laid out so that the base line of the bottom system of page 1 aligns with the base line of the bottom of page 2. The first page's header sometimes takes up more vertical space than necessary to make the spacing of the systems on that page more consistent with the system spacing of the subsequent pages.

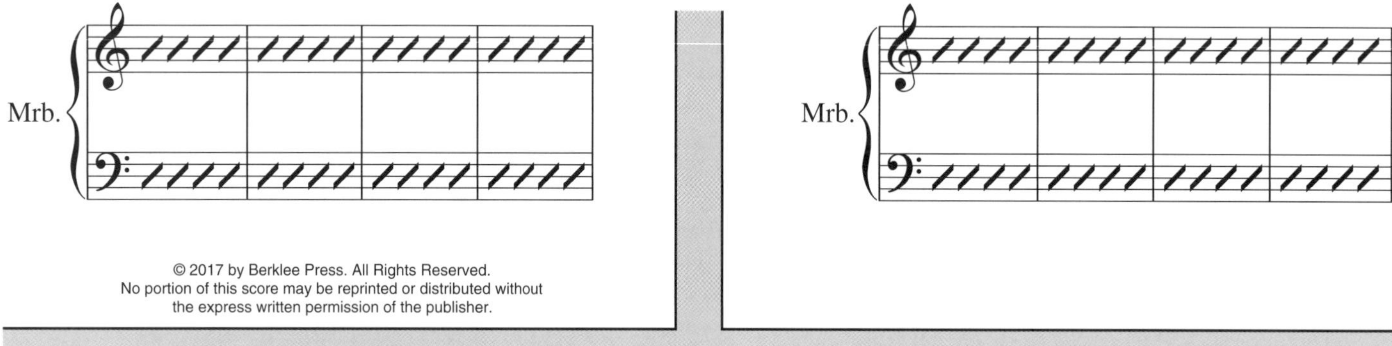

FIG. 9.6. Aligned Bottom Systems of Pages 1 and 2

Starting on page 2, in the header, even-numbered pages feature the number on the left, and odd numbered pages feature the number on the right. The title of the piece might be indicated in the header, centered, and a catalog number for the piece might appear in the footer. Alternatively, page numbers can be centered, either on the top or the bottom. There is an advantage to keeping all this information on top and in the corners, though, to avoid potential confusion between page numbers and notation elements, such as measure numbers, triplet markings, fingerings, etc.

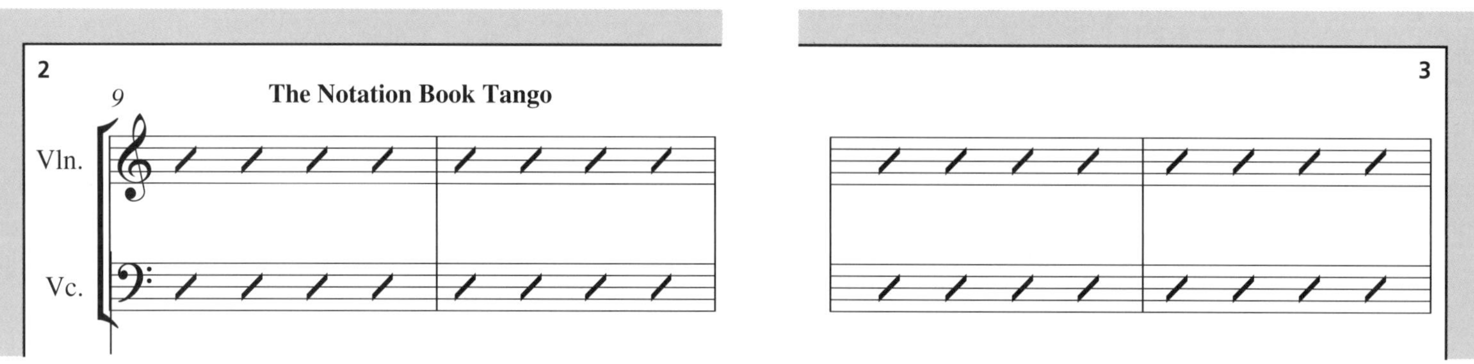

FIG. 9.7. Page Numbers on 2 (Verso) and 3 (Recto)

Condensed Scores

In a *condensed score*, staves with no notation for a complete system are hidden; an *optimized system* excludes staves for instruments that are not playing during those measures. This is a way to get more systems on a page and reduce the number of required page turns. The downside of score compression is that it can be confusing to have instruments come and go, and each system's layout and relationship to the ensemble will look different. The practice is therefore more common in study scores than in conductor scores, but you may see it anywhere. A condensed score takes every advantage to optimize systems and thus make the score take up the minimum number of pages possible.

In a condensed score, the first system might include a staff for every instrument of the ensemble, even if that instrument is tacet for the system. Alternatively, a complete instrument listing may be provided before the first page; then, only instruments that play need be shown in the first system.

Instrument Names: Transposition and Abbreviation

After the first system, it is common for staves to be labeled with abbreviated names. These abbreviations are somewhat standardized, though variations occur—even in the names of the instruments themselves.

Here is a list of full and abbreviated names for some common instruments. Variations occur, but these are common and clear. Of course, there are countless other instruments. If you can't find a respected source for its abbreviation, just keep it unique and clear, usually two or three characters.

Woodwinds	**WW.**
Piccolo	Picc.
Flute	Fl.
Clarinet	Cl., Clt.
Bass Clarinet	B. Cl., B. Clt.
Oboe	Ob.
English Horn	E. Hn., E.H.
Soprano Saxophone	S. Sax
Alto Saxophone	A. Sax
Tenor Saxophone	T. Sax
Baritone Saxophone	B. Sax
Bassoon	Bn.
Contrabassoon	C. Bn.
Harmonica	Harm.

Brass	**Br.**
Trumpet	Tp., Tpt.
Cornet	Cnt.
Flugelhorn	Flgl., Flghn.
French Horn, Horn in F	Hn., F. Hn.
Trombone	Tbn., Trb.
Bass Trombone	B. Tbn., Bs. Tbn., B. Trb.
Baritone Horn	Bar., B. Hn.
Euphonium	Euph.
Tuba	Tba.

Strings	**Stg.**
Violin	Vln.
Viola	Vla.
Cello, Violoncello	Vc., Vcl.
Contrabass (aka bass, double bass, acoustic bass, upright bass, string bass, not to mention doghouse and others . . . .)	Cb., Bs., D♭., A. Bs., Up. Bs., Str. Bs.
Harp	Hp.

Keyboards/Electronics	**Kb., Kbd.**
Piano	Pno.
Electronic Keyboard	E. Pno.
Synthesizer	Syn., Synth.
Organ	Org.
Theremin	Ther.

Plucked Strings	
Guitar	Gtr.
Electric Bass	E. Bs., Bass
Banjo	Bjo.
Mandolin	Mdn.
Ukulele	Uk., Uke.
Dobro	Dob.

Percussion	Perc.
Drum set	D.S., Drs., Ds., Drms.
Timpani	Timp.
Gong	G.
Cymbals	Cym.
Ride Cymbals	Ride
Crash Cymbals	Crash
China Cymbal	China
Hi-Hat	HH
Snare Drum	SD, S. Dr.
Bass Drum	BD, B. Dr., Kick
High Tom-Tom	Hi Tom
Medium Tom-Tom	Med. Tom
Low Tom-Tom	Low Tom
Floor Tom-Tom	Fl. Tom
Bells, Cowbell	Bls., C. Bl.
Glockenspiel	Glock, Glk.
Xylophone	Xyl.
Vibraphone	Vib.
Marimba	Mar., Mrb.

Voice	Vox., Voc.
Soprano	S, Sop.
Mezzo Soprano	Mezzo, M. Sop.
Alto	A, Alt.
Contralto	C. Alt.
Tenor	T, Ten.
Counter-Tenor	C. Ten.
Baritone	Bar., Bs.-Bar
Bass (Singer)	B, Bs.
Lead Vocalist(s)	Ld. Vox
Background Vocalist(s)	Bg. Vox
Female Vocalist(s)	Fem. Vox
Male Vocalist(s)	Male Vox
Vocal Percussion	Vox. Perc.

FIG. 9.8. Common Instruments and Abbreviations

In opera and musical theater scores, a vocal part may be named with the character's name and a suitable abbreviation: Z for Zerlina, Don G. for Don Giovanni. A common standard is to set these names in all uppercase: DON G.

Specific key names for instruments usually precede the instrument names and are included in the full name and abbreviation: B♭ Trumpet, C Trumpet, etc. The function of these note names is often confused. Specifically, they indicate the exact type of the instrument in use; a B♭ trumpet is a different machine than a C trumpet. A secondary benefit of these names is that they also often clarify the transposition. However, some instruments transpose, and the note name is typically left off of the instrument name, such as the baritone horn, which is in B♭, or the English horn, which is in F. Saxophones may or may not include the note; it's technically redundant, but you see it both ways: E♭ Alto Saxophone vs. Alto Saxophone. And then there's the confusing "B♭ Trombone," which never transposes. The B♭ just means that when the slide is in its default position, it plays a harmonic series based on the fundamental B♭. Yes, trombones in other keys exist, but they are rare—effectively extinct. Assume that any trombone is a B♭-based tenor trombone or bass trombone, both of which are nontransposing. And don't perpetuate the use of that "B♭ Trombone" tag, because it confuses people.

To a conductor, a key signature is the more reliable means of spotting an instrument's key transposition. The only way to know that an instrument transposes a perfect octave from where it's written (such as for double bass or guitar) is to study orchestration; the score itself will offer no help here.

You will see these note-name modifiers rendered either before the instrument name (F Horn) or after (Horn in F). It is easiest if all instrument names are structured the same way, so that the reader can easily spot those transpositions that are part of the name, as they are all in the same place, logically: B♭ Clarinet, F Horn.

My colleague/advisor/friend composer Ben Newhouse has a good idea: that we use the structure "B♭ Trumpet" (note first) to mean the instrument name, and the structure "Trumpet in B♭" (note last) to indicate transposition. That would be logical.

These standards for how instrument names are rendered are more our own personal wishful thinking than actual common practice, but I think that they are worth implementing. Let's start a movement, shall we? The "Ben Convention" for instrument names?

In a *transposed score*, each instrument is set in its transposed key. In a *score in C* (or "concert score"), the instruments are notated without key transpositions, though octave transpositions remain. The fact that it is a "score in C" should be prominently displayed in the header. One of the great miracles of music notation software is that scores can be toggled between transposed and nontransposed with a single mouse click. When you print a score in C, though, be sure it is clearly labeled as such. Perhaps now it's an obvious point, but the note-name modifiers before instrument names should be present even in a score in C. When it comes down to brass tacks, that initial letter is part of the physical instrument name, not an indication of the staff's transposition—particularly if we can all start using the Ben Convention.

Another common mistake among users of music notation software is to use the "out of the box" abbreviations for instrument names, which are often based on MIDI sounds rather than the real instrument name. So, the abbreviation "Ac. Gtr." might show up for a guitar, indicating "acoustic guitar." But conductors and other score readers nearly always would prefer the simpler "Gtr.," particularly if there is no need to distinguish between multiple guitars in the ensemble.

Instrument Family Order

Instrument staves within scores are organized and ordered by specific standard conventions: by family and by range within that family. Figure 9.14 shows some standard orders for various specific types of ensembles.

The general instrument families are: woodwinds, brass, percussion, strings, rhythm section, soloists, and vocal choir. This standard for organization has historical origins, more than logical or musical ones. So, flutes and saxophones are considered woodwinds even though they are made out of metal, and brass saxophones may use plastic reeds. Guitars aren't considered strings. Sousaphones are classified as brass, even though they are often made out of fiberglass. A synthesizer playing a string pad would be in the rhythm section, not the string section.

Within each family, the instruments are ordered in the score roughly by range: piccolo first (on top), then flute, all the way down to the contrabassoon. Similar instruments are also typically grouped together. So, the four saxophones are sub-grouped together within the woodwind section as a unit, even though the soprano sax has a range much like that of a clarinet and the bari sax range is like the bassoon.

Instrument groups, particularly in larger ensembles, are often independently connected together using brackets. There will typically be one bracket for the whole family and a secondary bracket for subgroups within that family. If a section temporarily splits into two staves, such as the violin I section dividing into two sections, those staves will be joined by a brace rather than a bracket. The brace is also used for a single instrument set on multiple staves, such as piano or marimba playing a grand staff.

Barlines also clarify instrument groups, connecting their staves together. Barlines break between instrument families and between pairs of grand staffs within a family (between electronic keyboard and piano, for example).

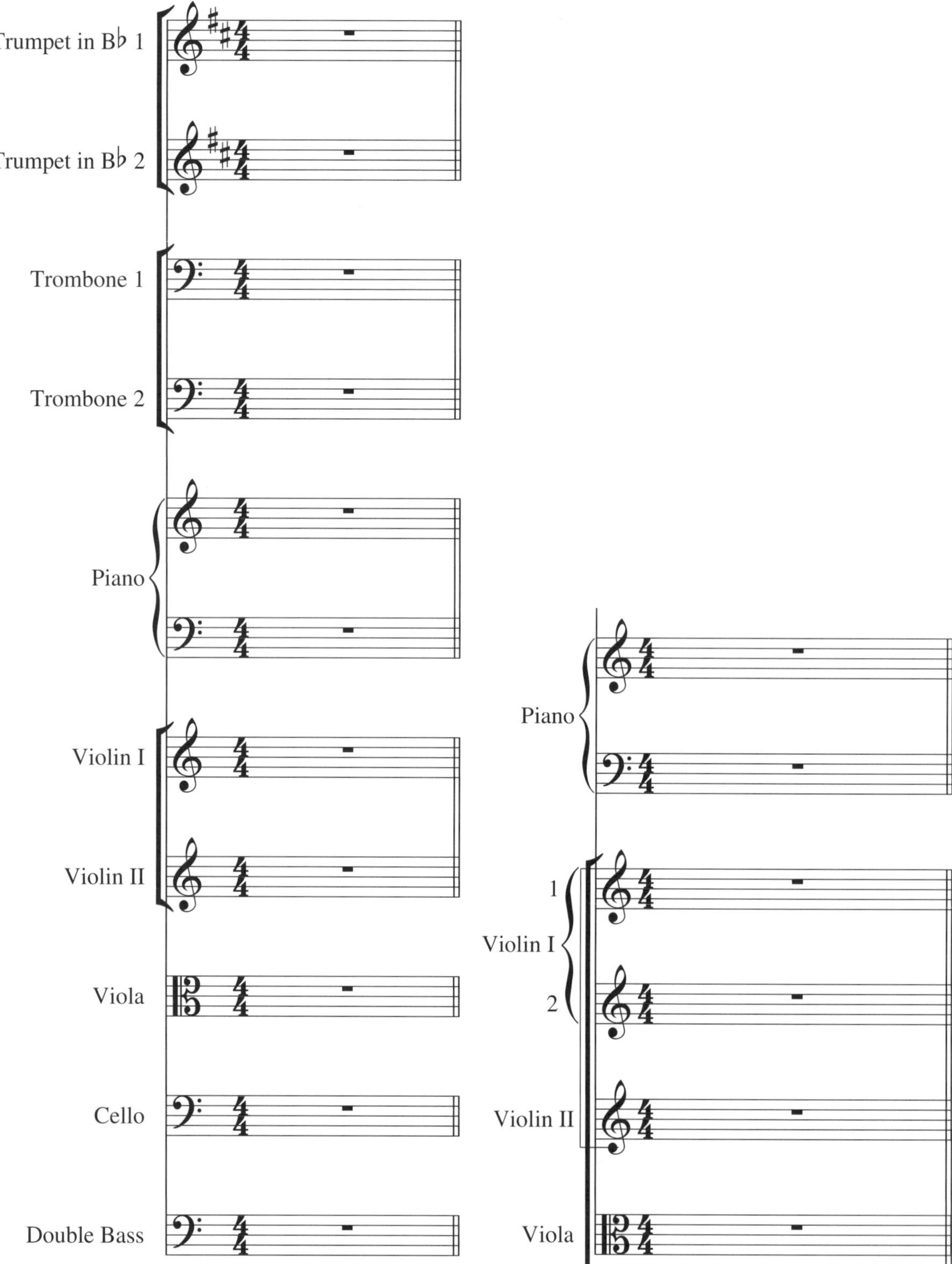

FIG. 9.9. Brackets, Braces, and Barlines

Sections may be divided into multiple staves, named with Roman numerals for subgroups on a part (Violin I, Violin II) or Arabic numerals for individuals on a part (Flute 1, Flute 2).

A smaller instrument group might include separate staves for each player, such as a pair of flutes or trumpets. However, they might share a single staff, if they usually play the same notes. If they split and play two different parts, they can still share a staff, with two voices, or temporarily read two staves. Similarly, a staff used for a larger section might sometimes be used for just a solo player, if the rest of the section stays out; mark it "Solo." When the staff returns to the full section playing the same notes, it is marked "a2" (*a due*—both players) or "tutti" (full section).

The instrument name should clarify that multiple individuals are sharing a staff. The first chair (Flute 1) reads the top voice; the second chair (Flute 2) reads the bottom voice. The label "divisi" (div.) can be used for multiphonic instruments, such as violin, to clarify that the notes are to be played by a divided section in two independent voices, rather than everyone playing the same interval or chord. The numerals can be stacked or separated with a comma.

FIG. 9.10. Two Flutes, One staff

When there are multiple staves for an instrument, each staff might get a complete name. Alternatively, the instrument name might appear just once, between the staves, and then each part gets a numeral: 1 and 2, or I and II for a large section. See figure 9.13 for various examples of how this can be done.

Redundancy Control

Scores easily grow complicated, with specific directions for every instrument. Redundant information should be excluded from the score, though included in individual parts so as to keep the score as clear and easily decipherable as possible. Small ensemble scores, such as for string quartet or choir and piano, may need information such as measure numbers, repeat endings, and tempo markings a single time for the whole ensemble, usually set above the top staff. Larger scores, such as for orchestra or concert band, generally feature such information on the top staff of each instrument family. It is unnecessary to restate this information on every staff, and doing so makes the score generally more intimidating, messy, and difficult to render clearly and correctly.

Information that need not be repeated for every staff includes:

- rehearsal letters
- bracketed repeat endings
- tempo markings
- measure numbers

Similarly, when instruments share notation, the score can be greatly simplified with the notation "col." (short for *colla*, meaning "with"). For example, if a trumpet and soprano sax are playing the same melody, you could just write it for the sax (top staff) and then use the word "col." in the trumpet staff. This omits some ink from the page and helps the conductor easily understand what is happening, without forcing him or her to read every note.

Our preference, at Berklee, is to use "col." only within a bracketed instrument family and when the notation is identical: same octave, same transposition, same clef. It's usually deployed for groups of three or more measures. You'll see variations of how this practice is implemented, but we've found that most conductors prefer to see unique notation spelled out rather than abbreviated. With the word "col." should be the name of the staff being mirrored. A wavy line shows how long the sharing lasts.

FIG. 9.11. Col. Notation

It is also worth considering whether two staves for independent players of the same instruments (Trumpets 1 and 2) can be combined into a single staff with multiple voices.

Time signatures are sometimes shared between staves in a conductor's score—set large and prominent, either once per instrument family or once every certain number of staves. This is a particularly common practice in film scores.

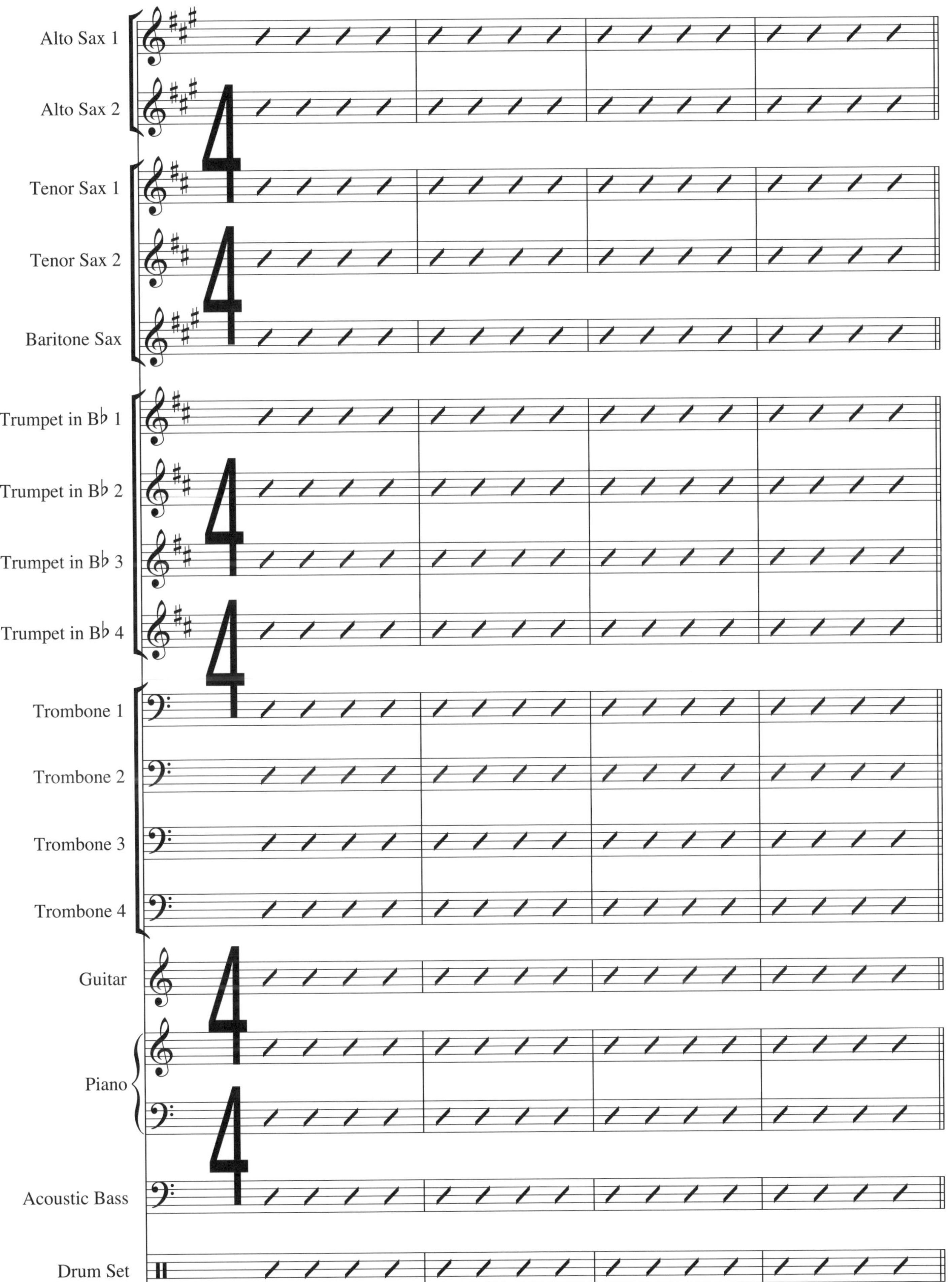

FIG. 9.12. Shared Time Signatures

Instrument Order

Many ensemble scores have standard instrumental orders. However, there are endless variations, particularly for large ensembles, regarding what their exact instrumentation will be. The instruments in a "standard orchestra" have varied dramatically over the past few centuries. Haydn didn't have a tuba, and Mahler didn't have a Theremin.

There is a basic score organization that has persisted, though. Families are ordered (top to bottom) woodwinds, brass, percussion, rhythm section (or just keyboards), choir, soloists, strings. Within each instrument family, the instruments are ordered by range, but similar instruments of a class (flute and piccolo, all clarinets, all saxophones) are subgrouped together within the family. In this example, the drum set is grouped with the rhythm section, rather than percussion, but you might see it either way. Also note that in this score, we have three possible staves called "bass": electric bass guitar in the rhythm section, bass singers in the choir, and acoustic bass in the string section. It's all about the bass! That said, it's helpful to have unique instrument names for each, in this circumstance.

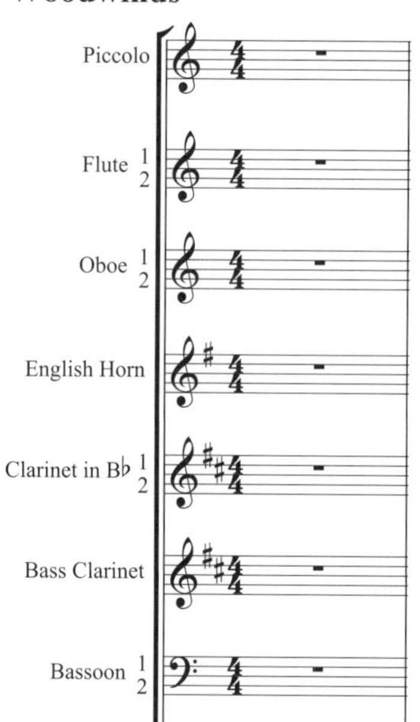

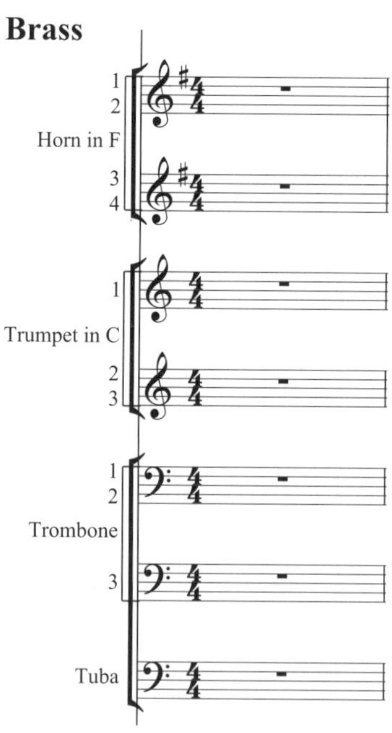

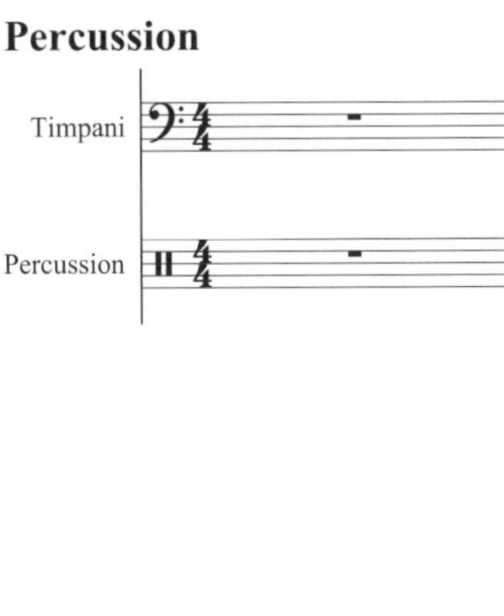

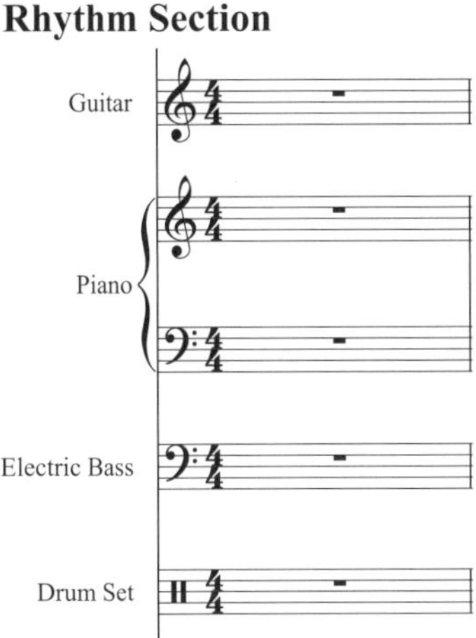

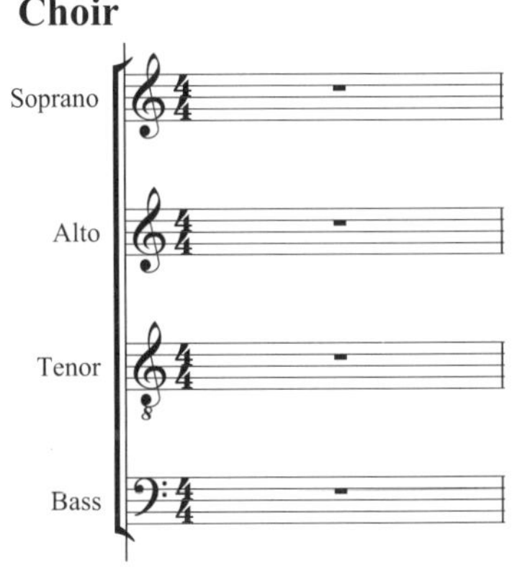

FIG. 9.13. Orchestral Instrument Family Order

Many contemporary ensembles have a generic "horns" section that groups all wind players in the same family, ordered by range.

Figure 9.14 shows common family orderings within some of the standard ensemble types. Of course, there are many other types of ensemble, but between these standards and the rules for ordering instruments within a family, you should be able to determine a logical and acceptable organization. Though the order of winds, brass, and strings is fairly consistent in the literature, the placement of percussion, keyboards, and voices varies.

If the rhythm section is an established group of guest artists, such as a rock band playing with an orchestra, scoring for the group should be kept intact and treated as a family. If the rhythm section instruments are simply ordinary members of the orchestra who are grooving, then they can be divided into their usual families: drum set with percussion, bass with strings, and then the guitar and piano above the strings as usual.

Orchestra	Concert Band	Jazz Band	Choir	Rhythm-Section Band
Woodwinds	Woodwinds	Woodwinds	Soloists	Lead Vocals
Brass	Brass	Brass	Choir	Background Vocal
Percussion	Keyboards/Comping Instruments	Rhythm Section	Keyboards	Guitar(s)
Rhythm Section	Rhythm Section	Pitched Percussion	Rhythm Section	Organ
Keyboards/ Comping Instruments	Pitched Percussion	Unpitched Percussion	Pitched Percussion	Synthesizer
Soloists	Unpitched Percussion		Unpitched Percussion	Piano
Choir				Bass
Strings				Drums

FIG. 9.14. Instrument Family Order

There are a few other score types that need mentioning, due to some special practices.

- **Film scores.** Film scores follow the organization for orchestral scores. They often include some staging cues, such as lead-in dialogue, to help the conductor synchronize with the picture. Scores designed for use in recording sessions are likely to number every measure centered under the bottom staff, enclosed in a box.
- **Piano/vocal scores.** Common in songbooks, these contain a vocal part above a piano part. Chord symbols with guitar fretboard diagrams may also be provided.
- **Piano/conductor scores.** These are piano versions of orchestral scores. They may be relatively heavily annotated with instrument names.
- **Hymnals.** Hymn notation is generally set on a pair of staves: soprano and alto on a single treble-clef staff, tenor and bass on a bass-clef staff. (Barbershop quartet notation is similar, but with tenor/lead on a treble-octave staff, and baritone and bass on a bass-clef staff.) The two voices may share the same stem, only dividing into two voices on the staff with opposing stems when they play different notes. Generally, just the first verse's lyrics are set under the notes, and subsequent verses are set in blocks of text below the notation, off the staff.

Other Ensemble Score Notation

We have mentioned various notation symbols throughout this book that have ramifications for ensemble scores. Here are two that warrant repeat mention. By coincidence, they both consist of two slashes—not to be confused with the unrelated two slashes for sixteenth notes or the two rhythm slashes to indicate improvisation in 2/4 time!

//	Caesura	A grand pause. The whole ensemble stops, and awaits the nod from a conductor or ensemble leader to continue.
[thick double slash symbol]	System Divider	Clarifies multiple systems on a page. Only necessary for large ensemble scores, particularly when tacet staves are hidden from some systems.

FIG. 9.15. Score Notation Symbols

FIG. 9.16. Caesura, System Divider, and Other Unrelated Two-Slash Symbols

PARTS

A *part* is the notation used by an individual musician in an ensemble. For purposes of this discussion, we'll consider three types of parts:

- Ensemble parts, such as for an orchestra, concert band, big band, etc., are generally printed on 12.5 x 19 paper. A part is just for a single instrument, though sometimes, two individuals will share a part, such as flutes 1 and 2.
- Marching band parts are printed on small paper, such as 5.5 x 7, so that they can fit into "flip folders" that attach to the instruments.
- Lead sheets, discussed in chapter 4, are usually instrument-generic parts, read by a variety of musicians. They tend to be relatively informal, and often are printed on whatever paper is on hand, such as 8.5 x 11 "letter" sized paper.

Some players "double" on multiple instruments. A single part might be for, say, saxophone and clarinet, performed by the same musician. When the player switches instruments, an indication such as "to Clarinet" is set during a rest, above the staff.

Individual instruments will often have extended periods of rest while their compatriots carry the music. A gong part, for example, might be tacet for most of a piece and only enter at the very end. It may mostly contain rests, which are ideally grouped in a multimeasure rest symbol.

Parts differ from full scores, in that they can make better use of the page through different symbols than would be seen on a conductor's score. Similarly, a part might have fingerings or other technical directions that would be unnecessary for a conductor to read. In this way, parts have both more and less information than full scores do.

Parts share these notation elements with the full score:

- page 1 headers and footers
- quantity of measures
- form designations (section headers, rehearsal letters, measure numbers, double barlines)
- tempo markings (including fermatas)
- notation keys specific to that part

Parts differ from scores in that they may include:

- multimeasure rests
- fingerings and other technical notes
- cue notes
- independent measure layout

Multimeasure Rests

Multimeasure rests can greatly reduce the amount of space a part requires. Break a multimeasure rest whenever there is a change in meter or tempo, or when there is a new formal section.

Here is a triangle part. Each section begins on a new system. Also, notice that in the second system, the 7-measure rest is longer than the 4-measure rest. All these layout choices makes this relatively sparse triangle part a little easier to follow and count.

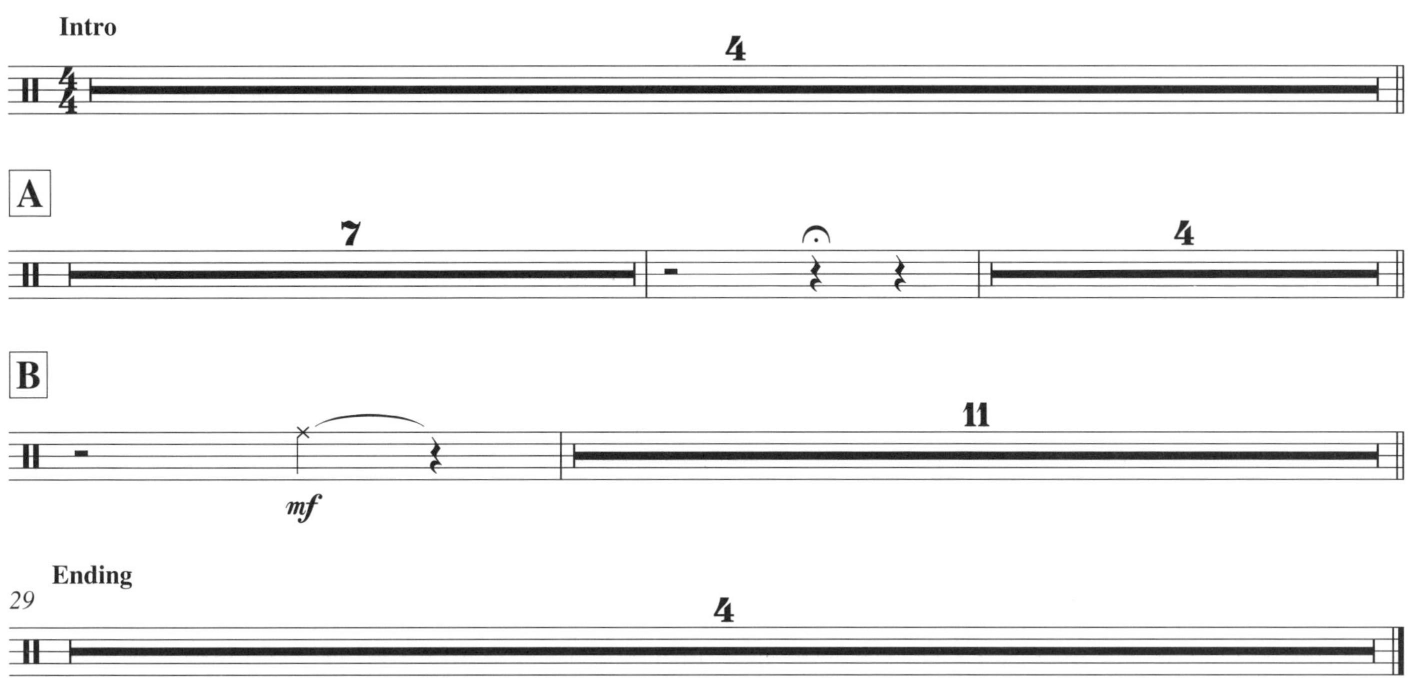

FIG. 9.17. Triangle Part with Multimeasure Rests

Cues

The challenge with parts, such as that in figure 9.17, is in paying the close attention required to come in on time when you've been laying out for quite a while. Cue notes are a great helper with this. These are distinctive parts played by other instruments that alert the player that their grand entrance is coming up. As a general rule, if there is a multimeasure rest of about eight or more bars, it's a good idea to include cue notes. In figure 9.17, they aren't necessary, as the conductor's breaking the fermata will serve as a wake-up call that we're getting close to our grand solo. However, if that fermata wasn't there, and we had a stretch of twelve measures, a cue would be helpful. Choose something easy for the player to hear. It could be something new by any instrument, or perhaps by an instrument close to home, such as the timpani, in this case. Cue notes may be set on their own staff, smaller (50 to 75 percent) than regular notation. Include the instrument name. Here, our triangle's entrance is clearly heralded by the timpani.

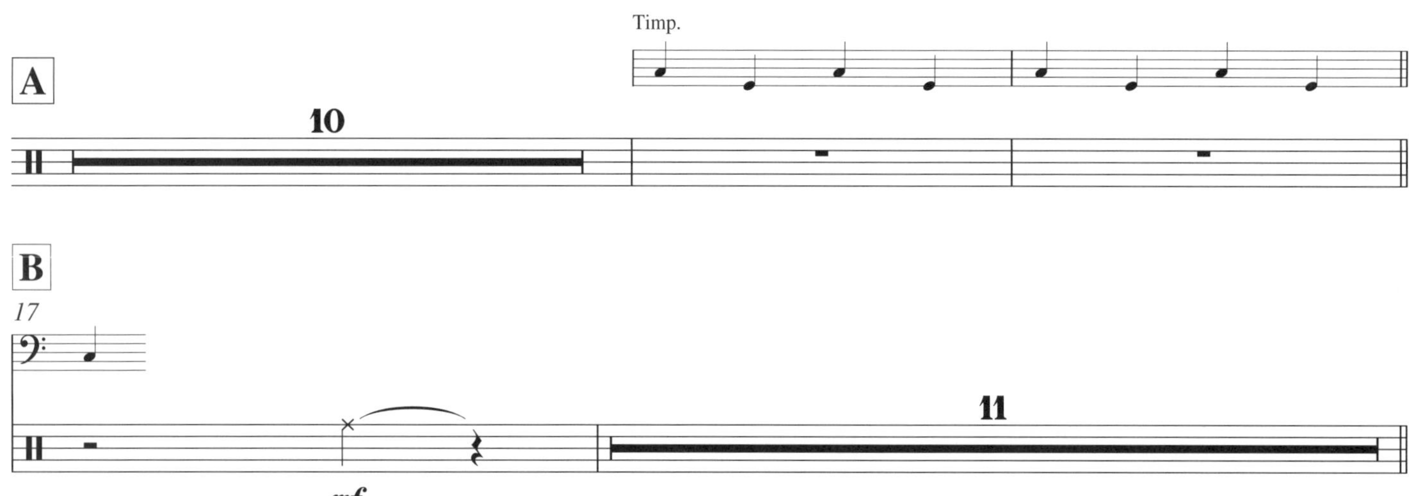

FIG. 9.18. Timpani Cue Notes

To make a sparse part like this more concise, a long initial rest symbol can be used. This symbol glosses over any change of meter, tempo, fermatas, formal organization, and such. After it, a measure number must mark the first measure played. It is particularly well suited to music analysis, rather than formal performance parts, as it relies on both the very careful attention of the player and conductor. It does make for a simpler part, though.

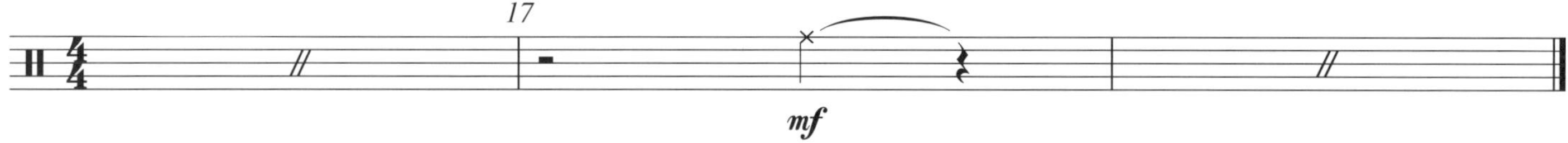

FIG. 9.19. Long Multimeasure Rest

Measure Repeats

Parts are also simplified and made concise by a variety of repeat symbols. They save space by clarifying repeated information. These are more common in rhythm section parts, but they are becoming more commonly accepted in the general literature.

⁒	Single-Measure Repeat	Repeat the most recently notated measure exactly. If there are several adjacent symbols, it is helpful to number every measure.
2 𝄎	Multiple-Measure Repeat	Repeat the most recently notated number of measures indicated. This is particularly common for clave patterns. The 2-bar repeat is most common, but you also see this for 4-bar patterns.
8 〰〰〰	Continuation Line	Continue the most recently notated measure for the number of bars indicated (8 bars, in this case). This is primarily used for drum sets repeating beat patterns. Minor variations in the pattern are acceptable, in some styles.
/ / / /	Time Slashes	Improvise. Each slash represents a beat of a measure. So, 4/4 time has four slashes per measure, 3/4 time has three slashes, 6/8 time felt in two has two slashes per measure, but six slashes if it is felt in six. These may be used both to indicate that the player creates an appropriate accompanying part or that the player improvises a featured solo. The word "solo" clarifies that there is a featured soloist during these measures.

FIG. 9.20. Measure Repeats

Here's a drum set part that uses all these symbols. It begins with an introduction where the drum set is tacet for the first four bars and then plays a two-measure pattern two times through. At letter A, the pattern is restated, as it begins a new section. The pattern is played three times, and then it is varied, starting out normally, but then playing a short fill for two beats into letter B. Letter B features a one-bar pattern that is played for sixteen bars, total, and the drummer has the liberty to vary it slightly, perhaps choosing a different drum or cymbal for an eighth note here or there. At C, the drum solos for eight bars. Then, at the coda, a one-bar pattern repeats three times, and the piece ends with a rolled cymbal.

FIG. 9.21. Drum Part with Measure Repeats

As you can see, these symbols clarify what the unique material is in the score. They are particularly useful for rhythm section parts, which tend to have a lot of repeated material. Besides reducing space and clarifying redundancy, they allow the player to focus on listening, interacting with their compatriots, and actually creating music, rather than being distracted by having their noses continually glued to the score.

CHAPTER 10

Writing About Music

Music writing is often technical, similar to writing about science or mathematics. There are many types of symbols and similar nomeclature to keep straight, and it is easy to craft our writing in ways that will confuse our reader.

There are a number of different types of music writing. Let's consider a few.

1. Technical instructions. How to play an instrument or apply a theoretical construct. Music instruction books use this approach.
2. Analysis. Some writing tries to uncover the magic behind the music by revealing the underlying patterns and relationships of elements that cause its effect.
3. Historical. Historical writing about music is a combination of technical writing and storytelling, revealing the cultural and historical contexts for the technical approaches being undertaken.
4. Review. Reviews of performances or recordings often include elements of all the above types of writing.

The challenge with all of these is to remain engaging while providing insight. Done poorly, technical and analytical writing, particularly, can become a mind-numbingly tedious trap, which is useless to everyone, and can even turn readers off learning about music generally—the opposite effect of what we're after. At its worst, analytical writing is like reading a phone book: it lists numbers, but doesn't reveal a higher truth, teach a useful technique, or tell a compelling story. Blah, blah, blah.

Examples make any writing come alive. If I point you to some real music—say, the song "Amazing Grace"—then the discussion suddenly becomes relevant and compelling. Examples keep it real.

The other side of good music writing, though, is in crafting the language so as to avoid being tedious or wordy.

Let's say that I want to point you to a note in a measure. Here are two ways to reference it. If you like, time yourself locating both notes.

Look at the and of the second beat of measure forty-two's bass clef staff, the note "C♯."

FIG. 10.1. Find the Note

Here's a revised version, finding a slightly different note. Time yourself finding this one too.

Find the D (circled) in bar 42: treble-clef staff, on the "and" of beat 1.

FIG. 10.2. Find Another Note

Why was the second one easier?

1. The unnecessary empty bars were omitted.
2. The target note was circled, and the directions mentioned this distinguishing mark.
3. Measure numbers were provided on every bar.
4. The sentence was better organized, using more numerals—particularly the one matching the measure and beat numbers.
5. After clarifying what we were looking for, we drilled down from general elements to specific ones: measure, clef, beat. It was a clear, logical path. The unusual logical function of the word "and" was set in quotation marks.

Crafting the text to connect to the example clearly and concisely makes it much easier to read, as does honing the exact notation being reviewed.

NUMERALS VS. ORDINALS VS. WORDS

Here are two more sentences:

A twelve-bar blues has three four-bar phrases.

A 12-bar blues has three 4-bar phrases.

In this example, the second one is easier to read, thanks to the surgical use of numerals. Two similar constructions (musical structure names identified by quantities of measures) were given numerals rather than words. The third number in that sentence (three) is logically different, so it gets a word instead of a numeral. Making this distinction in how numbers are rendered clarifies the meaning.

Generally speaking, words in sentences are the least jarring option: they are surrounded by their own kind. Numerals are a little more alien, and should generally be used more sparingly. However, as we have seen, they have the benefit of conciseness, and so using them can facilitate reading comprehension.

There are two other options: ordinals, in their numeric form (2nd) and their word form (second). The numeric ordinal form is a little more jarring than either a word or a numeral. Sometimes, though, they can be similarly useful in distinguishing different types of complex writing. For example:

> *On the second beat, slide your third finger from the fourth fret to the fifth fret.*
>
> *On beat 2, slide your third finger from the 4th fret to the 5th fret.*

Using those three forms for three different types of numbers, in this case, makes the reading easier. The ordinals show a clearer relationship between the two adjacent frets than would the words. Why not use just numerals for the frets? Because it is more idiomatic in the language to use the ordinal form. Nobody ever says "the 4 and 5 fret"—though they would easily say "the 4 and 5 of a major scale," and I would use numerals in the latter case.

Here is a chart showing the Berklee Press preference for when to use numerals, words, and ordinals for numeric values in music. We're not always completely consistent here and will temper these preferences to best suit the specific goals at hand. (A foolish consistency is the hobgoblin of little minds, and oh, how I hate being hobgobbled by my constant drive to find foolish consistency.) Usually, though, these preferences hold. General rule: If something is named for a numeral, or several numeric versions of something are being compared, then try to use the numeral or ordinal in text. For gear, if the industry seems to have a clear preference, go with that.

Scale or chord degrees	Numeral (flat 3)
Chord types	Word (seventh chord)
Chord numbers	Roman numeral (III)
Intervals	Word (fourth)
String quantities	Word (four-string arpeggio)
String numbers	Roman for orchestral strings (I string), circled numerals for guitar strings (①)
Fret numbers	Ordinal (4th fret)
Finger numbers	Ordinal or words, but numeral in notation (first finger, 1st finger)
Fretboard position numbers	Ordinal (5th fret)
Beat numbers	Numeral (beat 1)
Measure numbers	Numeral (bar 4)
Quantities of measures	Word (four measures)
Numbers indicating phrase lengths	Numeral or word (four-measure solo; 4-bar phrase), depending on context
Devices with channel names	Numeral (8-channel mixer)
Cable sizes	Word (quarter-inch cable)
Instrument types	Numeral (12-string guitar)

FIG. 10.3. Numerals, Ordinals, and Words

Capital vs. Lowercase

Rules for capitalization of musical terms can be a bit ornate. For example, it might seem inconsistent to lowercase jazz but capitalize Latin, or to lowercase scale names and then uppercase mode names (minor, Mixolydian). Many of these rules are due to the fact that some terms are derived from proper nouns. Others are more a matter of generally accepted practice that has evolved over a long time. Here are some of our capitalization preferences. They are not all universal preferences. For example, with chord names, some writers use uppercase letters for major chords and lowercase letters for minor chords. But you don't need to dig too deeply to see how a minor can make this a problem.

Notes	Uppercase (D)
Solfege syllables	Uppercase (Do, Re, Mi)
Scales	Lowercase (A minor)
Modes	Uppercase (A Mixolydian)
Chord degrees	Uppercase Roman (V)
Chord letters	Uppercase (Dmin)
Types of chords	Lowercase (major, minor, augmented, etc.)
Genres	Usually lowercase (jazz, rock, bossa, hip-hop) with some exceptions (Latin, R&B)

FIG. 10.4. Uppercase and Lowercase

Punctuation plays a role in music writing, and there are many ways to make this clearer. Note names, for instance, need not have quotation marks: play a D, don't play a "D." Another common one: putting a # before a number, as in "Play measure #3." We know that 3 is a number, and the # only hinders the reading comprehensibility and should be avoided. It goes back to my perpetual rant about omitting unnecessary ink from the page. Also, watch out for hyphenation. My spell-checker always wants me to erroneously hyphenate G string and C section. (Draw your own conclusions.)

When referencing short works, such as a song or a movement, set the title in quotation marks. For larger or multimovement works, such as symphonies, operas, film scores, albums, or tours, use italics.

- Sing "Misty" for me.
- Sing *The Wall* for me.

NOTATION EXCERPT GUIDELINES

We saw in figures 10.1 and 10.2 that the same notation example can be rendered in various ways. Here are some other ways you can make them clearer.

- Make sure measure numbers of the excerpt match that of the score. Watch out when using notation software programs, which may add extraneous measure numbers that don't relate to the example in its current context.
- When you have multiple lines beginning fresh examples, start each one with a time signature.
- Use a consistent barline ending scheme for excerpts. At Berklee Press, we end short technical illustrations with double barlines, and reserve the final barline for complete etudes or actual song ends.
- Left-align notation examples, rather than centering them on the page.

Figure Identification

When referencing notation examples in a book or article, it can be helpful to number them. The standard format is to use a two-part numbering system, with a chapter number followed by a sequential number within that chapter. Figures with multiple parts might have reference letters, such as (a) and (b) showing different versions of the arpeggio in figure 10.5. Using the letters can simplify the illustration by getting some of the text out of it. That said, using the actual words as labels would be fine in this case, as they are so short and there is plenty of room.

FIG. 10.5. C Major Arpeggio. (a) Ascending (b) Descending.

As you can see, figure captions can be four-part structures.

1. The label FIG. or Figure.
2. The chapter number.
3. The figure sequence number within that chapter. The figure number ends with a period.
4. The figure caption: a short title, set in title case, with the first letter of each word uppercase. The caption only ends in a period if there is also a legend.
5. A figure legend, which is a longer description or itemization of what's going on in the figure. Legends might include permissions information, a key to symbology, or other information. It is set in sentence case, and ends with a period.

Figures should always have captions; legends are optional. Avoid having legends without captions, though.

An article or blog post would just have a single numeral: *Figure 5.* In the text reference, write out the word "figure." In the actual figure, abbreviate it "Fig." At Berklee Press, our current house style is to set "FIG." all uppercase and bold (with the numeral). This is a unique style decision that we like because it makes it easy to find the figure numbers, but it is not a ubiquitous practice.

While referencing figures as described is a great help to readers trying to locate graphics associated with the discussion, they are not always necessary. A songbook or exercise workbook, for instance, might never reference figures by number, and so these labels are not needed.

That said, the two-part numbering scheme is helpful for organizing graphics file names. Numbering figures makes the book production process a lot easier. File names begin with the figure numbers, using underscores or hyphens instead of periods so that they are compatible with Windows operating systems: 10_5_CArpeggio.musx, for the Finale file name. Each figure should have its own notation file.

CONSISTENCY TOOLS

Keeping track of all these rules and preferences can be cumbersome, and if there are multiple people working on a project, it is important that they all use the same style choices. You don't want an author using one set of preferences, the editor using another, the three proofreaders using their own ways, the production manager using yet another system, and so on. You'd spend all your time crossing out each other's suggestions.

Here are some tools of the trade used by publishers to help implement consistent house style, preserve institutional knowledge, and generally speed up the publishing process and make the work go more efficiently.

1. Templates. A file template is a starting point for a project, such as a notation template for musical examples, a word processor template for starting a new chapter, or a DAW file for starting a new recording. It has all the preferences and libraries loaded into it, so that it's ready to go. Starting from a template greatly speeds up the creation process. We have many notation templates, particularly. Considering that a book can have hundreds of files associated with it, if you can save a couple minutes of setup on each one by starting with a template, that is obviously going to be a significant time savings.

   I use notation templates of all shapes and sizes. Some are very simple: four bars ending with a double barline, which I use for short examples. Others are longer, such as a template set up for extended string quartet works. If there is a chance that it will be used for an extended work, set it up to go on three pages, so that you can allow for the first page (title page), and then recto and verso pages (i.e., right-hand and left-hand pages of a spread), which will have different layouts for the page numbers. Four bars per system is a logical initial layout. You can always change it. It is easier to delete what you don't want than to create something new.

2. House style guide. Maintain a listing of all your house styles for notation preferences, terminology, punctuation, formatting, and so forth, and give it to everyone who will work on your projects. Be sure it has a version date, and whenever it is revised, give a new copy to whomever needs it.

3. Other style guides. It's helpful to name commercial publishing guides that are to be used as the definitive source for notation preferences, unless otherwise described in your house guide. We have such named references for text and for notation, and my hope is that this very book will serve that purpose. At Berklee Press, we use the following references as trusted resources for style preferences:

The Chicago Manual of Style. This is used widely by book publishers. Another popular guide is the *Associated Press Style Guide*, which is more optimized for journalism (including Web copy) than for books.

Music Notation: Preparing Scores and Parts, by Matthew Nicholl and Richard Grudzinski. Excellent resource for information about score preparation.

Music Notation, by Mark McGrain. We use this for handwriting style preferences, particularly on jazz charts.

Music Notation, by Gardner Read. A classic used particularly among many academic music departments in the "contemporary classical" tradition.

The Harvard Dictionary of Music. An excellent source for matters related to classical music.

4. Consistency Checklists. As you publish more, you will likely find that certain mistakes recur. Checklists can help you and your team catch mistakes that seem likely to creep in. Some checklists will be useful for all projects. Others will be more "ad hoc," developed for a special task. Here's an ad hoc checklist I developed for one of our bass books. I gave it to my assistant, who looked for these items on all eight of the book's chapters.

- ☐ S's for slides are always indicated. Use straight lines, not curves.
- ☐ Confirm PO don't have periods: not P.O.
- ☐ Time signatures and initial measure numbers should be set on excerpts.
- ☐ Indicate rakes with x not o; include the word Rake.
- ☐ Confirm eighth notes are beamed together on beats 1&2 and 3&4.

FIG. 10.6. Proofreader's Ad Hoc Checklist

All these tools will help you keep your writing clear, concise, and easier for your reader to understand.

AFTERWORD

If you know anything about music, you will almost certainly find something to disagree with me about in this book. And, if you are a member of the Berklee community, I can almost hear you muttering under your breath, "That's not how we do it here!"

The truth is, there is no single, universally accepted "correct" way that notation practices are executed. And even here at Berklee, we don't have complete consensus on quite a number of things.

I have come to see this as a strength. The music is what's important, not the way the music is notated. To be an effective musician out in the world, you need to be able to decipher notation styles. Being exposed to a diversity of options makes us all stronger—more flexible and resilient, and better equipped to work with other musicians all around the world. It's good that we may disagree—particularly if both of our arguments have merit.

Let me tell you two stories, from my thrilling life as an editor of music books. And I probably shouldn't reveal either one.

As editor in chief of Berklee Press, I try to find as wide a consensus as possible regarding both notating and discussing music. When a question arises, I usually check several well-respected, divergent sources in the literature to determine common practice. Then, I frequently consult my colleagues, often three to five smart, seasoned educators, to see whether there is consensus.

One day, I was working on a book—let's say it was a tuba book (it wasn't). A notation issue came up, with the author writing something in a way I hadn't seen before. So, I checked around. I looked at the literature, found some conflicting examples, and then trekked over to see the chair of the tuba department (Berklee doesn't have a tuba department), and asked for her advice. I asked her, "What's the standard 'Berklee' way we do this?"

She scratched her chin, said, "Hm, let me think. Oh, I know!" and she reached to her bookshelf and pulled out a book that (unbeknownst to her) I had actually edited—in fact, practically ghost-written—myself, a few years previously. She found an example of what we were discussing, rendered there in the way that I had learned it, and she presented it to me as the definitive answer.

At that moment, I lost any lingering faith I might have had in the sanctity of the printed page. When the issue had come up previously, it hadn't registered as a question, and so we published what that author thought it should be, which matched my own experience—so I didn't question it. Now, because it was published in a book, it became an illustration of the definitive "right way" to do it. A “rule” was born. (Note: I have never played the tuba. If I am the keeper of the definitive word about tuba notation, we are all in trouble!)

Okay, another story. In writing this very book, I did some research about how to notate something and checked a large number of scores, published over a century, for historical precedents. In my search, I noticed something unexpected: there was an unrelated “rule” that I’ve been spouting to my students for my whole career about how to render a certain other notation element, and in fact, the literature doesn’t consistently support my previously held opinion. Some well-respected publishers do it; others do not.

Perhaps I got my “rule” from a teacher long ago? I don’t remember. But I have been preaching it for twenty years, to perhaps hundreds of students, and there is a clear, easy counterargument against it. I’m not “wrong” in my preference about this issue, and in fact, I think my way has some merit. But I’m not “right,” either, in terms of reciting a universally held standard of common notation practice. The data just isn’t there to support it.

It is a “rule” that really doesn’t deserve to be a rule. And now, my old students are likely off telling their own students the same thing. “What’s the right way? Well, here’s the rule that my teacher gave me. . . .”

The point is, with both of these stories that I shouldn’t tell, there is a great diversity of practice in current use, and what’s “right” or “wrong” is not always universally believed. The best we can do is try to be clear and consisent, and to help our readers get at the music as best we can.

Language is something of a mess. To anyone who can claim that there are clear rules of written language, I would answer, “Though it’s tough, I ought to cut through the bough.” Say that aloud, and then justify the rules of English spelling and pronunciation, with your “rules.”

Music notation is a similar mess, but we muddle through.

I hope that you find this book to be helpful, as you consider these conundrums. And more importantly, I hope that it helps you to create some great music.

ABOUT THE AUTHOR

Photo by Patricia Gandolfo Mann

Jonathan Feist is editor in chief of Berklee Press, the official book publisher of Berklee College of Music, where he has edited and otherwise helped to produce hundreds of books, instructional videos, and online courses since 1998. He is the author and instructor of the Berklee Online course *Music Notation and Score Preparation using Finale*, which has had many hundreds of students since 2002. He is also author/instructor of the Berklee Online course *Project Management for Musicians*, a book of that same name, and several other books about music. He has had hundreds of articles about music published via About.com (where he served as "music education expert"), MakeMusic's Finale blog, *Keyboard Magazine*, Artist House Music, TakeNote (a magazine by Berklee Online), two editions of *The Songwriter's Market*, and through various other print and online media outlets.

Jonathan holds both a bachelor's and a master's degree in composition from New England Conservatory of Music, where he studied with Arthur Berger and William Thomas McKinley; he studied composition with Arthur Cunningham, before that. He lives in central Massachusetts with his wife Marci and sons Merlin and Forrest, plus a couple of beagles and a menagerie of barnyard creatures.

INDEX

C

E

F

G

M

Q

R

S

T

U

V

W

More Fine Publications

GUITAR

BEBOP GUITAR SOLOS
by Michael Kaplan
00121703 Book $14.99

BLUES GUITAR TECHNIQUE
by Michael Williams
50449623 Book/Online Audio $24.99

BERKLEE GUITAR CHORD DICTIONARY
by Rick Peckham
50449546 Jazz - Book $12.99
50449596 Rock - Book $12.99

BERKLEE GUITAR STYLE STUDIES
by Jim Kelly
00200377 Book/Online Media $24.99

CLASSICAL TECHNIQUE FOR THE MODERN GUITARIST
by Kim Perlak
00148781 Book/Online Audio $19.99

CONTEMPORARY JAZZ GUITAR SOLOS
by Michael Kaplan
00143596 .... $16.99

CREATIVE CHORDAL HARMONY FOR GUITAR
by Mick Goodrick and Tim Miller
50449613 Book/Online Audio $19.99

FUNK/R&B GUITAR
by Thaddeus Hogarth
50449569 Book/Online Audio $19.99

GUITAR CHOP SHOP - BUILDING ROCK/METAL TECHNIQUE
by Joe Stump
50449601 Book/Online Audio $19.99

GUITAR SWEEP PICKING
by Joe Stump
00151223 Book/Online Audio $19.99

INTRODUCTION TO JAZZ GUITAR
by Jane Miller
00125041 Book/Online Audio $19.99

JAZZ GUITAR FRETBOARD NAVIGATION
by Mark White
00154107 Book/Online Audio $19.99

JAZZ SWING GUITAR
by Jon Wheatley
00139935 Book/Online Audio $19.99

A MODERN METHOD FOR GUITAR*
by William Leavitt
Volume 1: Beginner
00137387 Book/Online Video $24.99
**Other volumes, media options, and supporting songbooks available.*

A MODERN METHOD FOR GUITAR SCALES
by Larry Baione
00199318 Book $9.99

Berklee Press publications feature material developed at the Berklee College of Music.
To browse the complete Berklee Press Catalog, go to
www.berkleepress.com

BASS

BASS LINES
Fingerstyle Funk
by Joe Santerre
50449542 Book/CD $19.95
Metal
by David Marvuglio
00122465 Book/Online Audio $19.99
Rock
by Joe Santerre
50449478 Book/CD $19.95

BERKLEE JAZZ BASS
by Rich Appleman, Whit Browne, and Bruce Gertz
50449636 Book/Online Audio $19.99

FUNK BASS FILLS
by Anthony Vitti
50449608 Book/CD $19.99

INSTANT BASS
by Danny Morris
50449502 Book/CD $9.99

VOICE

BELTING
by Jeannie Gagné
00124984 Book/Online Media $19.99

THE CONTEMPORARY SINGER - 2ND ED.
by Anne Peckham
50449595 Book/Online Audio $24.99

JAZZ VOCAL IMPROVISATION
by Mili Bermejo
00159290 Book/Online Audio $19.99

TIPS FOR SINGERS
by Carolyn Wilkins
50449557 Book/CD $19.95

VOCAL TECHNIQUE
featuring Anne Peckham
50448038 DVD $19.95

VOCAL WORKOUTS FOR THE CONTEMPORARY SINGER
by Anne Peckham
50448044 Book/Online Audio $24.99

YOUR SINGING VOICE
by Jeannie Gagné
50449619 Book/CD $29.99

WOODWINDS/BRASS

TRUMPET SOUND EFFECTS
by Craig Pederson & Ueli Dörig
00121626 Book/Online Audio $14.99

SAXOPHONE SOUND EFFECTS
by Ueli Dörig
50449628 Book/Online Audio $15.99

THE TECHNIQUE OF THE FLUTE: CHORD STUDIES, RHYTHM STUDIES
by Joseph Viola
00214012 Book $19.99

PIANO/KEYBOARD

BERKLEE JAZZ KEYBOARD HARMONY
by Suzanna Sifter
00138874 Book/Online Audio $24.99

BERKLEE JAZZ PIANO
by Ray Santisi
50448047 Book/Online Audio $19.99

BERKLEE JAZZ STANDARDS FOR SOLO PIANO
Arranged by Robert Christopherson, Hey Rim Jeon, Ross Ramsay, Tim Ray
00160482 Book/Online Audio $19.99

CHORD-SCALE IMPROVISATION FOR KEYBOARD
by Ross Ramsay
50449597 Book/CD $19.99

CONTEMPORARY PIANO TECHNIQUE
by Stephany Tiernan
50449545 Book/DVD $29.99

HAMMOND ORGAN COMPLETE
by Dave Limina
50449479 Book/CD $24.95

JAZZ PIANO COMPING
by Suzanne Davis
50449614 Book/CD $19.99

LATIN JAZZ PIANO IMPROVISATION
by Rebecca Cline
50449649 Book/CD $24.99

SOLO JAZZ PIANO - 2ND ED.
by Neil Olmstead
50449641 Book/CD $39.99

DRUMS

BEGINNING DJEMBE
by Michael Markus & Joe Galeota
00148210 Book/Online Video $16.99

BERKLEE JAZZ DRUMS
by Casey Scheuerell
50449612 Book/Online Audio $19.99

DRUM SET WARM-UPS
by Rod Morgenstein
50449465 Book $12.99

DRUM STUDIES
by Dave Vose
50449617 Book $12.99

A MANUAL FOR THE MODERN DRUMMER
by Alan Dawson & Don DeMichael
50449560 Book $14.99

MASTERING THE ART OF BRUSHES - 2ND EDITION
by Jon Hazilla
50449459 Book/Online Audio $19.99

PHRASING: ADVANCED RUDIMENTS FOR CREATIVE DRUMMING
by Russ Gold
00120209 Book/Online Media $19.99

WORLD JAZZ DRUMMING
by Mark Walker
50449568 Book/CD $22.99

STRINGS/ROOTS MUSIC

BERKLEE HARP
Chords, Styles, and Improvisation for Pedal and Lever Harp
by Felice Pomeranz
00144263 Book/Online Audio $19.99

BEYOND BLUEGRASS
Beyond Bluegrass Banjo
by Dave Hollander and Matt Glaser
50449610 Book/CD $19.99

Beyond Bluegrass Mandolin
by John McGann and Matt Glaser
50449609 Book/CD $19.99

Bluegrass Fiddle and Beyond
by Matt Glaser
50449602 Book/CD $19.99

EXPLORING CLASSICAL MANDOLIN
by August Watters
00125040 Book/Online Media $19.99

FIDDLE TUNES ON JAZZ CHANGES
by Matt Glaser
00120210 Book/Online Audio $16.99

THE IRISH CELLO BOOK
by Liz Davis Maxfield
50449652 Book/CD $24.99

JAZZ UKULELE
by Abe Lagrimas, Jr.
00121624 Book/Online Audio $19.99

BERKLEE PRACTICE METHOD

GET YOUR BAND TOGETHER
With additional volumes for other instruments, plus a teacher's guide.

Bass
by Rich Appleman, John Repucci and the Berklee Faculty
50449427 Book/CD $14.95

Drum Set
by Ron Savage, Casey Scheuerell and the Berklee Faculty
50449429 Book/CD $14.95

Guitar
by Larry Baione and the Berklee Faculty
50449426 Book/CD $16.99

Keyboard
by Russell Hoffmann, Paul Schmeling and the Berklee Faculty
50449428 Book/Online Audio $14.99

WELLNESS

MANAGE YOUR STRESS AND PAIN THROUGH MUSIC
by Dr. Suzanne B. Hanser and Dr. Susan E. Mandel
50449592 Book/CD $29.99

MUSICIAN'S YOGA
by Mia Olson
50449587 Book $17.99

THE NEW MUSIC THERAPIST'S HANDBOOK – 2ND EDITION
by Dr. Suzanne B. Hanser
50449424 Book $29.95

AUTOBIOGRAPHY

LEARNING TO LISTEN: THE JAZZ JOURNEY OF GARY BURTON
by Gary Burton
00117798 Book $27.99

MUSIC THEORY/EAR TRAINING/ IMPROVISATION

BEGINNING EAR TRAINING
by Gilson Schachnik
50449548 Book/CD $16.99

THE BERKLEE BOOK OF JAZZ HARMONY
by Joe Mulholland & Tom Hojnacki
00113755 Book/Online Audio $27.50

BERKLEE MUSIC THEORY – 2ND ED.
by Paul Schmeling

Rhythm, Scales Intervals
50449615 Book/Online Audio $24.99

Harmony
50449616 Book/CD $22.99

IMPROVISATION FOR CLASSICAL MUSICIANS
by Eugene Friesen with Wendy M. Friesen
50449637 Book/CD $24.99

REHARMONIZATION TECHNIQUES
by Randy Felts
50449496 Book $29.95

MUSIC BUSINESS

HOW TO GET A JOB IN THE MUSIC INDUSTRY – 3RD EDITION
by Keith Hatschek with Breanne Beseda
00130699 Book $27.99

MAKING MUSIC MAKE MONEY
by Eric Beall
50448009 Book $26.95

MUSIC LAW IN THE DIGITAL AGE – 2ND EDITION
by Allen Bargfrede
00148196 Book $19.99

MUSIC MARKETING
by Mike King
50449588 Book $24.99

PROJECT MANAGEMENT FOR MUSICIANS
by Jonathan Feist
50449659 Book $27.99

THE SELF-PROMOTING MUSICIAN – 3RD EDITION
by Peter Spellman
00119607 Book $24.99

MUSIC PRODUCTION & ENGINEERING

AUDIO MASTERING
by Jonathan Wyner
50449581 Book/CD $29.99

AUDIO POST PRODUCTION
by Mark Cross
50449627 Book $19.99

MIX MASTERS
by Maureen Droney
50448023 Book $24.95

THE SINGER-SONGWRITER'S GUIDE TO RECORDING IN THE HOME STUDIO
by Shane Adams
00148211 Book/Online Audio $16.99

UNDERSTANDING AUDIO – 2ND EDITION
by Daniel M. Thompson
00148197 Book $24.99

SONGWRITING, COMPOSING, ARRANGING

ARRANGING FOR HORNS
by Jerry Gates
00121625 Book/Online Audio $19.99

BEGINNING SONGWRITING
by Andrea Stolpe with Jan Stolpe
00138503 Book/Online Audio $19.99

BERKLEE CONTEMPORARY MUSIC NOTATION
by Jonathan Feist
00202547 Book $16.99

COMPLETE GUIDE TO FILM SCORING – 2ND ED.
by Richard Davis
50449607 .... $29.99

CONTEMPORARY COUNTERPOINT: THEORY & APPLICATION
by Beth Denisch
00147050 Book/Online Audio $19.99

JAZZ COMPOSITION
by Ted Pease
50448000 Book/Online Audio $39.99

MELODY IN SONGWRITING
by Jack Perricone
50449419 Book/CD $24.95

MODERN JAZZ VOICINGS
by Ted Pease and Ken Pullig
50449485 Book/Online Audio $24.99

MUSIC COMPOSITION FOR FILM AND TELEVISION
by Lalo Schifrin
50449604 Book $34.99

MUSIC NOTATION
Preparing Scores and Parts
by Matthew Nicholl and Richard Grudzinski
50449540 Book $16.99

MUSIC NOTATION
Theory and Technique for Music Notation
by Mark McGrain
50449399 Book $24.95

POPULAR LYRIC WRITING
by Andrea Stolpe
50449553 Book $15.99

SONGWRITING: ESSENTIAL GUIDE
Lyric and Form Structure
by Pat Pattison
50481582 Book $16.99

Rhyming
by Pat Pattison
00124366 2nd Ed. Book $17.99

SONGWRITING STRATEGIES
by Mark Simos
50449621 Book $22.99

THE SONGWRITER'S WORKSHOP
Harmony
by Jimmy Kachulis
50449519 Book/Online Audio $29.99

Melody
by Jimmy Kachulis
50449518 Book/CD $24.99

Prices subject to change without notice. Visit your local music dealer or bookstore, or go to **www.berkleepress.com**